COVID-19 and Social Protection

Steven Ratuva · Tara Ross ·
Yvonne Crichton-Hill · Arindam Basu ·
Patrick Vakaoti · Rosemarie Martin-Neuninger
Editors

COVID-19 and Social Protection

A Study in Human Resilience and Social Solidarity

palgrave
macmillan

Editors
Steven Ratuva
Faculty of Arts
University of Canterbury
Christchurch, New Zealand

Yvonne Crichton-Hill
University of Canterbury
Rolleston, Canterbury, New Zealand

Patrick Vakaoti
Sociology, Criminology
and Gender Studies Programme
University of Otago
Dunedin, Otago, New Zealand

Tara Ross
College of Arts
University of Canterbury
Lyttelton, Canterbury, New Zealand

Arindam Basu
School of Health Sciences
University of Canterbury
Sheffield, Canterbury, New Zealand

Rosemarie Martin-Neuninger
Macmillan Brown Centre
for Pacific Studies
University of Canterbury
Christchurch, Canterbury
New Zealand

ISBN 978-981-16-2947-1 ISBN 978-981-16-2948-8 (eBook)
https://doi.org/10.1007/978-981-16-2948-8

Cover illustration: Dot Nut Design

This Palgrave Macmillan imprint is published by the registered company Springer Nature Singapore Pte Ltd.
The registered company address is: 152 Beach Road, #21-01/04 Gateway East, Singapore 189721, Singapore

Contents

Notes on Contributors

Arindam Basu is an Associate Professor in Health Science at the University of Canterbury.

Jhon Urasti Blesia recently completed his PhD at the University of Canterbury, New Zealand and is now based in West Papua.

Yvonne Crichton-Hill is the Head of Social Work at the University of Canterbury.

Jovanie Camacho Espesor is a political anthropologist at the Mindanao State University, Philippines.

David Fielding is a Professor in the Department of Economics at the University of Otago.

Glenn Finau is an expert on indigenous and alternative accounting based at the University of Tasmania.

Teena M. Henderson is a Te Reo Maori Language Expert at the University of Canterbury, New Zealand.

Romitesh Kant University of the South Pacific, Fiji.

Stephen Knowles is a Professor in the Otago Business School of the University of Otago.

Efraim Lokden Fakultas Kedokteran, Universitas Cenderawasih, West Papua.

Richard F. Manning is an educationist and Senior Lecturer in the School of Education, University of Canterbury.

Joseph Martin is an Educationist at Northern Arizona University, USA.

Rosemarie Martin-Neuninger was a researcher for the Macmillan Brown Centre, University of Canterbury and is now at Stats NZ/Tatauranga Aotearoa.

Litea Meo-Sewabu is the Head of Social Work at the University of the South Pacific.

Nii-K Plange is a Professor of Interdisciplinary Research at the National University of Fiji.

Steven Ratuva is Director of the Macmillan Brown Center for Pacific Studies at the University of Canberra, New Zealand.

Jon Reyhner is a Professor at Northern Arizona University, USA.

Tara Ross is the Head of Journalism at the University of Canterbury.

Matthew Scobie is a Ngai Tahu scholar who specializes in indigenous and alternative accounting based at the Business Faculty, University of Canterbury.

Larry Steeves is an Indigenous Education Expert at the University of Regina, Canada.

Renny Sulelino Sekolah Tinggi Bio Sains Swadiri, West Papua.

Patrick Vakaoti is an Associate Professor in Sociology at the University of Otago.

Lori Whiteman is an Indigenous Education Expert at the University of Regina, Canada.

Jeffrey Willis completed his PhD at the University of Canterbury New Zealand and is an expert on climate change narratives and climate crisis in the Pacific.

List of Figures

List of Tables

CHAPTER 1

A Replay of the *War of the Worlds*? COVID-19 and Social Protection

Steven Ratuva

Introduction

Like Martians invading Earth in the book, *The War of the Worlds*, COVID-19 took the world by storm in unprecedented ways, causing havoc and pandemonium in its path of destruction. However, the ironic twist in H. G. Wells' story is that the invasion from outer space was defeated, not by human technological genius, but by pathogens—by infectious micro-organisms, much like COVID-19. Of course, the major difference between COVID-19 and *The War of the Worlds* is that the latter was fiction, a figment of human imagination, while the former is not. The current pandemic is a real nightmare, it is happening, it maims, kills, paralyzes economies and causes social chaos. Humanity has never seen anything so globally disruptive.

However, there is hope as human imagination, humanity's most powerful transformative tool, will eventually triumph, whether in the

S. Ratuva (✉)
Macmillan Brown Center for Pacific Studies, University of Canterbury, Christchurch, New Zealand
e-mail: steven.ratuva@canterbury.ac.nz

S. Ratuva et al. (eds.), *COVID-19 and Social Protection*, https://doi.org/10.1007/978-981-16-2948-8_1

form of vaccination (which, admittedly, brings new problems of inequality in terms of procurement, costs, logistics and coverage across countries, adding to the layers of problems) or the many stories of people using their powers of innovation and empathy to confront the pandemic and its consequences and transform lives and communities. So herein is a narrative both of tragedy and hope. This is what the present book is about. It is the story of the capacity of human agency to overcome adversity such as COVID-19 by building up resilience through innovative means of survival.

A pandemic is defined as an epidemic that has become worldwide in the extent of its contagion, across national boundaries and infecting a large number of people in many countries (Kelly 2011: 540). Pandemics are not new. Since the days of hunters and gatherers, communicable diseases had been rife and contributed to transforming the human capacity to respond to calamities. Some of the earliest recorded pandemics included one that was said to have infected Athens in AD 430, killing two-thirds of the population. The Antonine plague from AD 165 to AD 180 swept across the Roman Empire, even killing a Roman Emperor, Lucius Verus (McNeill 1976). Others included the Cyprian plague of AD 250 and the Justinian plague of AD 541, as well as the leprosy pandemic in Europe in the eleventh century. The great plague of London in 1665 was followed by a series of pandemics in the 1800s such as the first cholera pandemic of 1865, the third plague pandemic of 1855 and the Russian flu of 1889. In the twentieth century, a number of pandemics were prominent, including the Spanish flu of 1918, the Asian flu of 1957 and HIV/AIDS, which started in 1981, and in this century, we faced SARS in 2003 and now the current COVID-19 pandemic (Cartwright and Biddins 2020). Colonialism was also responsible for spreading various types of pandemic to colonized populations, and perhaps the most deadly of these saw the death of about 56 million Native Americans in the sixteenth and seventeenth centuries by diseases introduced by Spanish colonizers. In 1875, a measles pandemic that originated in Australia killed a total of 40,000 people in Fiji, about a third of the population. Significant numbers of colonized populations in Africa, Asia and the Pacific were decimated as a result of the Spanish flu and other diseases introduced from Europe.

Compared to former pandemics, COVID-19 is unpreceded both in terms of its global scale and impact. Tens of millions of people have been infected, and the numbers keep rising, hundreds of thousands have been killed, borders have been closed and economies paralyzed, causing untold misery for individuals, families and communities across the globe (Pawar 2020). One of the most immediate forms of response has been the implementation of social protection programmes, which include wage subsidy intervention by the government, food distribution, cash transfer and a whole range of other community-focused services that have been put in place by a range of players such as states, international organizations, civil society organizations and community organizations (Diwakar 2020; ILO 2020a). The speed with which COVID-19 became globalized is a result of extensive global interconnectedness through air travel. It is also the only pandemic to have infected all regions of the world at once. In an era of virtual communication, news and images of death and destruction reached other parts of the world in real time and people could make comparative assessments of their situation in relation to others. For once, all countries in the world became united in their common consciousness about a common threat, but different countries, for different reasons, utilized different approaches to address the pandemic.

This book has been written while the COVID-19 pandemic is still prevalent and the rate of infection is still increasing globally, and before the mass rollout of potentially game-changing vaccination. The book relates to the way local communities have devised ways of responding to the COVID-19 pandemic through various means of social protection and social solidarity economies. It examines through case studies and alternative modes of analysis the intersection between social protection and the social solidarity economy, particularly in relation to community-based responses to COVID-19.

COVID-19 and the Crisis of Neoliberalism: Rethinking Alternatives

In 2019, an international team of medical experts, led by the Nuclear Threat Initiative (NTI), the Johns Hopkins Center for Health Security (JHU) and The Economist Intelligence Unit (EIU) developed the Global Health Index (GHI), which amongst other things, ranked countries according to their levels of preparedness for pandemics (NTI et al. 2020). Touted as a 'ground-breaking index' by the authors themselves, the GHI ranked the United States (US) as number one, the United Kingdom as number two and the Netherlands as number three. This index suddenly became obsolete and a source of embarrassment when COVID-19 struck and revealed the first three ranked countries in the

GHI as amongst the worst performing in terms of COVID-19 responses, where countries in Africa, which were ranked very low in the index, were some of the highest performers. It was a clear case of epistemological incongruence between abstract academic metrification and social reality. The GHI was based largely on medical variables and failed to capture the wider socio-economic, cultural and political environment that impacts on heath conditions, human behaviour, policy outcomes and responses.

There are some important lessons here. Firstly, health issues should not be studied in isolation within the confinements of biological paradigms, but rather framed within broader interdisciplinary approaches that can better account for the interconnectedness between health and social conditions. The second issue is more methodological and relates to how the choice of inappropriate variables for the purpose of metrification could impact the outcomes. The GHI analysis did not consider significant social variables such as inequality, racism, ideology and political leadership, which were defining indicators in pushing the US down as the number six worst performer in the world as far as COVID-19 is concerned, a far cry from the number one status accorded by the GHI ranking. The point here is that while framing an index or a metricized algorithm may make sense in terms of providing a quantified snapshot of a situation at a particular point in time, it does not necessarily capture the subjective sentiments, intents and implicit biases of people. These lessons should also be guiding lights for how we understand social protection and the need to situate it in a changing social context, unequal social structure, as well as ideological and political context.

Often defined as programmes to address the situation of the most disadvantaged and vulnerable in society (Ratuva 2014), social protection has gone through significant policy reviews and academic debates about what it should be and what it should focus on. Part of the reason for this has to do with widespread neoliberal reforms driven by privatization, commodification and financialization of public goods, which have impacted wellbeing policy framing and implementation. The lessons of COVID-19 and the inability of neoliberal health systems to respond effectively, as we saw earlier in the case of the US, are compelling reasons as to why social protection needs to be redefined not in terms of the market imperatives that see social protection as a private commodity, but as a public good that serves human wellbeing first and foremost (Lazonick and O'Sullivan 2000). The neoliberal economic system has created an unequal and often racialized structure, which is reflected in disparity in access to health and social insurance and health programmes that often favour the interests of pharmaceutical and insurance corporations (Viana and Silva 2018).

A World Health Organization (WHO) study has shown that although there has been a growth in universal health coverage, inequality still remains as a major obstacle, with predominantly poor people having minimal or no access (WHO 2017). The neoliberal prescriptions in many countries have had a negative impact on social protection in many regions of the world, especially those targeted towards children (ILO 2020b). The disparities are between and within countries (van Doorslaer and Koolman 2004). The 2008 global crisis showed the fragility of the market economy and the need to rethink how communities can develop resilience (Mirowski 2013).

How we think about social protection as a form of direct assistance in times of crisis needs to be beyond just health and should incorporate other aspects such as development of opportunities and capacity in the areas of poverty, education, employment and other aspects of wellbeing (Walsham et al. 2019). Social protection needs to be framed in a holistic manner that includes not just protection, but also prevention, capacity building and transformation (Devereux and Sabates-Wheeler 2004).

There should also be a realization that there are diverse types of organizations such as multilateral, bilateral and private institutions, which frame social protection according to their specific interests and not just for universal human wellbeing (Waring et al. 2013). The ILO, whose mandate is to look after workers' rights, tends to be oriented towards labour market conditions and their impact on employees (ILO 2012). By contrast, the World Bank (WB) and the Asian Development Bank (ADB) (2011), which are global financial institutions driving austerity-based neoliberal economic reforms, tend to be involved in a rather uncomfortable balancing act between market-based principles and equity creation (Holmes and Jones 2009). The ADB has developed a Social Protection Index (SPI) to measure the depth and coverage of social protection using four variables: Social Protection Expenditure (SPEXP), Social Protection Coverage (SPCOV), Social Protection Distribution (SPDIST) and Social Protection Impact (SPIMP) (McKinley 2013).

The problem with the ADB system is that it does not take community-based and indigenous social protection systems into consideration, nor does it consider issues of systemic inequality and unequal access based on class, ethnicity and gender. This ideological and cultural bias is subconsciously embedded in the SPI formula, and while it may have policy value for the ADB, it does not fully reflect the intertwined and multi-dimensional complexities of culture, politics, economics and health. In a similar way, the framework used by the WB associates social protection with 'managing social risk' that might otherwise impact the market (Heltberg et al. 2008). The ADB and the WB's framing of social protection has been criticized for a parochial focus on the formal sector and formally employed people and for overlooking the significance of social protection in the community, including indigenous forms of social protection (Ratuva 2010). Beckert (2020: 319–320) takes the criticism further by stating that the optimism for growth and wealth promoted by financial institutions and the role of social protection as a means of market support is 'illusory' to say the least. The neoliberal assumption that social protection is part of the market's self-regulatory mechanism in levelling any anomalies (Hathaway 2020; Viana and Silva 2018) overlooks the pervasive power differentials, contradictions and inequalities in the market, including the specific rationale behind social protection (McCord 2009; Hickey 2007). To others, social protection, like any other economic activity, can be used to leverage state interests and domination (Darcy 2004; Harvey 2009; Harvey and Holmes 2007).

Moreover, it needs stressing that market-based social protection strategies vary considerably, ranging from the highly privatized system of health, education and other state services in the US to more state-based systems as in some European countries (Fullman et al. 2018). Despite its neoliberal economic strategy, Aotearoa New Zealand still maintains a state-subsidized and efficient public health system, and this is just one of the reasons for the country's commendable response to COVID-19. The contradiction between the idea of health as a social good and health as a private good continues to be a major dilemma in social protection (Viana and Silva 2018).

The call for more people-focused social protection is based on the principle of inclusivity and interconnections that take into consideration issues such as gender disparity, racism, conflict and other social issues at the family and community levels (Holmes and Jones 2009). In this regard, the idea of 'anticipatory' (preventive) and 'transformative' social protection proposed by Waring et al. (2013) is an alternative view that considers a human rights and gender-based perspective. This alternative intersects with the SSE, which has been growing in reach and relevance as a result of COVID-19. The lessons of the 2008 global crisis having now been replicated, especially in terms of how communities had to fall back on community-based social protection systems, there has been renewed interest in the search for alternative development strategies by development experts and international aid agencies (Slater and McCord 2009; Davies and McGregor 2009; Szreter 2009; Parks and Abbott 2009). To Szreter (2009: 290), the basis of this community-based social protection should be the 'endowment of mutually respecting and trusting relationships' and 'the quality of the set of relationships of a social group'. This needs to be anchored in local culture and framed by a sense of local space (Schiller and de Wet 2019). An important aspect of this is empowered relationships with indigenous cultures (Schiller and de Wet 2019). The relationship between community-based social protection and the SSE should be a basis for creating resilience and sustainability (Barrientos and Hinojosa-Valencia 2009; Devereux and Cipryk 2009; Köhler et al. 2009). Coupled with this is the need to allocate more power, capacity and resources to local communities (Norton et al. 2001; Shepherd et al. 2004).

The Social Solidarity Economy Alternative

COVID-19 has demonstrated the fragility of the market system which because of its narrow focus on private profit privileges a minority, because of its dependence on a life-long debt system ties people to the inescapable dictates of market imperatives, and because of its particular culture determines human identity and capacity by one's market value and relevance (Saad-Filho 2020). To sustain their paralyzed economies, states had to intervene to rescue corporations from collapse through wage subsidy and other strategies, and in countries where the capacity of the state was limited, people had to fend for themselves in the face of impending calamity (Roubini 2020). Many people in formal employment who, for most of their lives, relied on the capitalist mode of production for survival had to look for alternatives either by reinventing new community-based systems of economic survival or reverting to indigenous modes of survival. These constitute what is known as the social and solidarity economy (SSE), an alternative that has been promoted by the United Nations Inter-Agency Task Force on Social and Solidarity Economy (UNTFSSE), and which we will discuss in more detail below (UNTFSSE 2017, 2020).

The SSE has been part of many indigenous and local communities for a long time, and has been studied by sociologists and anthropologists, and latterly gained significance in policy research (Rafaelli 2017). While different definitions have been used by scholars over the years, the need to provide a unified, inclusive and representative definition led to this 2009 International Labour Organization (ILO) conference framing of SSE as a:

> ...concept designating enterprises and organizations, in particular cooperatives, mutual benefit societies, associations, foundations and social enterprises, which have the specific feature of producing goods, services and knowledge while pursuing both economic and social aims and fostering solidarity.

While this definition was aimed at 're-balancing economic, social and environmental objectives', it is only relevant to the semi-market and formal economy and still does not capture the realities of indigenous economies.

A significant aspect of the SSE is its focus on human wellbeing and ethics, rather than profit, which makes SSE-based strategies, policies and programmes increasingly popular in the worldwide response to worsening poverty, environmental degradation and climate change as a result of human activities (Rafaelli 2017). Also important is the way SSE draws the power of its meaning and moral force from people's histories, local culture and community worldviews as an alternative paradigm to neoliberal capitalism and some of its predatory practices (Laville 2010). For a number of years, international organizations such as the United National Development Program and the ILO, civil society organizations, scholars and grassroots communities themselves have joined hands to promote its use and significance in countries in the Global South. The UNTFSSE was set up in 2013 in response to the demands for greater involvement by international agencies to help mainstream the SSE into development and wellbeing programmes during the Rio+20 summit in June 2012. Some United Nations (UN) Member States have gone as far as forming an International Leading Group on Social and Solidarity Economy (ILGSSE) to promote the SSE as part of the global mainstream development component. However, despite these high-level global initiatives, there is still a large gap in terms of research and theorizing about the SSE in the Global South. The use of 'progressive' models from Western countries has continued to dominate the SSE narrative, but these may not necessarily be appropriate for marginalized communities in the Global South (Martinez et al. 2019: 1).

The link between the SSE and social protection also needs revisiting, especially given the ways in which COVID-19 has stimulated and inspired SSE and social protection strategies. For instance, reliance on kinship-based barter systems, which is an example of indigenous forms of social protection (as shown in Chapter 11), can be central to the SSE; examples in other chapters further demonstrate the synergies between the two concepts. The next section focuses more on alternative forms of social protection and how social protection is linked to the SSE in the broader framing of alternative wellbeing approaches in the context of COVID-19.

The Chapters

The COVID-19 crisis should be a basis for a more innovative look at interdisciplinary and integrated social protection approaches simultaneously to address climate change, inequality, health and other forms of wellbeing in a creatively adaptive and transformative way. This is an approach that has been suggested earlier by some scholars as a way of making social protection more connected with the SSE, more transformative and relevant to local realities (Davies et al. 2008; Raworth 2007; Heltberg et al. 2008). The chapters in the book attempt to do justice to this in various ways. They are configured to ensure that they are engaged in a process of interdisciplinary dialogue rather than being insulated from each other, to broaden and deepen the analysis and debates on COVID-19 and social protection. By bringing together chapters written by experts in different fields, the book also provides a trans-boundary space where authors share their research findings and analysis, unhindered by the limitations of artificial disciplinary lines. The desire to expand our understanding of the whole of society impact of COVID-19 in the areas of health, economy, social relations, politics, technology, media, culture and psychology has compelled us to think broadly and deeply about taking an inclusive, equity-based, people-centred, wellbeing-framed and participatory mode of understanding the pandemic, its consequences and different responses to it.

In Chapter 2, Arin Basu provides a view of social protection and social determinants of health in relation to COVID-19 and related disasters from an epidemiological perspective. Health of populations and individual health statuses are influenced by social position, and social situations determine the health of people. In this sense, health is not only a 'state', but also a resource that needs to be nurtured over people's lifetimes.

Poverty, or lack of material resources, impacts health adversely and in particular, may result in infectious diseases as people are forced to live in damp, crowded conditions. This is particularly relevant in the face of outbreaks of diseases that can shut down economies and force people into poverty where such conditions are exacerbated. The COVID-19 viral outbreak, the ongoing worldwide pandemic is a case in point. This has resulted in widespread lockdowns in different countries. While lockdown is used as a containment measure to control the spread of the virus and limit viral infection, it also has the downstream effect of shutting down parts of or whole economies, thus leading to further worsening of poverty and social distress. The chapter argues for the strengthening of social protection measures to protect vulnerable members of society from poverty-related adverse life events and circumstances. The chapter examines social protection policies and develops models to address what may happen and what needs to be done to strengthen social protection systems for securing the health and wellbeing of vulnerable populations in the face of unforeseen phenomena such as COVID-19.

In Chapter 3, Yvonne Crichton-Hill examines the impact of lockdown on family violence and discusses some of the relevant social protection approaches to address these. While lockdown was a 'scientific' national strategy to combat the spread of the infection, the consequences on some families were dramatic as perpetrators of family violence were locked together with victims, and high levels of stress and trauma simply escalated the violence in significant ways. The chapter explores the impact of lockdown measures on the occurrence of child abuse, intimate partner violence and elder abuse, social protection responses to family violence and considerations for an integrated social protection system.

Another consequence of COVID-19 was food insecurity as businesses closed and people lost their jobs and sources of income and thus their ability to buy food. In Chapter 4, Rosemarie Martin discusses the impacts of COVID-19 on food security by looking at emergency food systems in the form of food banks and policy responses. The pandemic exacerbated food insecurity amongst vulnerable groups, and those who lost employment were faced with the stark reality of reduced access to food and hunger. Many who previously did not need food aid joined food bank queues for the first time (in their thousands). This went hand in hand with increasing poverty and marginalization. While food banks may be a temporary measure, they do provide an immediate response to people's wellbeing as they rehabilitate themselves and look for other opportunities. For the unskilled and marginal groups and individuals, food banks have become part of their daily survival culture. The chapter also provides recommendations to improve food banks, which require holistic solutions and best practices. This includes the critical role of governments to support a diversity of food and social protection initiatives, reducing food insecurity by promoting food resilience and respecting food sovereignty.

Amongst the most affected social categories of people are young people. This is discussed by Patrick Vakaoti in Chapter 5. Since the pandemic, young people globally have been referred to as the 'lockdown generation'. This chapter talks about young people and the impact of the pandemic on tertiary education, work and wellbeing and the role of social protection mechanisms in addressing youth issues. The chapter builds on a piece in *The Big Q* titled 'How are young tertiary students that work faring in the wake of COVID-19?' written by the author himself and draws extensively from secondary sources, particularly academic blog posts and rapid assessment reports by various international agencies like the ILO and the ADB.

COVID-19 demonstrated how readily people can now share information through global interconnections of media networks and virtual modes of communication. It also underscored disparities in the way information is shared, which are reflective of deeper systemic inequalities within society. This is an issue explored by Tara Ross in Chapter 6 in which she critically examines communication inequalities in the context of the COVID-19 pandemic, as well as the role that media and digital technologies might play in a recovery. The COVID-19 pandemic has exacerbated the lack of access to digital and media technologies often faced by those socio-economically disadvantaged groups at greater risk of health problems from COVID-19. Media paywalls, for instance, exclude poorer communities from getting the most accurate health-related news and information, potentially making them more susceptible to misinformation and exacerbating their vulnerability in a health crisis. Contact tracing applications deployed by health agencies do not work for those who cannot afford or use a smartphone, while health information distributed through digital portals does not reach those who are digitally excluded. Given these challenges are likely to become more pronounced as the pandemic continues, it is vital that barriers to digital and media technologies are urgently addressed.

The impact of COVID-19 on Indigenous communities has been a major concern, especially because of the prior conditions of inequality and deprivation many have been subjected to through colonialism and even in the post-colonial era. Indigenous people are amongst the most infected groups because of their disadvantaged social conditions. This is an issue raised in Chapter 7 by a team of researchers consisting of Teena Henderson, Joseph Martin, Lori Whiteman, Richard Manning, Jon Reyhner and Larry Steeves. The chapter examines the impact of COVID-19 on Indigenous community resilience and schooling in New Zealand, the US and Canada. It revolves around three autoethnographies that recount experiences of indigenous peoples from Aotearoa New Zealand, the US and Canada. The first is an autoethnographic account by Teena Henderson, a Ngāi Tahu (Māori) academic from the University of Canterbury (Christchurch, New Zealand). Teena reflects on her tribe's experiences to suggest it must remain resilient and seek to be 'heard' by its Treaty partner (the Crown/New Zealand Government). This is followed by Joseph (Joe) Martin, a Navajo academic (Northern Arizona University) who shares his perspective and those of his close colleagues regarding significant challenges currently facing Navajo Nation leaders, administrators, teachers, parents and learners. Finally, Lori Whiteman (Dakota/Anishinabe; Treaty Education Alliance Executive Director) shares her concerns from rural Saskatchewan, particularly as they relate to the concepts of ambiguous loss and community resilience. The authors then combine as a full team to relate the key recurring themes that emerge from these narratives to international literature. This highlights the unique challenges and shared experiences facing many indigenous communities around the world, particularly those living in remote/rural areas.

The impact of COVID-19 on the elderly has been a major concern in many countries because of their vulnerability to infection as manifested by the fact that many rest homes became hotspots for the virus. Nii-K Plange examines the relationship between ageing, vulnerability and COVID-19 in Chapter 8. This chapter explores the challenges of the ageing populations in Pacific Island countries and their dependency on traditional family relations, despite the general shrinking of resources, including of able-bodied family members and how this presents a crisis of livelihood for ageing parents. In Fiji, government social protection schemes have proven inadequate, and this has opened up spaces for the resurgence of charity, reciprocity and the 'moral economy' as enduring Pacific values. Where then does social protection go from here? This is the question that the chapter tries to address.

The poor are amongst the most vulnerable to COVID-19 because of the way in which their conditions are exacerbated by the pandemic. In Chapter 9, Jovanie Camacho Espesor provides an analysis of the impact of COVID-19 on the poor in the Philippines and some of the country's social protection approaches. The Philippines has the highest number of COVID-19 cases in Southeast Asia. This chapter aims to explain the nature of vertical engagements of the national and local governments in the provision of social protection for the poor in the Philippines. The COVID-19 crisis has undeniably generated major economic repercussions that gravely affected disadvantaged and vulnerable populations, particularly ordinary workers. The Philippines national government takes the lead in managing the COVID-19 crisis and aiding the poor to cope with the adverse impacts of the pandemic. The chapter examines some key social protection programmes of the national and sub-national governments in the Philippines that are designed to manage and mitigate the detrimental socio-economic impacts of the COVID-19 pandemic. It argues that the pandemic has induced the Philippines government to reinforce its existing social protection architecture through the establishment of additional social security guarantees, especially for the poor.

In Chapter 10, Matthew Scobie examines how the notion of accountability as a form of cultural capital can be utilized as a part of responses to the pandemic. While the conventional economic effects of COVID-19 within the global capitalist economy are and will continue to be devastating, in Aotearoa New Zealand, Māori economies and responses have potential for imagining and implementing alternative futures. This chapter explores the potential for scaling out these economies and responses based on present practices and future possibilities, with a focus on the concept of accountability. The chapter first explores pre-colonial accountability structures by following Ngāi Tahu, Māori and indigenous thought and practice. This is to outline the original instructions of accountability, which Scobie discusses in terms of grounded accountability. The chapter briefly explores historical and contemporary perspectives on mutual aid to acknowledge the parallels between grounded accountability and mutual aid and then uses this framework to examine contemporary pandemic responses and future possibilities. The chapter then asks a number of guiding questions for future research and practice.

The paralysis of the market economy meant that for many, new alternative modes of survival that are resilient and sustainable had to be reinvented. In this aspect, many Pacific communities had to fall back on indigenous social solidarity economies, a form of which is direct reciprocity, commonly known as bartering. In Chapter 11, Glen Finau and Romitesh Kant provide an analysis of bartering as a form of resilience building during COVID-19, focusing on Fiji. With an ailing economy, lack of liquidity and inadequate government support, one would think that this would push Fijians into a situation of economic despair, increased crime and potential mass revolt. However, this has been far from the case. One of the most interesting developments in Fiji during COVID-19 has been the emergence of a barter economy facilitated by social media. The Barter for Better Fiji (BFBF) initiative is a Facebook page that was created by three Fijian women to help individuals in Fiji access essential goods such as groceries by bartering for other goods and services. The page has become a national and regional phenomenon, with outgrowths of the page also being created in other Pacific Island countries and in major economies with large Pacific Island communities. This chapter explores the re-emergence of Fiji's barter economy as an alternative form of community-based and internet-mediated social protection during the COVID-19 crisis.

Chapter 12 also provides a discussion of community responses to COVID-19, focusing on West Papuan students' responses to educational and economic challenges during the COVID-19 pandemic. The authors, Jhon Urasti Blesia, Efraim Lokden and Renny Sulelino provide an analysis of the interrelated pressures facing West Papuan students undertaking online learning while facing strains on their livelihoods during the COVID-19 pandemic. The chapter examines the impacts of the local government's health policy of increased social restrictions and educational institutions' termination of face-to-face learning interactions for West Papuan students. It presents the accounts of nine indigenous students enrolled at the local public university regarding their learning experiences and economic challenges. The chapter examines the difficulties faced by students in adapting to new learning methods, the lack of learning facilities and support and challenges from unclear communication of their learning activities. Students were also challenged by economic issues and the impacts of the pandemic on their families, communities and regional development. Besides the students' own efforts, the government, the university and the church have all contributed to addressing these challenges.

The responses to the pandemic by countries differed considerably with many industrialized economies struggling to come to terms with the unfolding calamity. The US is one of those countries whose response capacity has been criticized for being chaotic and unbecoming of a political, economic and technological superpower. Jeffery Willis provides an analysis of this in Chapter 13, focusing on the response of the United States Federal Government to the coronavirus crisis, in particular, the narrative constructed by Donald J. Trump. Since first coming to the attention of the global public in January 2020, few countries in the world have been as severely impacted by the novel coronavirus as the US. Though it holds just four percent of the world's total population, as of mid-2020, the US leads the world with a quarter of confirmed COVID-19 cases and deaths. Despite this dire situation, the administration of former President Trump has frequently downplayed the severity of the virus, and Trump himself has often relayed misinformation to the American public both about the virus itself and his administration's response to it. According to the author, independent analysis has ranked the US last in 'fact-based communications' about the coronavirus when compared to other nations with advanced economies. This chapter provides a chronological overview of how the coronavirus pandemic has unfolded in the US through to September 2020, with a particular focus on the various comments made by President Trump. By drawing on Trump's many public statements, the chapter pieces together the narrative that Trump has constructed about the coronavirus crisis and examines that narrative in light of the broader public health response of the US Federal Government to the pandemic. It argues that Trump's narrative has been erratic, divisive and misleading and that this, combined with a chaotic federal response to the crisis, has undermined public health in the US.

Mobilizing various forms of social capital to consolidate resilience is the subject of Chapter 14 by David Fielding and Stephen Knowles. Aotearoa New Zealand's Alert Level Four lockdown was one of the strictest in the world. The vast majority of New Zealanders not only approved of the restrictions, but also abided by them. The chapter argues that in a democratic society like New Zealand, it would not have been possible for the restrictions to be enforced without there being a high degree of social capital. It compares New Zealand's level of social capital to that of other countries and discusses why New Zealand having high social capital has been important in the fight against COVID-19. It also discusses some lessons from behavioural economics about the conditions under which strict lockdowns become more difficult to enforce, the longer the restrictions are in place.

The vulnerability of children to COVID-19 has been a major issue primarily because of their perceived vulnerability. In Chapter 15, Litea Meo-Sewabu examines the vulnerability of children in Fiji to the impact of COVID-19. The chapter focuses on two key questions. First, what makes children so vulnerable in the Fiji context? Second what are the social protection issues for children in Fiji? Both questions are explored in the context of COVID-19. Elements of child protection and social protection are identified and explored in the context of how children are socialized as Fijians and within the *Vanua* (the traditional cultural establishment). The discussion focuses on issues related to the family web of relationships and networks within the *Vanua*, which can have both positive and negative impacts for vulnerable children. The chapter further explores the contributions, the re-emergence and the reinforcement of the community-based economy, which provides the basis for social protection in the context of the *Vanua*. The chapter explores these community-based networks that have linked people together, as well as provided everyday citizens the opportunity to be of assistance to the most vulnerable in the community.

Conclusion: Some Final Words

Despite their technological advancement, the Martians in *The War of the Worlds* were ignorant of bacteria on planet Earth, and this was their main downfall as they were eliminated by virus-like creatures. The difference here with COVID-19 is that humans may once again be in control after the rollout of vaccination. However, this has not completely solved the problems because the same issues that worsened the pandemic such as inequality, self-interest and ignorance are still prevalent. Pharmaceutical corporations and other privateers have positioned themselves to make a 'killing' from the vaccines, and governments have used it as a means of vaccine nationalism as a way of promoting their respective global geopolitical standing. Despite this, there are some glimmers of hope because, as the book shows, there are community-based initiatives that rely fundamentally on and emphasize the human capacities to cooperate, transform, sustain and build resilience. Indigenous means of responses and resilience, which have sustained communities for ages have once again found relevance in a world dominated by failing neoliberal structures, norms and behaviours.

COVID-19 has caused untold destruction and misery. What started off as a health issue expanded and deepened into a society-wide tragedy, which enveloped every aspect of human existence, including the economy, food security, productivity, inequality, human rights, social relationships, political stability, psychological conditions, communication, education, health and our own sense of identity. The book examines just a small portion of this bigger, interrelated reality, and in a way, it is a work in progress project because the pandemic is still peaking in some countries such as the US, despite promises of the vaccine.

This is one of the first edited books in the social sciences to be written about COVID-19. It is written as snapshot assessment of the pandemic in its early stages, and with the understanding that the issues of social protection and the SSE are long term and both precede and outlive COVID-19. As such, the plan is to produce a follow-up publication that both reassesses the pandemic from a more distant vantage point and reassesses social protection and SSE in a post-COVID-19 environment.

The book also aims to encourage further debates about social protection and the SSE at a time when neoliberal market imperatives are still prominent in defining the norms of economic and social life. It provides a space for the voices of ordinary people to be heard and appreciated, not as irritants that undermine the march of progress as is often assumed by neoliberal ideologues, but as expressions of humanity urging us all to look for alternatives that call for equity and justice in a world where only a few wield power and wealth disproportionate to their size.

References

Asian Development Bank. 2011. *ADB and social protection: Challenges and opportunities*. Metro Manila.

Barrientos, Armando, and Leonith Hinojosa-Valencia. 2009. *A review of social protection in Latin America*. Brighton: Institute of Development Studies.

Beckert, Jens. 2020. The exhausted futures of neoliberalism: From promissory legitimacy to social anomy. *Journal of Cultural Economy* 13 (3): 318–330. https://doi.org/10.1080/17530350.2019.1574867.

Cartwright, Frederic, and Michael Biddins. 2020. *Disease and history: From ancient times to COVID-19*. Borough: Lume Books.

Darcy, James. 2004. *Conflict and social protection: Social protection in situations of violent conflict and its aftermath*. Theme Paper 5. London: Overseas Development Institute.

Davies, Mark, and Allister McGregor. 2009. Social protection responses to the financial crisis: What do we know. *IDS in Focus Policy Briefing* 7 (4).

Davies, Mark, Jennifer Leavy, Tom Mitchell, and Thom Tanner. 2008. Social protection and climate change adaption. *Report Prepared for the Commission on Climate Change and Development*. Brighton: Institute of Development Studies.

Devereux, Stephen, and Rachel Sabates-Wheeler. 2004. Transformative social protection. IDS Working Paper 232. Brighton: Institute of Development Studies.

Devereux, Stephen, and Rachel Cipryk. 2009. *Social protection in Sub-Saharan Africa: A regional review*. Brighton: Institute of Development Studies.

Diwakar, Vidya. 2020. From pandemics to poverty: Hotspots of vulnerability in times of crisis. Emerging analysis and ideas. ODI. https://www.odi.org/sites/odi.org.uk/files/resource-documents/coronavirus_from_pandemics_to_poverty3.pdf.

Fullman, Nancy, Rafael Lozano, Christopher J. L. Murray, Jamal Yearwood, Ryan M. Barber, Julian Chalek, Erika Eldrenkamp, and Chloe Shields. 2018. Measuring performance on the Healthcare Access and Quality Index for 195 countries and territories and selected subnational locations: A systematic analysis from the Global Burden of Disease Study 2016. *Lancet* 391: 2236–2271. https://doi.org/10.1016/S0140-6736(18)30994-2.

Harvey, Paul. 2009. Social protection in fragile states: Lessons learned. In *Promoting pro-poor growth: Social protection*, 183–196. Paris: ECD DAC.

Harvey, Paul, and Rebecca Holmes. 2007. *The potential for joint programmes for long-term cash transfers in unstable situations*. London: Overseas Development Institute.

Hathaway, Terry. 2020. Neoliberalism as corporate power. *Competition and Change* 24 (3–4): 315–337. https://doi.org/10.1177/1024529420910382.

Heltberg, Rasmus, Steen Lau Jorgensen, and Paul Bennett Siegel. 2008. *Climate change, human vulnerability, and social risk management*. Washington, DC: World Bank.

Hickey, Samuel. 2007. *Conceptualising the politics of social protection in Africa*. BWPI Working Paper 4. World Poverty Institute, University of Manchester.

Holmes, Rebecca, and Nicola Anne Jones. 2009. *Putting the social back into social protection: A framework for understanding the linkages between economic and social risks for poverty reduction*. London: Overseas Development Institute.

ILO. 2012. *Social protection for all: Building social protection floors and comprehensive social security systems*. Geneva.

ILO. 2020a. Social protection responses to the COVID-19 crisis: Country responses and policy considerations. In *Social protection spotlight, 23 April 2020 Issue*. Geneva.

ILO. 2020b. *Social protection responses to COVID-19 in Asia and the Pacific: The story so far and future considerations*. Geneva.

Kelly, Heath. 2011. The classic definition of a pandemic is not elusive. *Bulletin of the World Health Organization* 89: 540–541. https://doi.org/10.2471/BLT.11.088815.

Köhler, Gabriele, Marta Cali, and Mariana Stirbu. 2009. *Social protection in South Asia: A review*. Kathmandu: UNICEF Regional Office for South Asia.

Laville, Jean-Louis. 2010. The solidarity economy: An international movement. *RCCS Annual Review* 2: 3–41. https://doi.org/10.4000/rccsar.202.

Lazonick, William, and Mary O'Sullivan. 2000. Maximizing shareholder value: A new ideology for corporate governance. *Economy and Society* 29 (1): 13–35. https://doi.org/10.1080/030851400360541.

Martinez, Sara Calvo, Andrés Morales Pachón, José Maria Martin, and Valetín Molina Moreno. 2019. Solidarity economy, social enterprise, and innovation discourses: Understanding hybrid forms in postcolonial Colombia. *Social Sciences* 8 (7): 205. https://doi.org/10.3390/socsci8070205.

McCord, Anna. 2009. *Cash transfers and political economy in sub-Saharan Africa*. London: ODI.

McKinley, Terry. 2013. *The social protection index: Assessing results for Asia and the Pacific*. Metro Manila: Asian Development Bank.

McNeill, William. 1976. *Plagues and peoples*. New York: Bantam Doubleday Dell Publishing Group.

Mirowski, Philip. 2013. *Never let a serious crisis go to waste: How neoliberalism survived the financial meltdown*. London: Verso Books.

Norton, Andrew, Tim Conway, and Mick Foster. 2001. *Social protection concepts and approaches: Implications for policy and practice in international development*. London: ODI.

Nuclear Threat Initiative, Johns Hopkins University, and The Economist. 2020. *GHS index: Global health security index: Building collective action and accountability*. NTI. https://www.ghsindex.org/wp-content/uploads/2020/04/2019-Global-Health-Security-Index.pdf.

Parks, Will, and David Abbott. 2009. *Protecting Pacific Island children and women during economic and food crises: Working edition one for advocacy, debate and guidance*. Suva, Fiji: UNICEF Pacific and UNDP Pacific.

Pawar, Manohar. 2020. *The global impact of and responses to the COVID-19 pandemic*. New Delhi: Sage.

Rafaelli, Paola. 2017. Social and solidarity economy in a neoliberal context: Transformative or palliative? The case of an Argentinean worker cooperative.

Journal of Entrepreneurial and Organizational Diversity 5: 33–53. https://doi.org/10.5947/jeod.2016.003.
Ratuva, Steven. 2010. Back to basics: Towards integrated social protection for vulnerable groups in Vanuatu. *Pacific Economic Bulletin* 25 (3): 40–63.
Ratuva, Steven. 2014. 'Failed' or resilient subaltern communities? Pacific indigenous social protection systems in a neoliberal world. *Pacific Journalism Review: Te Koakoa* 20 (2): 40–58. https://doi.org/10.24135/pjr.v20i2.165.
Raworth, Kate. 2007. Adapting to climate change: What's needed in poor countries, and who should pay. *Oxfam Policy and Practice: Climate Change and Resilience* 3 (1): 42–88.
Roubini, Nouriel. 2020. Coronavirus pandemic has delivered the fastest, deepest economic shock in history. *The Guardian*, 25 March. https://www.theguardian.com/business/2020/mar/25/coronavirus-pandemic-has-delivered-the-fastest-deepest-economic-shock-in-history.
Saad-Filho, Alfredo. 2020. From COVID-19 to the end of neoliberalism. *Critical Sociology* 46 (4–5): 477–485. https://doi.org/10.1177/0896920520929966.
Schiller, Ulene, and Gideon de Wet. 2019. Indigenous cultural and social work practices creating inequalities among foster care adolescents in decision-making processes. *International Social Work* 62 (1): 22–34. https://doi.org/10.1177/0020872817710548.
Shepherd, Andrew, Rachel Marcus, and Armando Barrientos. 2004. *Policy paper on social protection*. London: UK Department for International Development (DFID).
Slater, Rachel, and Anna McCord. 2009. *Social protection, rural development and food security: Issues paper on the role of social protection in rural development*. London: Overseas Development Institute.
Szreter, Simon. 2009. *The new political economy: The importance of social capital*. In Juan Somavia (Ed.), *The global financial crisis and its impact on the work of the global financial system*. Geneva: UN System Chief Executives Board for Coordination.
UNTFSSE. 2017. Social and solidarity economy as a means to implement the SDGs: Partnerships to bridge the financing gap. https://www.un.org/esa/ffd/wp-content/uploads/2017/03/UN-Inter-Agency-Task-Force-on-Social-and-Solidarity-Economy-submission_May2017.pdf. Accessed 31 October 2020.
UNTFSSE. 2020. What role for the social and solidarity economy in the post COVID-19 crisis recovery. https://www.ilo.org/wcmsp5/groups/public/---ed_emp/---emp_ent/---coop/documents/publication/wcms_748794.pdf.
van Doorslaer, Eddy, and Xander Koolman. 2004. Explaining the differences in income-related health inequalities across European countries. *Health Economy* 13 (7): 609–628. https://doi.org/10.1002/hec.918.

Viana, Ana Luiza d'Ávila, and Hudson Pacifico da Silva. 2018. Neoliberal meritocracy and financial capitalism: Consequences for social protection and health. *Ciencia and saude coletiva* 23 (7): 2107–2117. https://doi.org/10.1590/1413-81232018237.07582018.

Walsham, Matthew, Hannah Kuper, Lena Morgon Banks, and Karl Blanchet. 2019. Social protection for people with disabilities in Africa and Asia: A review of programmes for low-and middle-income countries. *Oxford Development Studies* 47 (1): 97–112. https://doi.org/10.1080/13600818.2018.1515903.

Waring, Marilyn, Anit N. Mukherjee, Elizabeth Reid, and Meena Shivdas. 2013. *Anticipatory social protection: Claiming dignity and rights*. London: Commonwealth Secretariat.

WHO. 2017. *World health statistics 2017: Monitoring health for the Sustainable Development Goals*. Geneva.

CHAPTER 2

Social Protection and Social Determinants of Health in COVID-19 and Related Disasters: What Can We Do About Them?

Arindam Basu

Introduction

Health of the populations and individual health statuses are influenced by their social position and social situations determine health of people. In this sense, health is not only a 'state' but also a resource that needs to be nurtured over people's lifetimes. Poverty, or lack of material resources impact health adversely and in particular, result in infectious diseases as people are forced to live in damp, crowded conditions. This is particularly relevant in the face of outbreaks of diseases that can shut down economies and force people into poverty where such conditions exacerbate.

The SARS-COV-2 viral outbreak is a currently ongoing pandemic worldwide is a case in point. This has resulted in widespread lockdowns in different countries. While lockdown are used as containment measures

A. Basu (✉)
School of Health Sciences, University of Canterbury, Sheffield, Canterbury, New Zealand
e-mail: arindam.basu@canterbury.ac.nz

S. Ratuva et al. (eds.), *COVID-19 and Social Protection*,
https://doi.org/10.1007/978-981-16-2948-8_2

to control the spread of the virus and limit viral infection, it also has the downstream effect of shutting down part or whole economies, thus leading to further worsening of poverty and social distress. The World Bank has estimated that in the wake of COVID-19, 60–70 million more poor people will be added to the pool of already existent poor population around the world, due to emergence of noveau poor.

So what needs to be done? One possible way to address the problem of poverty and ill-health of societies in the wake of COVID-19 is to strengthen social protection measures. Social protection refers to the funds catering to the mix of programmes and policies governments establish to protect the vulnerable members of the society from poverty-related adverse life events and circumstances. These programmes prevent and mitigate adverse consequences of poverty by providing a scaffold so that people can lead a sustainable healthy life and maintain their mental, physical and social well-being. Beyond such protection, such programmes ensure inclusive and sustainable growth.

Hence, the goal of this chapter is to examine social protection policies and develop models to address what may happen and what needs to be done to strengthen social protection systems for securing the health and well-being of vulnerable populations in the face of unforeseen phenomena such as natural disasters and outbreaks that threaten the structure of existent social protection and threaten the sustainability of the target populations.

Inequality, Inequity and Social Determinants of Health

The World Health Organisation (WHO) defines health in terms of a state of complete physical, mental and social well-being (*Frequently Asked Questions* 1948). As knowledge has accumulated since 1948, this definition, scholars in the field have critiqued this definition of health as it emphasised medicalisation of health and 'completeness'. The Ottawa Charter has thus redefined the concept of health in holistic terms and resources that include peace, shelter, education, availability of food and social justice (*WHO | The Ottawa Charter for Health Promotion* 1986). Huber et al. argue that while the original definition of health might have been useful to conceptualise health as a state of well-being back in 1948, such a framing of health has lost its relevance in the twenty-first century (Huber et al. 2011). Be that as it may, if we frame health both as a resource and as a state, it helps us to conceptualise how social systems and changes over time can drive peoples' health. Here, let us consider poverty as one such driver, and how unprecedented pandemics, in our case, COVID-19 can alter the state and affect health as a resource.

The World Bank defines a person as poor if they can afford to spend less than US $1.95 per day, and on this basis, the Bank has estimated that worldwide, 50–60 million such people exist. They contend that after the COVID-19 pandemic, the number of poor people worldwide will likely increase by about 70 million as more people will be added to the pool of poor people, dubbing such noveau poor people as 'new poor' (The World Bank 2020).

Poverty is associated with a number of related downstream effects. Denavas-walt et al. state based on US census data that about 29% of poor people aged 25 years or older do not complete high school, and another 15% of people may have completed high school, but do not attain higher education. Data published by the World Bank for the time period between 1990 and 2014 indicate over 50% of the world's poor live in Sub-Saharan Africa and South Asia. Further,while the proportion of poor people worldwide has dropped in the three decades starting in the 1990s, poverty has increased in Sub-Saharan Africa and as of 2014 and beyond, they remain the poorest region of the world.

Lack of material resources leads to loss of an individual's or a community's social status. In turn, this leads to worsening of their health and wellness. This speaks to the framing of health as a resource. Consider for example, in New Zealand, death rates from cancers of urinary bladder, breast cancer among women, cervical cancer, colorectal cancer and cancers of the head and neck are higher among poor people than among the non-poor (Table 2.1).

Table 2.1 Differences in cancer rates for selected cancers reproduced from the cancer trends document (Blakely et al. 2012)

Cancer site	*Summary of excess death rates (%)*
Bladder cancer	15
Female breast cancer	28
Cervical cancer	25
Colorectal cancer	13
Head and neck cancer	28

Poor people tend to live in houses that are dark and damp, and there is also a risk of overcrowding. As a result, in poor households the risk of infectious diseases is high. In particular, spread of those diseases that spread via cough and sputum when people are close to each other, are particularly high. This is why among the poor people, illnesses and hospitalisation rates due to respiratory infections that are propagated among close contacts are high (Table 2.2).

Worldwide, poverty accounts for a significant burden of mental illnesses, heart diseases, tuberculosis, malaria and HIV/AIDS. The term 'burden' here refers to a composite of two-related concepts: how much deaths are attributed to diseases that lead to loss of life and therefore lost time, and how much illnesses lead to people staying in hospitals and homes where they cannot participate in active life and there results in not only loss of productivity but also loss of time contributed to public life and earning. From this perspective, among poor people, tuberculosis, malaria and HIV/AIDS add significantly to burden of illnesses and also are manifestations of poverty-associated public health problems (Table 2.3). Poverty adds significantly to the global burden of diseases and disability.

As can be seen in Fig. 2.1, poverty acts through a number of different pathways and results in both unequal distribution of health and wellness and inequitable access to healthcare. Poor people end up with less than optimum material resources and poverty is a root cause of unequal distribution of resources among the members of the society. This is intuitive, but poverty also leads to loss of one's right to health. This is because

Table 2.2 Hospitalisations due to close contact infectious diseases (CCID) in New Zealand and their relationships with ethnicity and deprivation data (Baker et al. 2010, p. 10)

Cause of hospitalisation and parameter	*Ethnicity difference figures (%)*
All CCID hospitalisation, all ages	European: 23.6 Māori: 29.1 Pasifika: 32.9
All CCID hospitalisations, under five	European: 54.9 Māori: 65.1 Pasifika: 68.9
All CCID hospitalisations, all ages	NZ Deprivation Index 1–2: 16.6 NZ Deprivation Index 9–10: 21.0

Table 2.3 Evidence on the association between poverty and illnesses, based on United Nations Population Fund (2002)

Parameter	*Value*
Life expectancy at birth	Least developed countries: 50 years Most developed countries: 77 years
Pregnancy-related death rates	600 times higher in poorer countries compared with richer countries
Case load of HIV/AIDS	38.5 million in Developing Countries 1.5 million in Developed Countries

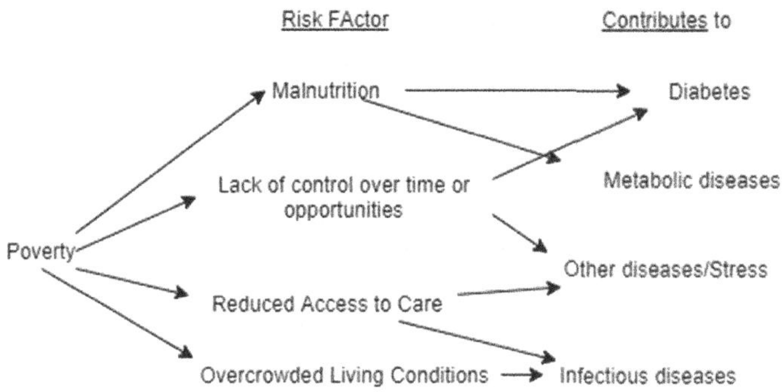

Fig. 2.1 Pathways of poverty causing diseases

poverty leads to situations where people's access to health and health care services are hampered because of their lack of material resources and lack of time that would be needed to access health services. A poor person does not have the flexibility of foregoing earning so that the person can attend a clinic when ill. A poor person may not have access to transportation or flexibility of working hours adjustment so that they can access health services. As a result, access to care for poor people are inequitable because in these situations, for such people, their access to care is determined by their social status, and not on the basis of their clinical, physiological or biologically driven urgency or need. For example, if a poor person suffers from diabetes and needs care in an outpatients department of a hospital that only offers a fixed time window (say between 9 a.m. and 12 p.m.) for consulting, a poor person working inflexible hours is much less likely to attend such clinics as opposed to a relatively well-off white-collar worker who can adjust working hours. This sets up a poor person to suffer much worse health outcome than a better-off person. Thus parameters other than biological, pathological or clinical urgency determine which members of the society can access and utilise healthcare. Lou Ann Aday and Ronal Andersen, while theorising about behavioural access to health care, termed such access to care as inequitable access to care level of access to care (Aday and Andersen 1974).

Such lack of access implies that even though governments and local authorities may indiscriminately make available the healthcare facilities and care to every member of the society without regard to their ability to access them, in reality such access may never happen in the context of inequitable access to health services. An inequitable health system does not guarantee that everyone will be equally able to access and utilise such services, for the mere availability of a resource does not guarantee its utilisation.

Such lack of access to care has other implications. For example, the burden of heart disease such as high blood pressure and chronic heart failure is high among the poor (Kwan et al. 2016). However, these diseases can be effectively controlled if people were to receive care provided in outpatients services; in turn, this would reduce resource utilisation for inpatient care in hospitals saving the health system time and resources such as services of expert cardiologists. Unfortunately, for reasons we have discussed earlier in this chapter such services may be out of bounds for many poor people. In particular, people with heart diseases who work day-shifts with few opportunities to take leave from work, or those who work long or inflexible work hours cannot afford to attend outpatients departments for ambulatory care; such people are likely to be poor. At the other end of the spectrum, many people such as middle-level managers, or those whose jobs allow them enough flexibility so that they can attend outpatients departments for their treatment have a higher chance of survival and less complications and risk of hospitalisation. In this way, poverty leads to inequitable access to heart health are and perpetuates heart disease burden in the society. This example illustrates how poverty, and resultant social inequality and inequitable access, account for and complicate health outcomes for individuals and populations. Following COVID-19 pandemic, we believe that this disparity will further accentuate. Besides, they will be complicated following climate-related emergencies, mass displacement of people, wars and many other environmental disasters such as floods, wildfires and further epidemics. In this way, lack of material resources, people becoming poor on account of such deficiencies, social inequality and vulnerability to further distress form a vicious cycle.

Individual and societal vulnerability to adversity worsen population health outcomes. What is vulnerability after all? Kristie Ebi et al. (2006) provide a working definition of vulnerability in the context of environmental health where it is widely discussed. They define vulnerability in terms of sensitivity—the extent to which health and health outcomes depend on the changing life circumstances. In the context of a pandemic as in COVID-19, a further catastrophic flood and natural emergency on the top of it can have disastrous health and poverty consequences. First, a flood or forest fire or an earthquake leads to people being displaced. This displacement leads to overcrowding, and overcrowding in turn can lead to new and in case of pre-existing infections, worsening of the epidemic characterised by respiratory infection in face of person to person transmission when they are in close proximity.. Further, a disaster on the top of COVID-19 will likely also lead to stress-related worsening of depression and anxiety and risks of heart disease. As a result, when populations face unprecedented disasters, the most vulnerable in the society are likely to suffer from the highest burden of diseases and disabilities, not only because of their limited access to care services, but also because poor people have low health resources to deal with emergency situations. Such worsening of health conditions in times of the COVID-19 pandemic poses significant challenges to both public health communities and health policy makers worldwide.

Emergence of COVID-19 and How This Pandemic Can Worsen Inequality-Related Diseases

The Story of COVID-19

In December of 2019, an outbreak of viral respiratory illnesses emerged in the Hubei province of China and subsequently over 2020, this outbreak spread across the world (*WHO | Pneumonia of Unknown Cause—China*, 2020). This disease is caused by exposure to coronavirus SARS-COV-2 believed to originate in a wet market in Wuhan. From first infection to manifestation of symptoms, a variable number of days occur, and many individuals are asymptomatic, but can pass the infection on to others. The disease itself is characterised by a dry hacking cough and fever, spreading droplets in the air and thus transmitting the viral particles in droplets to people nearby or unprotected and who are in close contact; thus the infection itself spreads via respiratory droplets and fomites on surfaces and is highly contagious: in the initial phases of the outbreak, one person can transmit the virus to anywhere between two to three people (Wang et al. 2020). The virus has a variable incubation period of about five days, and an average reproduction number, i.e. the number of persons an infected person can in turn infect is about 2.5 (He et al. 2020; Lauer et al. 2020; McAloon et al. 2020; Nishiura et al. 2020; Park et al. 2020; Singhal 2020; Tindale et al. 2020; Wang et al. 2020) (Table 2.4).

Hennegan et al. have estimated that between five and 80% people are asymptomatic (*COVID-19* 2020). Although the characteristic of this viral outbreak is similar in nature to the influenza pandemic of 1918, its magnitude and impact is more pervasive. The WHO declared COVID-19 a public health emergency of international concern (PHEIC) on 30th January and followed up with a formal declaration of pandemic on 11th March (Cucinotta and Vanelli 2020).

By November, over 45 million people have been confirmed with the disease and over a million people have died from this infection already (WHO 2020). An effective vaccine is not yet available (Corey et al. 2020). Given what is known about the transmission of the virus, to protect the vulnerable members of the public from viral infection, governments around the world have put in place country-wide social distancing and some countries have enforced 'lockdowns' where they have allowed very limited opportunities for people to interact face to face with each other, and people have largely been confined home. This has led to unforeseen situations with worsening poverty, job losses and economic downturn in many countries that have had protracted lockdowns.

Table 2.4 Average incubation period of COVID-19

Author	*Estimates of incubation period*
Lauer (2020)	5.1
Nishiura (2020)	4.6
He (2020)	5.2
McAloon (2020)	5.1
Singhal (2020)	2–14 days
Park (2020)	4–6 days
Velavan	3 days (Range: 0–24 days)
Tindale (2020)	7.1
Wang (2020)	6.4 (Range: 0–24 days)

Anderson et al. has argued that using lockdown as a control strategy, governments may be able to limit the spread of the disease, but they may not be able to salvage economic fallouts (Anderson et al. 2020). In the six months since the declaration of pandemic by The WHO, commercial air travel is down by 55%, most airports around the world are closed to the public traffic, borders between countries are virtually shut down (other than allowing repatriation or special flights), and tourism and hospitality in most countries have severely suffered (Petchenik 2020). On the other hand, e-commerce and information technology services such as remote videoconferencing usage have increased worldwide by over 77% (Koetsier 2020).

Lockdowns have adversely affected businesses that rely on face to face transactions and reduced commercial activities have resulted in job losses. Yet, due to reliance on the internet for conducting online transactions such as virtual meetings, online commerce and those who work in networking and videoconferencing, have experienced growth. On the other hand, relatively low-paid jobs of barbers, waiters and couriers and others whose trade involve close contact with clients are at high risk of contracting COVID-19. Note that they are also lower paid than white collar workers whose work can be accomplished online. Because of this, COVID-19 has effectively perpetuated poverty and inequality so that white collar better paid workers continue to retain their jobs while blue collar workers whose jobs depend on face to face transactions tend to suffer loss of their trades and income. Even among those with white collar jobs, not everyone has benefitted equally; Campello et al. have reported that COVID-19 has resulted in drops of corporate hiring in 2020 across the board; this implies that some sectors have indeed flourished while other trades have suffered (Campello et al. 2020).

Another challenge of COVID-19 is organisation and provision of available health services. As addressing the COVID-19 pandemic is urgent for healthcare organisations worldwide, in countries that have a heavy burden of COVID-19, admission to many departments such as cancer care units is either curtailed or practices such as those in cancer wards are significantly altered (*Cancer, Coronavirus Are a Dangerous Mix, New Studies Find* 2020; Søreide et al. 2020). As a result, in several countries, vital public health activities have either been underfunded or are being stalled. This is further likely to accentuate disparity in care provision.

One can nevertheless argue that the gamut of socioeconomic and population health impacts of COVID-19 has not been fully realised.

Based on early signs, it is anticipated that this will lead to the emergence of millions more poor people; poverty will in turn intensify social disparity and inequality, and Hogan et al. (2020) have estimated that following the COVID-19 pandemic, prevalence of HIV/AIDS, tuberculosis and malaria will increase by 10%, 20% and 36% worldwide, indicating that diseases and conditions associated with health inequity will increase (Hogan et al. 2020).

How Might COVID-19 Exacerbate Poverty and Social Inequality and What Can We Do?

As we have argued in the preceding sections, COVID-19 will exacerbate poverty, worsen inequality and inequity of access to health services, and in this way worsen health and well-being of populations across the world. While the world grapples with unforeseen challenges, there are also mechanisms in place that are aimed to mitigate such challenges. We turn to a discussion of those issues next as poverty is not new and has been at the forefront of the policy makers' minds in their framing of millennium development goals and sustainability.

At the turn of the century, when the United Nations framed the millennium development goals (MDGs) and later in 2015, when they adopted sustainable development indicators, reduction of poverty was a major theme (dpicampaigns 2020). In accordance with this, they emphasised the role of social protection as it was obvious that building resources and allowing people to access such resources alone were not enough to achieve sustainable development. It was equally important to build 'scaffolds' so that economically and socially weaker sections of the society can be protected against the effects of poverty and vulnerability that results from these shocks (Asian Development Bank 2011). Social protection itself can mitigate adverse impacts of social determinants of health and can help in addressing inequality and inequities that exist in access to healthcare.

The Role of Social Protection in Mitigating the Adverse Effects of Poverty

Essentially, social protection refers to funds that countries and societies set aside for the poor and vulnerable populations although this benefits everyone, regardless of their economic status. Social protection in essence refers to an overall suite of strategies and policies that governments and societies adopt to reduce poverty and reduce vulnerability of the people so that their lives and livelihoods are protected against adversity. This includes mitigation of different types of risks that people face, steps that governments and societies can take to increase people's resilience and build capacity, and increase their participation in the labour market. Five entities make up social protection, including reduction of (1) poverty, (2) vulnerability of people when they fall into adverse circumstances, (3) risk (4) promoting participation of people in the labour force of the society and (5) capacity enhancement.

Social insurance refers to social contributory schemes between governments and their citizenries. These are meant to mitigate the risks people face due to life circumstances. These include unemployment benefits, old age pensions and provision of health insurance. Social assistance refers to the transfer of funds (cash/non-cash) to the needy. Importantly, such transfers are endowments and not loans, usually in the form of child welfare payments, elderly benefits, healthcare assistance, disability benefits and other miscellaneous social benefits. Finally, labour market-related social protection measures are those that are aimed at enabling people to secure employment, increasing the size of the workforce, or getting people to either enter or stay in the workforce. These are usually in the form of cash or food for work and provision of training so that people can skill themselves to be workforce-ready, beyond traditional school or college education.

In summary, the following ten entities constitute the space of social protection:

1. Unemployment benefits (social insurance)
2. Old age pension (social insurance)
3. Health insurance (social insurance)
4. Child welfare (social assistance)
5. Elderly benefits (social assistance)
6. Healthcare assistance (social assistance)
7. Disability benefits (social assistance)
8. Disaster reliefs (social assistance)
9. Cash/food for work (labour market)
10. Training (labour market)

Estimation of Social Protection: Social Protection Indicator

Each government provides for these 10 items, and the expenditure in these entities is measurable so that one can directly compare different countries, and even within countries, different regions as to their performances. The Asian Development Bank, for instance, has developed a series of formulae to compare the overall and sectoral expenses, referred to as social protection indicators. The base indicator is the amount of money spent as fraction of the per capita GDP of a country divided over the number of eligible beneficiaries. These are further subdivided into various units such as indicators for women versus men, poor versus non-poor and over each of the three entities: that of social insurance, social assistance and labour market programmes. In general, social insurance and social assistance receive the bulk of the financing, and very little is spent for labour market programmes, and that too is mostly spent in cash or food for work, rather than skill development programmes worldwide.

There can be a number of possible configurations here. Some countries can thinly spread out the payment over a large proportion of the population, although each payee may not receive a lot of money as payment. This is the case with the more developed countries with larger payment bases in Asia-Pacific such as Japan and Korea (Asian Development Bank 2011). On the other end of the spectrum are other countries such as Bangladesh, India and generally, the countries within South Asia, who tend to pay out a smaller fraction of all eligible payees, but when they pay out, the payment is "deep" although the spread is thin (op.cit.).

These indicators enable policy makers to understand how social protection disbursements are distributed among the general members of the public, the various ways such payments are distributed, the depth and breadth of the disbursements, how different groups receive them based on their financial status, and how individuals receive the funds based on their gender. In each case, international or sectoral comparisons make use of the country's GDP and identify the relevant population. The underlying assumption in social protection is that, by allocating and actually paying out funds in the specific areas (social insurance, social assistance and labour market programmes), policy makers have ensured that appropriate utilisation of the services available is taking place, and that risks are mitigated based on available resources. However, these allocations ignore how individuals within each of these categories are benefitted;

these disbursement formulae also do not take into account informal, more qualitative ways in which social support networks enable social protection. In particular, such informal networks of support are moot to understand how communities maintain resilience in the face of uncertainties faced in pandemics and disasters.

How do we know that social protection measures are working in the way they should? One can argue that if social protection measures were to work as they are intended, then in those areas of the world or those economies and those countries that enjoy high levels of social protection, we would see a reduction in incidence of tuberculosis, HIV/AIDS and malaria. In contrast, in countries where social protection is not prevalent or low, we would see high rates of diseases attributed to poverty and malnutrition.

Further, one can argue that countries that have robust social protection policies in place will be better off in managing the pandemic (Gerard et al. 2020). Indeed, countries within strong social protection measures such as Taiwan and New Zealand have shown better control of the epidemic while United States and India, two countries with relatively lower social protection for vulnerable populations have seen large number of cases and repeated lockdown measures. At the same time, burden of COVID-19 appears to be low in Africa, and part of this low burden might be explained on the basis of low levels of testing in this part of the world due to resource constraints and therefore, the full impact of COVID-19 may not have been realised.

Conclusion

In conclusion, it is anticipated that by its nature and how the world has responded to COVID-19 so far, poverty and its downstream effects on public health will be exacerbated. In this sense, COVID-19 presents an unprecedented challenge to health systems and governance worldwide, in particular, achievement of millennium and sustainable development goals. While such challenges are new, globally, as we have strengthened and systematically addressed the challenge of poverty using social protection, the challenge can be met. More work is needed to stage a response using social protection and to measure the successes of social protection to mitigate the adverse impacts of this pandemic.

References

Aday, Lou Ann, and Ronald Andersen. 1974. A framework for the study of access to medical care. *Health Services Research* 9 (3): 208.

Anderson, Ronald M., H. Heesterbeek, D. Klinkenberg, and T.D. Hollingsworth. 2020. How will country-based mitigation measures influence the course of the COVID-19 epidemic? *The Lancet*: S0140673620305675. https://doi.org/10.1016/S0140-6736(20)30567-5.

Asian Development Bank (ed.). 2011. *The revised social protection index*. Asian Development Bank.

Baker, Michael, L. Telfar Barnard, J. Zhang, T. Lanumata, M. Keall, A. Verrall, and P. Howden-Chapman. 2010. *Close-contact infectious diseases in New Zealand: Trends and ethnic inequalities in hospitalisations, 1989 to 2008*. Wellington: University of Otago; He Kāinga Oranga. http://www.healthyhousing.org.nz/wp-content/uploads/2010/06/Close-contact-IDs-2nd-edition1.pdf.

Blakely, Tony, and M. Soeberg. 2012. *Cancer trends: Trends in cancer survival by ethnic and socioeconomic group : New Zealand, 1991–2004*. New Zealand: Ministry of Health. https://www.health.govt.nz/system/files/documents/publications/cancer-trends-survival-ethnic-socioeconomic-1991-2004_1.pdf.

Campello, Marcia, G. Kankanhalli, and P. Muthukrishnan. 2020. Corporate hiring under COVID-19: Labor market concentration, downskilling, and income inequality. Working Paper No. 27208; Working Paper Series. National Bureau of Economic Research. https://doi.org/10.3386/w27208.

Cancer, coronavirus are a dangerous mix, new studies find. 2020. Hosted, May 28. https://hosted.ap.org/standardspeaker/article/22e14f21fcf5935307a5a0b3810ae20e/cancer-coronavirus-are-dangerous-mix-new-studies-find.

Corey, L., J.R. Mascola, A.S. Fauci, and F.S. Collins. 2020. A strategic approach to COVID-19 vaccine R&D. *Science* 368 (6494): 948–950.

COVID-19: What proportion are asymptomatic?. 2020. CEBM. https://www.cebm.net/covid-19/covid-19-what-proportion-are-asymptomatic/.

Cucinotta, D., and M. Vanelli. 2020. WHO declares COVID-19 a pandemic. *Acta Bio-Medica: Atenei Parmensis* 91 (1): 157–160. https://doi.org/10.23750/abm.v91i1.9397.

dpicampaigns. 2020. Take action for the sustainable development goals. United Nations Sustainable Development. https://www.un.org/sustainabledevelopment/sustainable-development-goals/.

Ebi, Kristie L., Kovats R. Sari, and Menne Bettina. 2006. An approach for assessing human health vulnerability and public health interventions to adapt to climate change. *Environmental Health Perspectives* 114 (12): 1930–1934. https://doi.org/10.1289/ehp.8430.

Frequently asked questions. 1948. https://www.who.int/about/who-we-are/frequently-asked-questions.

Gerard, F., C. Imbert, and K. Orkin. 2020. Social protection response to the COVID-19 crisis: Options for developing countries. *Oxford Review of Economic Policy* 36 (suppl. 1): S281–S296.

He, F., Y. Deng, and W. Li. 2020. Coronavirus disease 2019: What we know? *Journal of Medical Virology* 92 (7): 719–725. https://doi.org/10.1002/jmv.25766.

Hogan, Alexandra B., Britta L. Jewell, Ellie Sherrard-Smith, Juan F. Vesga, Oliver J. Watson, Charles Whittaker, Arran Hamlet, Jennifer A. Smith, Peter Winskill, Robert Verity, Marc Baguelin, John A. Lees, Lilith K. Whittles, Kylie E.C. Ainslie, Samir Bhatt, Adhiratha Boonyasiri, Nicholas F. Brazeau, Lorenzo Cattarino, Laura V. Cooper, Helen Coupland, Gina Cuomo-Dannenburg, Amy Dighe, Bimandra A. Djaafara, Christl A. Donnelly, Jeff W. Eaton, Sabine L. van Elsland, Richard G. FitzJohn, Han Fu, Katy A.M. Gaythorpe, William Green, David J. Haw, Sarah Hayes, Wes Hinsley, Natsuko Imai, Daniel J. Laydon, Tara D. Mangal, Thomas A. Mellan, Swapnil Mishra, Gemma Nedjati-Gilani, Kris V. Parag, Hayley A. Thompson, H. Juliette T. Unwin, Michaela A.C. Vollmer, Caroline E. Walters, Haowei Wang, Yuanrong Wang, Xiaoyue Xi, Neil M. Ferguson, Lucy C. Okell, Thomas S. Churcher, Nimalan Arinaminpathy, Azra C. Ghani, Patrick G.T. Walker, Timothy B. Hallett. 2020. Potential impact of the COVID-19 pandemic on HIV, tuberculosis, and malaria in low-income and middle-income countries: A modelling study. *The Lancet Global Health* 8 (9): e1132–e1141. https://doi.org/10.1016/S2214-109X(20)30288-6.

Huber, M., J. A. Knottnerus, L. Green, H.v.d. Horst, A.R. Jadad, D. Kromhout, B. Leonard, K. Lorig, M.I. Loureiro, J. W.M.v.d. Meer, P. Schnabel, R. Smith, C.v. Weel, and H. Smid. 2011. How should we define health? *BMJ* 343(jul26 2), d4163–d4163. https://doi.org/10.1136/bmj.d4163.

Koetsier, J. 2020. COVID-19 accelerated E-commerce growth '4 to 6 years'. *Forbes*. https://www.forbes.com/sites/johnkoetsier/2020/06/12/covid-19-accelerated-e-commerce-growth-4-to-6-years/.

Kwan, G.F., B.M. Mayosi, A.O. Mocumbi, J.J. Miranda, M. Ezzati, Y. Jain, G. Robles, E.J. Benjamin, S.V. Subramanian, and G. Bukhman. 2016. Endemic cardiovascular diseases of the poorest billion. *Circulation* 133 (24): 2561–2575. https://doi.org/10.1161/circulationaha.116.008731.

Lauer, S.A., K.H. Grantz, Q. Bi, F.K. Jones, Q. Zheng, H.R. Meredith, A.S. Azman, N.G. Reich, and J. Lessler. 2020. The incubation period of coronavirus disease 2019 (COVID-19) from publicly reported confirmed cases: Estimation and application. *Annals of Internal Medicine*. https://doi.org/10.7326/M20-0504.

McAloon, C., Á. Collins, K. Hunt, A. Barber, A.W. Byrne, F. Butler, M. Casey, J. Griffin, E. Lane, D. McEvoy, P. Wall, M. Green, L. O'Grady, and S.J. More. 2020. Incubation period of COVID-19: A rapid systematic review and meta-analysis of observational research. *British Medical Journal Open* 10 (8): e039652. https://doi.org/10.1136/bmjopen-2020-039652.

Nishiura, H., T. Kobayashi, T. Miyama, A. Suzuki, S. Jung, K. Hayashi, R. Kinoshita, Y. Yang, B. Yuan, A.R. Akhmetzhanov, and N.M. Linton. 2020. Estimation of the asymptomatic ratio of novel coronavirus infections (COVID-19) [Preprint]. *Epidemiology*. https://doi.org/10.1101/2020.02.03.20020248.

Park, M., A.R. Cook, J.T. Lim, Y. Sun, and B.L. Dickens. 2020. A Systematic review of COVID-19 epidemiology based on current evidence. *Journal of Clinical Medicine* 9 (4): 967. https://doi.org/10.3390/jcm9040967.

Petchenik, I. 2020. Charting the decline in air traffic caused by COVID-19. *Flightradar24 Blog*, March 29. https://www.flightradar24.com/blog/charting-the-decline-in-air-traffic-caused-by-covid-19/.

Singhal, T. 2020. A review of coronavirus disease-2019 (COVID-19). *The Indian Journal of Pediatrics* 87 (4): 281–286. https://doi.org/10.1007/s12098-020-03263-6.

Søreide, K., J. Hallet, J.B. Matthews, A.A. Schnitzbauer, P.D. Line, P.B.S. Lai, J. Otero, D. Callegaro, S.G. Warner, N.N. Baxter, C.S.C. Teh, J. Ng-Kamstra, J.G. Meara, L. Hagander, and L. Lorenzon. 2020. Immediate and long-term impact of the COVID-19 pandemic on delivery of surgical services. *The British Journal of Surgery*. https://doi.org/10.1002/bjs.11670.

The World Bank. 2020. *Projected poverty impacts of COVID-19 (coronavirus)* [Text/HTML]. World Bank. https://www.worldbank.org/en/topic/poverty/brief/projected-poverty-impacts-of-COVID-19.

Tindale, L., M. Coombe, J.E. Stockdale, E. Garlock, W.Y.V. Lau, M. Saraswat, Y.-H.B. Lee, L. Zhang, D. Chen, J. Wallinga, and C. Colijn. 2020. Transmission interval estimates suggest pre-symptomatic spread of COVID-19 [Preprint]. *Epidemiology*. https://doi.org/10.1101/2020.03.03.20029983.

United Nations Population Fund. 2002. *The state of world population 2002: People, poverty and possibilites*. UNFPA.

Wang, C., P.W. Horby, F.G. Hayden, and G.F. Gao. 2020. A novel coronavirus outbreak of global health concern. *The Lancet* 395 (10223): 470–473. https://doi.org/10.1016/S0140-6736(20)30185-9.

WHO. 2020. *Coronavirus*. https://www.who.int/westernpacific/health-topics/coronavirus.

WHO | Pneumonia of unknown cause—China. 2020. WHO; World Health Organization. http://www.who.int/csr/don/05-january-2020-pneumonia-of-unknown-cause-china/en/.

WHO | The Ottawa Charter for Health Promotion. 1986. WHO; World Health Organization. http://www.who.int/healthpromotion/conferences/previous/ottawa/en/.

CHAPTER 3

Lockdowns, Family Violence and Social Protection

Yvonne Crichton-Hill

Introduction

Family violence, in all its forms, is an important public health and welfare issue. Family violence has a negative impact on family systems, communities and societies. We know that many intersecting factors cause family violence, and that responses to family violence are varied. There is no single internationally agreed definition of family violence; in some contexts, the term 'family violence' is used interchangeably with 'domestic violence', while in other environments, domestic violence is used to refer to violence in intimate relationships. For the purposes of this chapter, family violence refers to various forms of violence that occur within families, including intimate partner violence, elder abuse, child abuse and neglect, violence between siblings and adolescent violence toward parents. This chapter will focus on child abuse and neglect, intimate partner violence and elder abuse.

Y. Crichton-Hill (✉)
University of Canterbury, Christchurch, New Zealand
e-mail: yvonne.crichton-hill@canterbury.ac.nz

S. Ratuva et al. (eds.), *COVID-19 and Social Protection*,
https://doi.org/10.1007/978-981-16-2948-8_3

Social protection policies and programs aim to reduce the impact of poverty and exclusion and thus are intended to 'buffer individuals from shocks and equip them to improve their livelihoods and create opportunities to build a better life for themselves and their families' (World Bank 2012, p. i). Devereux and Sabates-Wheeler (2004) conceptualize social protection in terms of four response categories, including *protective measures* that provide income and social service support to those unable to work; *preventative measures* that aim to prevent deprivation via social insurance or social safety nets for the economically vulnerable, for example, in the form of unemployment benefits; *promotive measures* that aim to enhance incomes, for example, via microfinancing; and *transformative measures* that address inequity and include marginalized groups in collective action to enhance social justice and social equity. Across the world, the form that social protection policies take varies widely in terms of the type of intervention and whether the intervention is delivered by the public or private sector. According to the Devereux and Sabates-Wheeler social protection framework, family violence would be addressed under transformative measures.

In order to address how social protection systems can best respond to family violence, we deal first with the COVID-19 pandemic context.

Current Context

As the seriousness of the COVID-19 crisis expanded across the globe, many countries entered various degrees of lockdown, which essentially required that people stay in their homes as much as possible and only leave their homes for essential activities, such as medical care or grocery shopping. Households maintained physical distance from other households, including from extended family. Those engaged in essential services were able to move outside of their household bubble.

Social isolation was a useful strategy employed by many nations in response to the COVID-19 pandemic, but the requirement of families to live in an isolated bubble can create a breeding ground for violence as families experience increasing economic and psychological stress. Violence in families during COVID-19 has been termed 'the shadow pandemic' (UN Women 2020). Emerging data suggests that, around the world, family violence is likely to increase due to lockdown conditions (UN Women 2020; Usher et al. 2020). However, family violence statistics must be treated with caution especially as statistical data collected is often based on family violence reporting, which is traditionally under-reported with reporting shown to have decreased even further in some places during the COVID-19 pandemic (UNICEF 2020). Before proceeding to an exploration of the social protection response to family violence in a COVID-19 context, it is important to provide an overview of child abuse and neglect, intimate partner violence and elder abuse.

Child Abuse and Neglect

Reports suggest that parents experience stress and parental demands during lockdown conditions that can lead to parental burnout (Griffith 2020). Parental burnout is a sustained response to parental stress, that is, the usual stressors associated with parenting. Parental stress includes concerns about children's behavior, worries about health, or everyday tasks associated with parenting (Mikolajczak et al. 2018). Parental stress is transient. Parental burnout, on the other hand, is more persistent and consists of three elements: pronounced exhaustion, which can impact emotion regulation; increased lack of involvement with children; and parents feeling inadequate in their role as parents (Mikolajczak et al. 2018). During lockdown, in many places around the world, parents were expected to home–school children, while at the same time, maintain job productivity by working from home. Parents who were essential workers and continued to work outside of the home may have felt concerned about the risk of contracting coronavirus. Some parents lost their jobs and were, therefore, under pressure financially. These factors intersected with the COVID-19 lockdown context where parents were unable to access informal or formal supports, which may have reduced the risk of parental burnout. Literature suggests that parental burnout, such as that experienced by many parents during lockdown, increases the risk that child abuse and neglect may occur (Mikolajczak et al. 2018; Miragoli et al. 2020; Rodriguez 2010).

Extant child abuse literature highlights how the accumulation of multiple risk factors in a child's environment, such as conflict in the home, parental criminality, parental stress and burnout and parental mental illness, increase the likelihood of negative impacts on wellbeing across the life span (Bonomi et al. 2008; Felitti 2009; Felitti et al. 1998; Herrenkohl et al. 2013). It can, therefore, be assumed that the COVID-19 pandemic and ensuing lockdown restrictions are another risk factor likely to negatively impact child development and wellbeing.

In New Zealand, women reported to not for profit and government organizations that children during lockdown had experienced a range of violence by their caregiver, including emotional and verbal abuse, neglect (including rejection of medical treatment) and were prevented from engaging in opportunities for learning online (New Zealand Human Rights Commission 2020). In the United Kingdom (UK), there have been increased calls to child help lines (Green 2020) and reports of an increase in the incidence of abusive head trauma at a London hospital (Sidpra et al. 2020). A global report on preventing violence against children (World Health Organization 2020b) states that, with 1.5 billion children impacted by school closures and families facing heightened levels of anxiety and stress while cut off from formal and informal supports, COVID-19 has changed the prevalence of child abuse. It is expected that stabilized rates of child abuse and neglect will be higher than pre COVID-19.

Intimate Partner Violence (IPV)

There is a profusion of literature that underlines the prevalence of IPV with violence against women by an intimate partner recognized as one of the most common forms of violence throughout the world, cutting across boundaries of culture and class (World Health Organization 2013). Global estimates are that '35.6% of women have ever experienced either non-partner sexual violence or physical or sexual violence by an intimate partner, or both' (World Health Organization 2013, p. 20). In other words, prior to the COVID-19 pandemic, it was estimated that one in three women had experienced intimate partner violence. It is known that when natural disasters have occurred there has been an ensuing increase in intimate partner violence reporting and that the risk of violence is increased for women who are migrants or refugees, living in high conflict areas, who have disabilities, are from minority groups and who are living in poverty (Gillum 2019; Kofman and Garfin 2020; World Health Organization 2020a). The impacts of the COVID-19 pandemic are unique because of the introduction of restrictive physical distancing lockdown conditions, which have raised concerns about the likelihood of increased vulnerabilities for women in violent relationships during forced isolation (Sánchez et al. 2020). Perpetrators may use COVID-19 as a form of coercive control (Stark 2009), enhancing a women's fears about COVID-19 by telling her that they have the virus and will infect them, threatening to cough over family members, or preventing access to soap and hand sanitizer, or on the other hand, by forcing excessive handwashing (Fielding 2020; World Health Organization 2020a). The forced isolation is likely to be devastating for many women trapped in violent relationships.

An Australian online survey conducted in May 2020 asked women about their experience of IPV in the three months prior to the survey; that is, in the early stages of the COVID-19 pandemic in Australia (Boxall et al. 2020). Approximately 66% of women who had experienced IPV prior to the pandemic indicated that violence had started or escalated during the three-month period. Many women also indicated that they were unable to seek help due to concerns about their safety. The authors concluded that the pandemic lockdown restrictions, stress and economic worries likely contributed to an increase in IPV. A study in the UK found that 54.8% of women living with the perpetrator reported feeling more afraid during lockdown, while 61.3% said that the violence had worsened during the pandemic, and 25.8% of women stated that they could not access IPV support (Women's Aid 2020).

Elder Abuse

The percentage of older people in the world population is growing, and this means there is likely to be a rise in the number of older persons with disabilities and who are mentally, physically and financially at risk (Ho et al. 2017). Alongside a growing older population is the recognition that elder abuse is a serious health and social problem facing many of the world's societies. The World Health Organization defines elder abuse as:

> a single or repeated act, or lack of appropriate action, occurring within any relationship where there is an expectation of trust, which causes harm or distress to an older person (aged 60 years and older). It includes physical, sexual, psychological/emotional abuse; financial and material abuse; abandonment; neglect; and serious loss of dignity and respect. (World Health Organization 2020c)

A meta-analysis of elder abuse studies from 2002 to 2015 found that, globally, approximately one out of every six older persons has experienced abuse; this figure totals approximately '141 million victims of elder abuse annually' (Yon et al. 2017, p. 152). Despite the global prevalence of elder abuse, less attention has been paid to this form of family violence than other forms, such as child abuse and neglect and intimate partner violence. Additionally, there is a lack of data on elder abuse from low- and middle-income countries and from Asian and African nations (Yon et al. 2017).

COVID-19 has had a particularly damaging impact on older persons as evidenced by the high mortality rate of older persons in long-term care facilities and hospitals as a result of the virus (Ouslander and Grabowski 2020; Sun et al. 2020; Yang et al. 2020). Older persons who remain in their homes during lockdown conditions may experience loneliness and social isolation (Brooke and Jackson 2020), and for those who are living with stressed caregivers or family members and dependent on their support, there is a risk of elder abuse (Han and Mosqueda 2020; Makaroun et al. 2020; Pegorari et al. 2020). Additionally, the financial uncertainty presented by COVID-19 may result in people attempting inappropriately to gain access to older persons' savings to offset their own financial damages (Elman et al. 2020).

To conclude this section, the literature identifies that physical distancing and social isolation has exacerbated vulnerability, and, therefore, the risk of family violence during the pandemic is increased. In the next section, factors that have influenced the development of health and social services provision are explored.

Social Protection Responses to Family Violence

As noted earlier, traditionally, social protection can be viewed as a kind of 'safety net' to support sectors of the population who are susceptible to income deprivation by providing targeted, short-term income support or cash transfers (Sabates-Wheeler et al. 2009). Social protection discourses emphasize the right to live a violence free life, however, COVID-19 and the ensuing lockdown restrictions have resulted in an increased risk of violence and vulnerability. This interplay between dominant ideas about social protection and the actuality of social protection provision in pandemics raises questions as to whether social protection responses at the time of a pandemic enhance equity and access or are barriers to people getting the assistance they need.

Governments around the world put in place measures to protect populations from the virus and also to prevent health systems from collapsing. This required populations to have faith in the state's ability to protect

(Dasgupta et al. 2020). However, to understand global health provision, one must appreciate the influence of neoliberalism and its focus on individual rights, increased competition, increased accountabilities of organizations and an increased focus on risk. Neoliberalism sits at odds with collective responses to health issues and clearly places power in the hands of governments and elites (Kim et al. 2019). The upshot of a neoliberal doctrine, suggests Dasgupta et al. (2020), is a global health system that, for years, has been under-resourced, inequitable in terms of access to health services and medicines and lacking in strong relationships with communities. Additionally, it has been argued that the global health response has been driven by wealthy nations in a particular part of the world; as Byass (2013, p. 1) suggested, 'global health, despite its rapid growth, so far remains a largely northern concept'. Furthermore, framing health as an individual responsibility neglects the powerful influence of social, economic and political contexts on health and wellbeing. The impact of framing health in this way is that interventions and solutions to the health problem are individual programs of behavioral change. It is hardly surprising, therefore, that the response to COVID-19 has put health systems under greater pressure, bringing into central focus the complex connection between health and wellbeing and the physical, social and economic environment (Barton and Grant 2006).

The broader social services sector across the globe has also been influenced by neoliberal aims where, over time, the drive to achieve social justice has been cast aside for the primary aims of limiting expenditure, reducing regulation and reducing the role of the state in people's lives (Ferguson et al. 2005). Social services are thus molded by managerialism and consequently restricted in terms of how and what services are delivered (Garrett 2009). To summarize the matter:

> neoliberal policies emphasized self-funding of access to services (with an effective increase in the contribution of service users to social expenditure), actions focused on the poorer segments of society, decentralization of service provision and management, separation of functions (funding and provision, for example), and competition between different service providers (schools, hospitals, etc.). (Viana and da Silva 2018, p. 2110)

With the onset of COVID-19, health and social services that may have already been under-resourced have been greatly pressured with many organizations hampered in terms of the services they could deliver to struggling families and communities. In particular, the physical distancing and lockdown requirements have posed challenges to those working in the violence field.

Fragmented health and social service systems responding to family violence are in competition for limited resources. The impact of managerialism on professionals working in the family violence field has been apparent in the constraints placed on innovative practice, the reduction of professional autonomy in decision making and the risk averse culture that pervades violence work with families and communities (Chenoweth and McAuliffe, 2017). In fragmented systems, families who experience violence receive inadequate services and may experience formal helping systems as stigmatizing and exclusionary.

So how do already fragmented and under-resourced health and social services systems responsible for implementing social protection policies address family violence in a pandemic context? The next section explores considerations for an integrated response system.

Transformative Measures

The three forms of family violence addressed in this chapter are interconnected, but there are also differences that justify nuanced and targeted social protection responses. For example, one social protection intervention for women in violent relationships, in low- to middle-income countries, is the provision of cash transfers and economic strengthening programs. This is sensible because we know that economic strengthening is connected with reductions in IPV (Peterman et al. 2020). On the other hand, it is unclear as to whether safety net economic support actually reduces child abuse and neglect as this area is under-researched (Peterman et al. 2017). Therefore, a one-size-fits-all family violence approach to social protection is not likely to adequately address needs. Nevertheless, circumstances, such as lockdown, that further isolate people experiencing family violence from formal and informal supports are worrying as they increase the invisibility of the occurrence of violence (Pfitzner et al. 2020). Therefore, it is useful to consider general responses that could fall under Devereux and Sabates-Wheeler's (2004) definition of *transformative measures* that can contribute to reducing inequity of access for people experiencing family violence.

Integration of Family Violence Services with First Point of Contact Services

When health and social services are under pressure during a pandemic and when, typically, it is even more difficult to gain access to people who are experiencing violence, it is important to take every opportunity to screen for and respond to violence. There are two ways that this could happen. Family violence services could be integrated with first point of contact, essential health and social services. This would be a way for those experiencing family violence to alert professionals to their situation. Another way of gaining access to those experiencing violence is for essential health and social service professionals to screen for family violence with every patient or client. This measure requires sufficient numbers of professionals to carry out family violence screening, and those professionals need to be competent to deal sensitively with potential victims and perpetrators of family violence. These professionals would also need to have a good knowledge of steps to take, including referral processes, if violence screening results in positive identification of violence.

Targeted Support

Targeted support could be provided to communities who are identified as especially vulnerable to family violence (Campbell and Jones 2016). The barriers facing populations who are from marginalized ethnic and cultural backgrounds and who experience economic and social challenges are likely to be enhanced in a COVID-19 pandemic context. The impact of colonization, that is, the effect of the collective loss of land, language and kinship systems of support, on indigenous communities must also be recognized, both in terms of colonization's intersection with family violence and the ensuing enhanced vulnerability for indigenous populations in times of disaster (Blagg et al. 2015; Ministry of Social Development 2020). Social protection measures, therefore, should target interventions with especially vulnerable communities.

Community Education and Mobilization

In non-pandemic times, engagement with communities would involve face-to-face community meetings with key community champions with the aim of educating communities about family violence and empowering them to be actively involved in developing responses to family violence. During lockdown, community champions could still be engaged, via technology or phone, in a process of determining the best approach to family violence within their communities. Unfortunately, there is always the potential for community champions to be engaged in community mobilization strategies without any financial contribution for their work. To prevent exploitation, community champions should be adequately financially resourced for their efforts.

Social media campaigns might accompany community mobilization. With enforced lockdown, social media has a greater role to play. In the same way that social media has been used to disseminate medical information during the pandemic (Gottlieb et al. 2020), social media can be used to share information about family violence and the discreet ways that people can access services without the knowledge of their abusers (Bradbury-Jones and Isham 2020).

Post Lockdown

Efforts to address family violence must continue to engage communities in continued planning about family violence education and responses to violence. Additionally, services that were in place to respond to violence prior to lockdown should be strengthened to deal with the likely increased occurrence of family violence in communities post lockdown in the pandemic context.

While the considerations noted here highlight the importance of appropriate funding and resourcing, there is a danger that dedicated family violence resources are, during the pandemic, directed toward the COVID-19 medical response, further increasing the likelihood of injury and death from family violence.

The suggestions here can contribute somewhat toward transformation in terms of equity and social justice, but there is evidence that integration of services alone is not enough to reduce family violence (Family Violence Death Review Committee 2017). What is needed is an approach that is more systems focused (Carne et al. 2019) and that addresses relationships of power at the individual level, but also organizationally and globally. A transformative approach to social protection recognizes this connection between inequity of access and power. Ultimately, transformation in social protection terms, whether during a pandemic setting or not, is not only about more equitably financing community efforts to respond to family violence. It must also be about including communities impacted by family violence at the decision making table, both to mobilize their agency and self-determination and to promote resistance to the way things have been done before.

Conclusion

Considerations for how to respond to family violence are multi-disciplinary and incorporate ideas about human rights, the dynamics of power, gender, culturally responsive practice and legal and policy frame-works. Preliminary information suggests that child abuse, intimate partner violence and elder abuse has increased with the onset of the COVID-19 pandemic and stay-at-home restrictions. The pandemic has influenced how and what information families and communities receive about available family violence services and access to those services and the ability of organizations to actually deliver services.

While there are opportunities to improve the social protection response in a pandemic setting, systems of response in many countries were already fragmented and struggling to cope with rates of family violence prior to COVID-19. The pandemic has only exacerbated system failures. Social protection measures could have a transformational impact on the family violence response landscape if those communities most impacted are key actors in system change.

References

Barton, Hugh, and Marcus Grant. 2006. A health map for the local human habitat. *The Journal of the Royal Society for the Promotion of Health* 126 (6): 252–253. https://doi.org/10.1177/1466424006070466.

Blagg, Harry, Nicole Bluett-Boyd, and Emma Williams. 2015. Innovative models in addressing iolence against indigenous women: State of knowledge paper. *ANROWS Lanscapes*.

Bonomi, Amy E., Elizabeth Cannon, Melissa Anderson, Frederick Rivara, and Robert Thompson. 2008. Association between self-reported health and physical and/or sexual abuse experienced before age 18. *Child Abuse & Neglect* 32 (7) (July 1): 693–701. https://doi.org/10.1016/j.chiabu.2007.10.004.

Boxall, Hayley, Anthony Morgan, and Rick Brown. 2020. The prevalence of domestic violence among women during the COVID-19 pandemic. *Statistical Bulletin* 28.

Bradbury-Jones, Caroline, and Louise Isham. 2020. The pandemic paradox: The consequences of COVID-19 on domestic violence. *Journal of Clinical Nursing* 29 (13–14): 2047–2049. https://doi.org/10.1111/jocn.15296.

Brooke, Joanne, and Debra Jackson. 2020. Older people and COVID-19: Isolation, risk and ageism. *Journal of Clinical Nursing* 29 (13–14): 2044–2046. https://doi.org/10.1111/jocn.15274.

Byass, Peter. 2013. *Is global health really global?*, January 6 (Supplement S5).

Campbell, Lesley, and Susie Jones. 2016. An innovative response to family violence after the Canterbury earthquake events: Canterbury family violence collaboration's achievements, successes, and challenges. *Australasian Journal of Disaster and Trauma Studies* 20 (People in Disasters Special Issue): 89–100.

Carne, Sarah, David Rees, Nicola Paton, and Janet Fanslow. 2019. Using systems thinking to address intimate partner violence and child abuse in New Zealand.

Chenoweth, Lesley, and Donna McAuliffe. 2017. *The road to social work and human service practice*, 5th ed. South Melbourne, VIC: Cengage.

Dasgupta, Jashodhara, et al. 2020. Axes of alienation: Applying an intersectional lens on the social contract during the pandemic response to protect sexual and reproductive rights and health. *International Journal for Equity in Health* 19 (1): 1–5. https://doi.org/10.1186/s12939-020-01245-w.

Devereux, Stephen, and Rachel Sabates-Wheeler. 2004. Transformative social protection. IDS Working Papers (232), 30.

Elman, Alyssa, et al. 2020. Effects of the COVID-19 outbreak on elder mistreatment and response in New York City: Initial lessons. *Journal of Applied Gerontology* 39 (7): 690–699. https://doi.org/10.1177/0733464820924853.

Family Violence Death Review Committee. 2017. *Family Violence Death Review Committee. Fifth Report: January 2009 to December 2015*. Wellington: Family Violence Death Review Committee.

Felitti, Vincent. 2009. Adverse childhood experiences and adult health. *Academic Pediatrics* 9 (3): 131–132. https://doi.org/10.1016/j.acap.2009.03.00.1.

Felitti, Vincent, et al. 1998. Relationship of childhood abuse and household dysfunction to many of the leading causes of death in adults: The adverse childhood experiences (ace) study. *American Journal of Preventive Medicine* 14 (4): 245–258. https://doi.org/10.1016/S0749-3797(98)00017-8.

Ferguson, Iain, Michael Lavalette, and Elisabeth Whitmore. 2005. *Globalisation, global justice and social work*. London: Routledge.

Fielding, Sarah. 2020. In quarantine with an abuser: Surge in domestic violence reports linked to coronavirus. *The Guardian International Addition*, April 3. Retrieved from https://www.theguardian.com/us-news/2020/apr/03/coronavirus-quarantine-abuse-domestic-violence.

Garrett, Paul. 2009. *Transforming' children's services?: Social work, neoliberalism and the 'modern' world*. Maidenhead, UK: Open University Press.

Gillum, Tamika. 2019. The intersection of intimate partner violence and poverty in Black communities. *Aggression and Violent Behavior* 46 (May 1): 37–44. https://doi.org/10.1016/j.avb.2019.01.008.

Gottlieb, Michael, and S. Sean Dyer. 2020. Information and disinformation: Social media in the COVID-19 crisis. *Academic Emergency Medicine* 27 (7): 640–641. https://doi.org/10.1111/acem.14036.

Green, Peter. 2020. Risks to children and young people during COVID-19 pandemic. *BMJ* 369: m1669. https://doi.org/10.1136/bmj.m1669.

Griffith, Annette. 2020. Parental burnout and child maltreatment during the COVID-19 pandemic. *Journal of Family Violence* (June 23). https://doi.org/10.1007/s10896-020-00172-2.

Han, Duke, and Laura Mosqueda. 2020. Elder abuse in the COVID-19 era. *Journal of the American Geriatrics Society (JAGS)* 68 (7): 1386–1387. https://doi.org/10.1111/jgs.16496.

Herrenkohl, Todd, et al. 2013. Developmental impacts of child abuse and neglect related to adult mental health, substance use, and physical health. *Journal of Family Violence* 28 (2) (February 1): 191–199. https://doi.org/10.1007/s10896-012-9474-9.

Ho, Cyrus, Siow-Yi. Wong, Marcus Chiu, and Roger Ho. 2017. Global prevalence of elder abuse: A meta-analysis and meta-regression. *East Asian Archives of Psychiatry* 27 (2): 43–55.

Kim, Hani, Uros Novakovic, Carles Muntaner, and Michael Hawkes. 2019. A critical assessment of the ideological underpinnings of current practice in global health and their historical origins. *Global Health Action* 12 (1): 1651017. https://doi.org/10.1080/16549716.2019.1651017.

Kofman, Yasmin, and Dana Garfin. 2020. Home is not always a haven: The domestic violence crisis amid the COVID-19 pandemic. *Psychological Trauma: Theory, Research, Practice, and Policy* 12 (S1): S199–S201. https://doi.org/10.1037/tra0000866.

Makaroun, Lena, Rachel Bachrach, and Ann-Marie. Rosland. 2020. Elder abuse in the time of COVID-19—Increased risks for older adults and their caregivers. *American Journal of Geriatric Psychiatry* 28 (8): 876–880.

Mikolajczak, Moira, et al. 2018. Consequences of parental burnout: Its specific effect on child neglect and violence. *Child Abuse & Neglect* 80 (June 1): 134–145. https://doi.org/10.1016/j.chiabu.2018.03.025.

Ministry of Social Development. 2020. *E Tū Whānau mahere rautaki: Framework for change 2019–2023*. Wellington: Ministry of Social Development.

Miragoli, Sarah, Luca Milani, Paulo Di Blasio, and Elena Camisasca. 2020. Difficulties in emotion regulation in child abuse potential: Gender differences in parents. *Child Abuse & Neglect* 106 (August 1): 104529. https://doi.org/10.1016/j.chiabu.2020.104529.

New Zealand Human Rights Commission. 2020. Submission of the New Zealand Human Rights Commission for the Special Rapporteur on violence against women, its causes and consequences. The impact of COVID-19 and the increase of domestic violence against women.

Ouslander, Joseph, and David Grabowski. 2020. COVID-19 in nursing homes: Calming the perfect storm. *Journal of the American Geriatrics Society* 68 (10): 2153–2162. https://doi.org/10.1111/jgs.16784.

Pegorari, Maycon, et al. 2020. Covid-19: Perspectives and initiatives in older adults health context in Brazil. *Ciência & Saude Coletiva* 25 (9): 3459–3464. https://doi.org/10.1590/1413-81232020259.21622020.

Peterman, Amber, et al. 2017. Understanding the linkages between social safety nets and childhood violence: A review of the evidence from low- and middle-income countries. *Health Policy and Planning* 32 (7): 1049–1071. https://doi.org/10.1093/heapol/czx033.

Peterman, Amber, et al. 2020. Pandemics and violence against women and children. CGD Working Paper 528.

Pfitzner, Naomi, Kate Fitz-Gibbon, and Jacqui True. 2020. *Responding to the 'shadow pandemic': Practitioner views on the nature of and responses to violence against women in Victoria, Australia during the COVID-19 restrictions.* Victoria: Monash Gender and Family Violence Prevention Centre, Monash University.

Rodriguez, Christina. 2010. Parent-child aggression: Association with child abuse potential and parenting styles. *Violence and Victims* 25 (6): 728–741. https://doi.org/10.1891/0886-6708.25.6.728.

Sabates-Wheeler, Rachel, Stephen Devereux, and Anthony Hodges. 2009. Taking the long view: What does a child focus add to social protection? *IDS Bulletin* 40 (1): 109–119. https://doi.org/10.1111/j.1759-5436.2009.00015.x.

Sánchez, Odette, Diama Vale, Larissa Rodrigues, and Fernanda Surita. 2020. Violence against women during the COVID-19 pandemic: An integrative review. *International Journal of Gynecology & Obstetrics* 151 (2): 180–187. https://doi.org/10.1002/ijgo.13365.

Sidpra, Jai, et al. 2020. Rise in the incidence of abusive head trauma during the COVID-19 pandemic. *Archives of Disease in Childhood* (Arch Dis Child) 106 (3): e14. https://doi.org/10.1136/archdischild-2020-319872.

Stark, Evan. 2009. *Coercive control: The entrapment of women in personal life.* New York;Oxford: Oxford University Press.

Sun, Haiying, et al. 2020. Risk factors for mortality in 244 older adults with COVID-19 in Wuhan, China: A retrospective study. *Journal of the American Geriatrics Society* 68 (6): E19–E23. https://doi.org/10.1111/jgs.16533.

UN Women. 2020. COVID-19 and ending violence against women and girls. In *United Nations Entity for Gender Equality and the Empowerment of Women.* UN Women.

UNICEF. 2020. *Moving beyond the numbers: What the COVID-19 pandemic means for the safety of women and girls*. UNICEF.

Usher, Kim, et al. 2020. Family violence and COVID-19: Increased vulnerability and reduced options for support. *International Journal of Mental Health Nursing* 29 (4): 549–552. https://doi.org/10.1111/inm.12735.

Viana, Ana, and Hudson da Silva. 2018. Neoliberal meritocracy and financial capitalism: Consequences for social protection and health. *Ciência & Saude Coletiva* 23 (7): 2107–2118. https://doi.org/10.1590/1413-81232018237.07582018.

Women's Aid. 2020. *A perfect storm: The impact of the Covid-19 pandemic on domestic abuse survivors and the services supporting them*. Bristol: Women's Aid.

World Bank. 2012. *Resilience, equity, and opportunity: The World Bank's social protection and labor strategy 2012–2022*.

World Health Organization. 2013. *Global and regional estimates of violence against women: Prevalence and health effects of intimate partner violence and non-partner sexual violence*. Italy: World Health Organization.

World Health Organization. 2020a. COVID-19 and violence against women. What the health sector/system can do.

World Health Organization. 2020b. *Global status report on preventing violence against children 2020*. Geneva: World Health Organization.

World Health Organization. 2020c. Violence Info. Elder Abuse. Retrieved 19 October 2020, from https://apps.who.int/violence-info/elder-abuse.

Yang, Jing, et al. 2020. Prevalence of comorbidities and its effects in patients infected with SARS-CoV-2: A systematic review and meta-analysis. *International Journal of Infectious Diseases* 94 (May 1): 91–95. https://doi.org/10.1016/j.ijid.2020.03.017.

Yon, Yongjie, Christopher Mikton, Zachary Gassoumis, and Kathleen Wilber. 2017. Elder abuse prevalence in community settings: A systematic review and meta-analysis. *The Lancet Global Health* 5 (2): e147–e156. https://doi.org/10.1016/S2214-109X(17)30006-2.

CHAPTER 4

The Impacts of COVID-19 on Food Security: Emergency Food Systems (Food Banks) and Policy Responses

Rosemarie Martin-Neuninger

Introduction

In 2020, the global spread of COVID-19 forced many governments to take drastic measures to limit the virus's spread. These measures included introducing restrictions that caused unforeseen disturbances to our global, local and regional food systems.[1] Although there was no global scarcity in food, there were some short-term problems in distributing food to those who need it the most, both on national and international levels. Farmers, distributors, producers, consumer- and

[1] A food system includes 'growing, harvesting, packing, processing, transforming, marketing, consuming and disposing of food. The most common food system is the agro-industrial food system that is global. It is dominated by a few multinational corporations through vertical integration. This is a very complex system with a long supply chain and it has a lot of processed foods' (CFS 2016).

R. Martin-Neuninger (✉)
Macmillan Brown Centre for Pacific Studies, University of Canterbury, Christchurch, Canterbury, New Zealand
e-mail: rosemarie.martin@canterbury.ac.nz

S. Ratuva et al. (eds.), *COVID-19 and Social Protection*,
https://doi.org/10.1007/978-981-16-2948-8_4

packaged-goods companies, and retailers were suddenly facing new challenges, a situation that at the time of writing, was still evolving in many parts of the world. The rapidly rising numbers of infections and hospitalisations saw many countries and territories around the world implementing physical distancing measures. Lockdowns, quarantines and curfews had to be enforced on a regular basis to reduce contact between people and to minimise the spread of the virus. During these times, numerous countries had workplace closure measures in place, and some businesses and marketplaces were forced to close. Many vendors were not allowed to sell their goods, many businesses remained unable to restore operations to full capacity and many businesses went into liquidation.

Under these measures, food production and distribution became harder due to economic threats to business viability, disruptions in the shipping and aviation industries, movement restrictions, border closures and restrictions on exports of food staples. In some countries, farmers had to throw away their crops, farmers were dumping milk or burying perishable food, and meat processing plants and food markets were forced to close due to disruptions in the supply chain (UN 2020). Another issue was that when countries were forced into lockdowns, panic buying (Sterman and Dogan 2015) and unnecessary stockpiling resulted in temporary fluctuations in food prices and shortages of food as shops could not re-stock fast enough to keep up with increased demand (Martin-Neuninger and Ruby 2020), leaving many without adequate resources to access appropriate food. In particular, those living in urban centres have struggled to access fresh and nutritious food as they are unable to get their food from local markets (UN 2020). Governments around the world had to act swiftly and adopted emergency financial measures. They developed stimulus packages to support businesses and workers who lost jobs as a way to avoid what is expected to be the worst economic crisis since the Great Depression of the 1930s (IMF 2020). All these are clear indicators as to how fragile our food systems are and how unforeseen disturbances such as the COVID-19 pandemic can worsen the food insecurity issue on a global scale. If no action is taken, 270 million people around the world will face starvation by the end of 2020 (WFP 2020c).

With the above facts in mind, in this chapter, I aim to provide an overview of how COVID-19 has made our food systems more fragile and how this has contributed to the growth of poverty and inequality and placed vulnerable populations into food insecurity. In this article, I will use grey literature, web-based material and news to provide a snapshot of the effects that COVID-19 has had around the world on food security. I will also use emergency food systems, in this case food banks, as a case study and highlight sustainable solutions that are more complex than merely increasing yields and facilitating trade. Recommendations for reducing and improving food banks are provided, along with recommendations on ways of re-thinking social protection mechanisms to make resilient, sustainable changes that respect food sovereignty and benefit the most vulnerable. I frame these recommendations within a post-colonialist framework of food sovereignty (Gandhi 2019; Deepak 2014).

The Issue of Global Food Security Before the COVID-19 Pandemic

In 2019, with many people around the world already affected by food insecurity, specifically in regions of Africa, Latin America, the Caribbean, and Western Asia, hunger was on the rise (FAO et al. 2019). Even in wealthier parts of the world, including North America and Europe, around 8% of the population was already experiencing moderate food insecurity before the COVID-19 pandemic, which has now put them at a higher risk of malnutrition and poor health (FAO et al. 2019). One person in nine was not able to access secure, safe and nutritious food to sustain themselves (WHH 2020). Many people have not been able to afford the high costs of healthy diets, which has contributed to wasting, overweight, stunting and malnutrition (WFP 2020a; FAO et al. 2020). In 2020, approximately 212 million people were chronically food-insecure with 95 million acutely food-insecure in the Central African Republic, Ethiopia, Zimbabwe, Nigeria, Iraq, Yemen, Armenia, Democratic People's Republic Korea, Bangladesh, Venezuela and Haiti. Many of them have been suffering from acute hunger, chronic hunger and hidden hunger (WHH 2020). Similarly, more than 144 million children are stunted and approximately 47 million are wasted (WHO 2020b) and sadly, a child dies every ten seconds from the effects of hunger (WHH 2020). UNICEF has predicted that an additional 6.7 million children under five could suffer from wasting in 2020 due to COVID-19 (UNISEF 2020). One of the major issues is limited access to social protection mechanisms (for example, social assistance, social insurance, social care services and labour market programmes) and if there are no appropriate measures in place, the most vulnerable and marginalised people they will most likely fall further into poverty and food insecurity (ILO 2020).

Not only have countries been affected by food insecurity, malnutrition and obesity, but also by inequality, climate change, resource scarcity, environmental degradation, conflicts/wars and pandemics, which themselves contribute to food insecurity (Dury et al. 2019) (see Fig. 4.1). Some predict that the economic consequences and their long-term repercussions will be far more devastating than the COVID-19 pandemic itself (WFP 2020a). Ironically, although so many people globally are suffering from hunger, it is estimated that 1.3 billion tons of food that is produced is lost or wasted around the world (FAO 2011).

In 2019, many people around the world had already been affected by food insecurity and in the regions of Africa, Latin America, the Caribbean and Western Asia, hunger was on the rise (FAO et al. 2019). In addition, many households had been facing a reduction in purchasing power due to the consequences of economic shocks (FAO et al. 2019). According to the FAO et al. (2019), most countries (52 out of 65) where undernourishment had been growing were 'highly dependent on primary commodities for export and/or imports'. Parts of East Africa and South Asia were facing severe food shortages caused by climate change and in El Salvador, many people needed immediate food assistance due to tropical storms (WFP 2020b). Many Asian and African countries, including

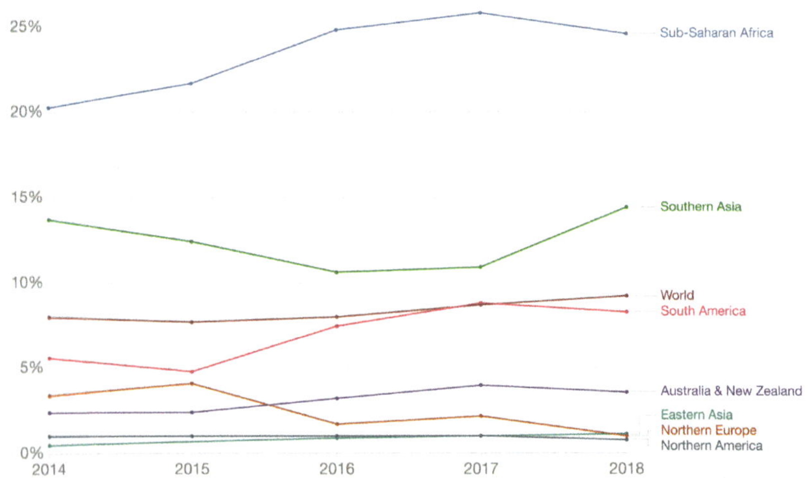

Fig. 4.1 Share of population with severe food insecurity, 2014 to 2018 (Roser and Ritchie 2013) (Figure created by the author)

Kenya, Ethiopia, Uganda, Somalia, Eritrea, India, Pakistan, Iran, Yemen, Oman and Saudi Arabia, have been affected by desert locust (Schistocerca gregaria) outbreaks. These outbreaks have been threatening the food system, having severe consequences on small farmers and informal workers across many regions. Tens of thousands of hectares of crops have been destroyed and farmers are now struggling with emerging environmental and health problems (Njagi 2020).

Before COVID-19 struck, there had been debates about the nature of food security[2] and the methods to combat it. Neoliberal 'productionist' paradigms (Patel 2009; Lang and Barling 2012; Fouilleux et al. 2017) focussed on under-consumption as the core issue and suggested increasing production and liberalising trade as the solutions to provide increased affordable food to those who were suffering shortages. In recent years, this view has been challenged by those arguing the need to address a complex array of problems in addition to production (Lang and Barling 2012). Such other problems might include sustainability (the long-term effects of production on communities and the environment), resilience (the ability of food systems to withstand shocks) and food sovereignty (the rights of producers and citizens over their food and food systems).

Global Food Security Since the COVID-19 Pandemic

The impact of COVID-19 has highlighted the need to address food security more than ever. This pandemic is a crisis that is threatening food security for millions of people globally. It is true that COVID-19 has worsened many social, environmental and economic issues, including food insecurity, but it is also important to recognise that these issues had already existed before the pandemic started (see Fig. 4.2). There is an urgent need to establish and expand social protection systems, in particular for poor and marginalised populations, without lapsing into the productionist paradigm as happened after the global food shocks in 2008 (Lang and Barling 2012).

[2] "Food security exists when all people, at all times, have physical and economic access to sufficient, safe and nutritious food that meets their dietary needs and food preferences for an active and healthy life" (FAO 2006).

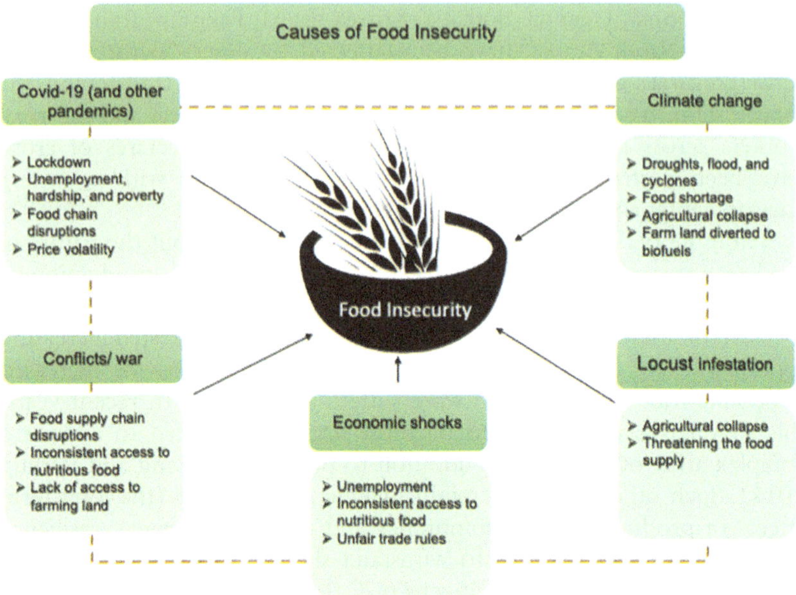

Fig. 4.2 Causes of food insecurity (Figure created by the author)

In the context of COVID-19, it has also become clear that our current food systems are fragile, and that it is vital to make these more resilient[3] to disturbances (natural, political or economic shocks). According to Tendall et al. (2015, p. 19), food system resilience is the 'capacity over time of a food system and its units at multiple levels, to provide sufficient, appropriate and accessible food to all, in the face of various and even unforeseen disturbances'. Globally, there is a need for policy makers to act and to work in solidarity on short- and long-term solutions (WEF 2020) to prevent a 'global emergency' (UN 2020) that will have long-lasting impacts on humanity. All forms of shocks, but in particular COVID-19, have shown us that many countries have struggled to adapt to the disruptions in the food supply chain. According to CGIAR (2020), the COVID-19 pandemic:

[3] The concept of resilience originated in ecology (Holling 1973).

> Will create an additional shock to the resilience of global, regional, and local food systems, through increased disease incidence and reduction in productivity as households care for themselves and family members and miss out on income opportunities due to COVID-19 distancing restrictions.

Ensuring that poor people and those in vulnerable situations have access to safe, nutritious and sufficient food is one of the key aims of the Sustainable Development Goals (SDGs). Since the COVID-19 pandemic, it has been estimated that by the end of 2020, an additional 130 million people could be suffering from chronic hunger (FAO 2020b). It is expected that world hunger is going to exceed 840 million by 2030 (FAO et al. 2020), presenting a major concern about how to guarantee food security in the future. With the rising numbers of hunger and malnutrition and the negative impacts that COVID-19 has had, the SDG of zero hunger by 2030 is unlikely to be met as hunger will rise (IFPRI 2020).

Unemployment, COVID-19 and Food Security

The impacts of COVID-19 on food insecurity are due to a number of factors. The COVID-19 pandemic has seen a major increase in unemployment as work opportunities have disappeared. In the second quarter of 2020, there had been a decline in global working hours of 14% (up from the previous estimates of 10.7%), which is equivalent to 400 million full-time jobs (ILO 2020). Millions of people have lost their jobs and will require an alternative way to support themselves, and sectors dominated by women will be particularly affected. According to WFP (2020b), Africa and Latin America will experience the highest decline in earnings by informal workers. Income shocks will most likely have a negative impact on people's wellbeing and the poor will take the heaviest burden. Many of these households have become jobless and they might find it difficult as they do not have any savings and are not able to borrow money from the bank or from family members. The situation is most alarming in Africa where pre-existing shocks or crises have been the main cause of acute food insecurity, and many people are malnourished, weak and vulnerable to disease. Many people in Africa (19.1%) are undernourished, compared to Asia (8.3%) and Latin America and the Caribbean (7.4%) (FAO 2020a). If these trends continue, then Africa will become home to more than half of the world's chronically hungry by 2030. These individuals live in poor, rural areas (for example, Ethiopia, Kenya and Somalia), and they are highly dependent on agricultural production, seasonal jobs in agriculture, fishing or pastoralism (FAO 2020d). The FAO (2020d) has suggested that disruptions in the food supply chain can have similar devastating consequences as during the 2014 West Africa Ebola outbreak where people went hungry. It is estimated that in Africa, between five million and 29 million people will be pushed below the extreme poverty line (US$1.90) and that 'for the majority of Africans, at this moment, the fear of hunger is greater than the fear of COVID-19' (GFN 2020f). Losses of jobs and income will cost more lives than the lockdown itself as governments are not distributing food or providing compensation packages to those affected.

Impacts of COVID-19 on Access to Food

In many countries, the fear of food insecurity due to COVID-19 led to mass hysteria as people thought that they would run out of food and toilet paper. Panic buying, stockpiling and hoarding by those who can afford to have created empty shelves in supermarkets, which has consequently caused food insecurity amongst vulnerable groups. A preliminary report of the New Food Foundation shows that in Great Britain, more than three million people (6%) had someone in their household go hungry at some point during the first lockdown in the United Kingdom (UK) (Loopstra 2020). According to Loopstra (2020), the number of adults who are food-insecure in Great Britain has quadrupled under the COVID-19 lockdown. Gradually, it will become more difficult for people to access nutritious food, and we will see a drastic change in food consumption patterns (Sanderson et al. 2020). An increase in food waste was also reported in several countries. Spain reported that during the lockdown, household food waste increased by 12% (Aldaco et al. 2020), while others were hungry and became dependant on emergency food systems such as food banks. In order to address the growing food insecurity issue during the pandemic, food banks have been taking care of vulnerable people and their basic needs by providing essential items. In the next section, I will provide a snapshot to demonstrate how food banks have supported vulnerable people during the COVID-19 pandemic.

The Response of Food Banks to the COVID-19 Crisis

As a result of COVID-19, some countries have started to respond with large programmes to support their citizens and residents. Countries such as Argentina, Australia, Denmark, France, Germany, Ireland, New Zealand, Norway, Singapore, Sweden and the UK have also put in place policies to protect lives, jobs and incomes. These twelve countries were the first to set a standard on how governments can support workers. Notably, COVID-19 is causing distress and destitution as many governments are still not putting appropriate social protection measures in place to address food insecurity. Since the start of the COVID-19 pandemic, food banks around the world have been stepping in to feed families and people facing economic and social devastation. In London, food banks had increased demand from those on no or low income (for example, the elderly, disabled people, rough sleepers, asylum seekers and migrants) and were struggling to cope with the demand (Mayor of London 2020). A similar situation has been unfolding in many other countries around the world, which saw leaders of the major international networks for food banks such as the European Food Banks Federation (FEBA), Feeding America (FA) and the Global Food Banking Network (GFN)[4] calling for 'urgent, strengthened, and sustained' action to help the critical work of food banks in response to the COVID-19 pandemic (GFN 2020a).

In many countries, the demand for food aid from food banks has been growing exponentially. The increase in food bank users might be blamed on the failure of welfare state reform, although some governments have argued for less state intervention and are pleased to see an increase in food bank use (BBC 2017). The COVID-19 pandemic has shown that in many countries, there are many problems with the current benefits system. There have been long waits for people to access benefits, which left many with no money to put food on the table for themselves and their families. Often, these benefits were also not sufficient for families to live on. This means that states are passing on the responsibility of caring for our most vulnerable populations to the third sector and charities (Lambie-Mumford and Silvasti 2020).

[4] The GFN network is providing food relief in 51 countries in six continents. More than 22 million people received food and hygiene products since the COVID-19 pandemic started. Their partners include Bank of America, General Mills, Kellogg's, Pepsico, and many others (2020h).

The GFN has been supporting food banks in many countries, and they have experienced a 50–100 per cent+ increase in demand (GFN 2020i). In Canada, the demand for food banks has increased up to 20% on average (Britneff 2020). In Addis Ababa, 1000 food banks have been established in response to a predicted decrease in food security (ILO 2020). Compared to April 2019, the Trussell Trust in the UK reported an increase of 89% including a 107% increase in the number of children needing emergency food parcels (Revie 2020). In New Zealand, the demand for food banks also increased dramatically with the greatest rises in Auckland, Northland and Christchurch (The Salvation Army 2020). The Wellington City Mission reported an increase in demand of 400% in seven days during the national lockdown (Wellington City Mission 2020), while other places in Wellington and in Palmerston North have had increases of over 900% (Robson 2020). In New Zealand, the country's largest indoor stadium in Auckland was transformed into a food bank to support thousands of households who were struggling to get food (nzherald 2020). Food banks around the world are 'stretched', and food bank users are at severe risk of hunger for an unknown period of time (GFN 2020g).

In many places, the problem of increased demand is exacerbated by a decrease in donations. Decreased donations may be due to reduced food resources of individuals (GFN 2020b) concerned by their own lack of food security and of supermarkets as they have reduced stocks due to panic buying (GFN 2020g). This seems ironic given that producers were having to throw away food that they were not able to distribute. It reveals a problem within the food distribution system. In the United States (US), resources at food banks are limited as food retailers, wholesalers and manufacturers are unable to donate extra food (NBC News 2020; Net News 2020). In New Zealand, The Wellington City Mission reported a decline in food donations and in volunteer numbers (Newshub 2020). In London, food banks were struggling to cope as they were in high demand, but had insufficient food donations from supermarkets and were also lacking in help from volunteers (London Government 2020). Most GFN members (90%) indicated that they urgently needed more food as donations were not sufficient. A large number (86%) said that there was an urgent need for funds, while some (21%) indicated that they needed more employees or volunteers (GFN 2020d). This shows the dramatic increase in demand but also how food banks are hardly coping with this crisis.

As a response to the growing demand, food banks have been seeking increased donations. In New Zealand, the Salvation Army called for financial donations through 'The Foodbank Project' on their website to support their food banks, which resulted in an increase in donations (The Salvation Army 2020). At the start of the lockdown, small independent vegetable growers across the county started to donate their produce to food banks as they were unable to sell them, as their usual retail outlets had closed to enable physical distancing (Gilbertson 2020). In the US and UK, private companies, including supermarkets, made donations to food banks of food and money (wtap 2020; The Trussell Trust 2020) although overall, supermarkets are making less donations of staple foods than before the pandemic. In Chile, food banks are working together with wholesalers to make up for a shortage in donations (GFN 2020b). It is clear that the food industry became involved with donations to help those in need.

Governments have also provided funding to food banks. The Canadian government provided $100 million in funding to food banks and other food security groups (Trudeau 2020). In New Zealand, food banks were classified as 'essential services', which allowed them to continue operating during the lockdown. The government supported food banks by providing funding to food banks as part of the COVID-19 response (Ministry of Social Developement 2020). In Auckland, a large government-funded foodbank was established to deliver around 5000 parcels per week. While the funding for food was covered by the national government, the local council took charge of operating the food bank (Blake-Persen 2020). In London, the government asked the public to make donations to support food banks (London Government 2020), and local councils have been funding food banks for some years before the start of the pandemic (BBC News 2020). The COVID-19 crisis has brought about both a need for immediate change to cope with the ongoing situations, as well as an opportunity for long-term changes.

Food banks have needed to adjust their operations, so that staff and users can adhere to the physical distancing and staff-wellbeing requirements of the lockdown. In the US, the GFN is working closely with their members and advising them to use the WHO's food safety guide (GFN 2020c; WHO 2020a). Feeding America food banks are implementing online orders for beneficiaries, and those who are in self-isolation have established mobile and drive-through facilities to enforce physical distancing, while other food banks are preparing kits of essential supplies to distribute to families (GFN 2020c). In New Zealand, The Salvation Army was operating with precautions, including physical distancing and the use of disinfectant and sanitisers. Dunedin's three main food banks are operating under lockdown conditions, handling inquiries by telephone and making deliveries, rather than having people visit the individual food banks (Gibb 2020). In Argentina, some food banks are delivering meal bags to families to cook at home. In France and in Norway, food banks have introduced new hygiene protocols (for example, all staff have to wash their hands with soap or antibacterial hand sanitiser, surfaces need to be cleaned, trucks need to be disinfected at the end of each journey, charities can only pick up food one at a time and visits to food banks need to be pre-scheduled). Food banks in Australia are providing mental health support and using videoconferencing wherever possible. The food bank in Japan has recommended having short 15 minute meetings via Zoom/Skype, so that everyone is kept in the loop of key developments. GFN's Latin America team held a webinar with the food banks in the region titled 'How to manage stress in times of disaster'. They have been using WhatsApp and Zoom to stay in touch with colleagues (GFN 2020b). This response from Food banks and temporary financial aid from governments have been the major tools in addressing food security during COVID-19.

The Need for Policy Change in Response to the COVID-19 Food Security Crisis

There is a need to prepare worldwide for the next global pandemic, which might be more severe than COVID-19 (Jia and Wu 2020), as well as dealing with the ongoing effects of the current pandemic. Ensuring food supply for the most marginalised and vulnerable people should be equally important for governments as responding to the direct health emergency of the COVID-19 pandemic. COVID-19 has had a low impact on food systems, so far. However, international organisations are warning about future food security problems as a result of the current pandemic (IFPRI 2020). There is currently no global scarcity in food, but there are short-term problems in distributing food to those who need it, both on national and international levels. There are also long-term issues of sustainability, non-communicable diseases such as obesity, and of food waste that also need to be addressed.

The United Nations (UN) is urging countries to implement emergency measures in their respective countries and to protect food supplies. Such measures include on-site health measures, implementing sick-leave policies, physical distancing instructions and improving capabilities amongst all food system workers (FAO 2020b). Global measures to improve international trade such as lowered tariffs and import taxes were also suggested, so as to ensure food security in all countries. Such free trade measures may help in the short term. I note, however, that these measures are contrary to the ideals of food sovereignty expressed by farmers' and peasants' organisations (Patel 2009), which argue that free trade agreements diminish the rights producers have over the food they produce. The Food and Land Use (FOLU) coalition (an organisation of businesses and government organisations) has argued for maintaining open trade to keep food supplies flowing, scaling support to the most vulnerable by income, food protection support within and between nations, and to invest in more resilient food systems. These measures should mitigate the effects on the most heavily impacted populations: low-income countries and those who rely on international trade for their food supply. These challenges can only be tackled if countries work together and collaborate (OECD 2020).

Effective social protection systems are crucial to look after the poor and vulnerable, particularly in times of crisis. Prior to the COVID-19 crisis, many countries around the world had already been providing assistance to those living in poverty, elderly individuals, and those with disabilities. However, this crisis has impacted many people who had not been in need of aid in the past. The World Bank (2020) has suggested that social protection systems are limited in many countries and require significant upgrading. As of April 10, 2020, a total of 126 countries have introduced or adapted social protection and jobs programmes in response to COVID-19. The most widely used innovation has been cash transfer programmes (143 programmes in 81 countries). Many of these countries have launched new programmes, including Burkina Faso ($10 million cash transfer programme for fruit and vegetable sellers), Columbia (one-off payment of $108 for informal workers), Egypt (one-off monetary compensation for three months for those working in construction, ports, agriculture, fishing, plumbing and electricians), El Salvador (will give $300 to about 1.5 million households in the informal economy), Madagascar (unconditional cash transfers will be given out for April and May to around 150,000 households) and Haiti (one-off cash transfer will be given to about 1.5 million households) (Gentilini et al.). The World Bank group will distribute up to $160 billion over the next 15 months to support families and businesses, restore income, preserve livelihoods, compensate for price hikes, help countries enhance the preparedness of their social protection systems and build resilience against future crises (The World Bank 2020).

While measures such as cash transfers and distribution of food present a short-term crisis response, the food security issues resulting from the COVID-19 crisis present an opportunity to re-think food security policies and the role of social protection. In order to cope with future shocks and to solve ongoing food insecurity, governments and other organisations could make longer term structural changes to protect the poorest and most vulnerable, taking into account sustainability, resilience and food sovereignty.

Reducing the Need for Food Banks: The Way Forward

Sustainable structural changes to the food system should reduce the need for food banks. The COVID-19 pandemic has dramatically increased the number of food bank users globally. In this section, we provide some recommendations that emphasise the need for governments and policy makers to improve domestic policies, so that the need for food banks is reduced. The drastic increase in food bank users shows that countries should consider working on a preventative approach and build social security systems that are reliable for people who are suffering from hunger due to a crisis that might be out of their control such as unemployment, benefit payment delays or reductions, health issues or bereavement. Many people simply cannot afford to eat healthily due to the increasing food prices, and this needs to change.

Healthy food prices continued to rise during the COVID-19 pandemic. Globally, the cost of basic foods such as cereals, sorghum, barley, maize and rice has risen (FAO 2020e). For example, vegetable prices have also been on the rise, which in New Zealand, saw courgettes and cucumbers reaching record high prices (Stats NZ 2020). On a global scale, there is an urgent need to review and increase minimum wages. These need to be realistic, so that everyone is able to pay their living expenses and can afford nutritious foods. Furthermore, food security should be high on the political agenda, and countries need to have a concrete plan on how to address this. According to the chief executive of the Trussell Trust in the UK:

> Food isn't the answer to people needing food banks. Food can't be used to cover the cost of heating, lighting, rent or mortgages and food won't help a family buy school shoes, period products or bus tickets. (Revie 2020)

Governments need to do more, so that everyone can cover the costs of living and afford healthy and nutritious food. Food insecurity has been found to be higher in places with higher food prices, (Gregory and Coleman-Jensen 2013), so policies to lower food prices should be considered. Traditional methods of reducing food prices include trade liberalisation, but these are generally regarded as reducing food sovereignty as they expose local consumers to the effects of international conditions such as price fluctuations (Deepak 2014). However, promotion of competition between local food producers could help reduce food prices in countries subjected to local or global monopolies. The introduction of living wages is also required, which leads to lower inequality and lower food insecurity (Pollard and Booth 2019). Income needs to be in line with the costs of living and food prices need to be realistic. This would increase the sovereignty of individuals to buy their own food, rather than depend on handouts. There is also the urgent need to build resilience and resilience-based policies to address food insecurity (FAO 2020c) and continue working towards the UN SDGs. To ensure that food is not wasted unnecessarily, food rescue organisations should work closely with supermarkets, restaurants, cafes and hotels to pick up food that is not needed. In order for cities to improve community health, there should be more emphasis in promoting community gardens and urban agriculture—these are the local policies that would address food sovereignty most directly.

In order to mitigate the growing food insecurity of the urban poor, there is a need to re-build local food economies in a way that protects and rebuilds agricultural diversity (Norberg-Hodge et al. 2002). Diversity of food sources will produce resilience as with multiple food sources, if one is lost, others can compensate (Dombroski et al. 2020). Local farmers would benefit as they would receive a bigger share of the money spent on food, while consumers would be provided with healthier and nutritious foods at affordable prices, increasing food sovereignty in local communities. Improving land tenure security to smallholders will also improve resilience and food security. At the same time, greenhouse gas emissions, food miles and agricultural chemicals could be reduced. Less storage, packaging, refrigeration and artificial additives would be needed, and rural economies and communities around the globe would be helped to revive (Norberg-Hodge et al. 2002). Agricultural landscapes in urban systems (urban agriculture) can provide good infrastructure, access to labour and low transport costs for local food distribution within short food supply chains. Making shorter supply chains should increase resilience to shocks such as pandemics by reducing food system complexity. Consequently, food chains will be less vulnerable to the perturbations to one part. Urban agriculture will need to increase its productivity as smallholders are not as productive as large commercial farmers. This might be addressed by including future food production systems such as vertical farming where conditions can be optimised to significantly increase yields (Al-Chalabi 2015; Benke and Tomkins 2017). Breeding high-yield crops that have a low climate impact will also improve food security and sustainability.

Another way to build resilience could be for example, by adapting farming models such as community supported agriculture (subscription farming or farm shares) where community members receive a share of local harvest (Toth et al. 2016). Food markets could be created to enable local producers to trade with local consumers, which will need to be subsidised by the state (Malan 2015). For such schemes, households can build resilience by self-supply and may use a household's own land or growing space (backyards, rooftops and balconies), or by sharing land within a community (community gardens). These will have to be integrated into development systems and could include school feeding schemes. It is also recommended that community kitchens and groups are encouraged to combine resources for purchasing food at reduced cost and to cook together. This will contribute to a social safety net. These changes, including the growth of small and medium enterprises in the food system, are known as inclusive food supply systems. Including poor and marginalised people within their own food systems can increase their economic wellbeing, empower them in decision-making processes, contributing to food sovereignty and political stability, as well as making their food supply more resilient (IFPRI 2020). Increasing the proportion of the agricultural labour force comprised of women is also predicted to increase crop yields and reduce hunger (Fischer et al. 2014).

The main conclusion of this section is that national and local governments should support a diversity of food and social protection initiatives, reducing food insecurity by promoting food resilience and respecting food sovereignty.

Food Banks: Suggestions for Improvement

While mitigating the need for food banks is vital, the need for food banks will still remain, at some level. It is therefore important to improve the efficiency and effectiveness of food banks, especially their ability to respond in times of shock. The following changes have been suggested for the future of food banks: using technologies to help them operate more efficiently, including apps for vehicle routing; systems to allocate the donated food to different charities (Aleksandrov et al. 2015); applying lean logistical practices to food banks (Glover et al. 2014); and mapping demand (Hindle and Vidgen 2018). Individual food banks could work closely with organisations such as the GFN in order to share best practices during shocks (GFN). Food banks can become GFN members, which also gives access to funding in emergencies, as well as technical support (GFN 2020e).

Conclusion

This chapter has shown how COVID-19 and the associated response disrupted global food systems and made food security an international concern. The award of the Nobel Peace prize to the United Nations humanitarian organisation World Food Programme (WFP) in 2020 for feeding millions of people during the COVID-19 pandemic shows that the importance of this issue is being recognised at the international level. In response to the disruption, there were many changes and adaptations. Authorities in countries such as New Zealand mapped the diversity of the food system and brought community food organisations and others together as never before (Dombroski et al. 2020). The government removed barriers to food access, and jump-started a national food rescue system. It will take some time, however, until we have a clear understating of the true long-term impacts of COVID-19.

The economic consequences of COVID-19 call for the urgent need for governments to take action; delivering short-term economic support packages is not sufficient to tackle food insecurity. The global food system was facing serious challenges before the COVID-19 pandemic, which have now worsened. Food is a fundamental need and a right, and everyone should have access to good and healthy food (WHO 2019). Holistic solutions and best practices are needed. It is increasingly clear that COVID-19 has reinforced the existing issue of food insecurity on a global scale and that urgent action is needed from governments around the globe. Both governments and emergency food systems such as food banks must ensure diverse forms of social protection, respecting food sovereignty in order to address the food insecurity issue. I have provided recommendations for governments and other organisations such as diversifying food sources, strengthening international co-operation and enabling local producers and consumers to regain food sovereignty through local community production. This should result in a resilient food system. However, there is a need for future research into community food security based on diverse forms of social protection, in order to investigate and test these options in greater detail and with rigour.

The food resilience approach will enable countries to cope with shocks, complexity and uncertainty (Tendall et al. 2015). In order to measure the impact of improvements to food systems, I recommend using tools such as the Community Economy Return on Investment tool, which includes non-monetary returns on social investments in measuring system change (Dombroski et al. 2018). Examples of such returns include financial, environmental and social dimensions, with an eye to community wellbeing and diverse possible forms of food security.

References

Al-Chalabi, Malek. 2015. Vertical farming: Skyscraper sustainability? *Sustainable Cities and Society* 18: 74–77.

Aldaco, R, D. Hoehn, J. Laso, M. Margallo, J. Ruiz-Salmón, J. Cristobal, R. Kahhat, P. Villanueva-Rey, A. Bala, and L. Batlle-Bayer. 2020. Food waste management during the COVID-19 outbreak: A holistic climate, economic and nutritional approach. *Science of The Total Environment* 742: 140524.

Aleksandrov, Martin, Haris Aziz, Serge Gaspers, and Toby Walsh. 2015. Online fair division: Analysing a food bank problem. *arXiv preprint*: arXiv:1502.07571.

BBC. 2017. Jacob Rees-Mogg: Food banks 'rather uplifting'. BBC. Accessed 13 April. https://www.bbc.com/news/uk-politics-41264965.

BBC News. 2020. Councils spending £3m on food poverty and food banks. Accessed 17 April. https://www.bbc.com/news/uk-26369558.

Benke, Kurt, and Bruce Tomkins. 2017. 'Future food-production systems: Vertical farming and controlled-environment agriculture. *Sustainability: Science Practice and Policy* 13: 13–26.

Blake-Persen, N. 2020. Auckland's Spark Arena becomes huge foodbank during lockdown. Accessed 17 April. https://www.rnz.co.nz/national/programmes/checkpoint/audio/2018741875/auckland-s-spark-arena-becomes-huge-foodbank-during-lockdown.

Britneff, Beatrice Britneff. 2020. Food banks' demand surges amid COVID-19. Now they worry about long-term pressures. Global News. Accessed 20 April. https://globalnews.ca/news/6816023/food-bank-demand-covid-19-long-term-worry/.

CFS. 2016. Committee on World Secuirty. Accessed 15 August. http://www.fao.org/cfs/home/blog/blog-articles/article/en/c/448182/.

CGIAR. 2020. Covid-19 and global trade implications for food systems and health diets. Accessed 20 August. http://a4nh.cgiar.org/2020/05/20/covid-19-and-global-trade-implications-for-food-systems-and-healthy-diets/.

Deepak, Anne C. 2014. A postcolonial feminist social work perspective on global food insecurity. *Affilia* 29: 153–164.

Dombroski, K, G. Diprose, D. Conradson, S. Healy, and A. Watkins. 2018. When cultivate thrives: Developing criteria for community economy return on investment. *Christchurch, NZ: National Science Challenge* 11.

Dombroski, K., G. Diprose, E. Sharp, R. Graham, L. Lee, M. Scobie, S. Richardson, A. Watkins, and R. Martin-Neuninger. 2020. Food for people in place: Reimagining resilient food systems for economic recovery. *Journal of Sustsainability* 12 (22): 9369.

Dury, S., P. Bendjebbar, E. Hainzelin, T. Giordano, and N. Bricas. 2019 Food Systems at risk: New trends and challenges. In *Rome, Montpellier*. Brussels: FAO, CIRAD and European Commission.

FAO. 2006. Policy brief. Accessed 20 August. http://www.fao.org/fileadmin/templates/faoitaly/documents/pdf/pdf_Food_Security_Cocept_Note.pdf.

FAO. 2011. Global food losses and food waste. In *Extent, causes and prevention*. Rome.

FAO. 2020a. As more go hungry and malnutrition persists, achieving Zero Hunger by 2030 in doubt, UN report warns. Accessed 7 September. http://www.fao.org/news/story/en/item/1297810/icode/.

FAO. 2020b. A battle plan for ensuring global food supplies during the COVID-19 crisis. Accessed 31 August. http://www.fao.org/news/story/en/item/1297810/icode/.

FAO. 2020c. Building resilience for food security and nutrition. Accessed 23 April. http://www.fao.org/neareast/perspectives/building-resilience/en/.

FAO. 2020d. Hunger and food insecurity. Accessed 7 September. http://www.fao.org/hunger/en/.

FAO. 2020e. International prices of wheat and maize rose sharply in September but those of rice edged down. Accessed 12 October. http://www.fao.org/giews/food-prices/international-prices/detail/en/c/1313809/.
FAO, IFAD, UNICEF, WFP, and WHO. 2019. *The state of food security and nutrition in the world 2019: Safeguarding against economic slowdowns and downturns*. Rome: FAO.
FAO, IFAD, UNICEF, WFP, and WHO. 2020. *The state of food security and nutrition in the world 2020: Transforming food systems for affordable healthy diets*. Rome: FAO.
Fischer, R.A., Derek Byerlee, and Greg Edmeades. 2014. Crop yields and global food security. *ACIAR: Canberra, ACT*: 8–11.
Fouilleux, Eve, Nicolas Bricas, and Arlène Alpha. 2017. 'Feeding 9 billion people': Global food security debates and the productionist trap. *Journal of European Public Policy* 24: 1658–1677.
Gandhi, Leela. 2019. *Postcolonial theory: A critical introduction*. Columbia University Press.
Gentilini, U., M. Almenfi, I. Orton, and P. Dale. 2020. Social protection and jobs responses to COVID-19: A real-time review of country measure. Accessed 11 August. http://www.ugogentilini.net/wp-content/uploads/2020/04/Country-SP-COVID-responses_April10.pdf.
GFN. 2020a. The COVID-19 pandemic is deepening the hunger crisis. Food banks can't do it alone. Accessed 23 June. https://www.foodbanking.org/international-call-to-action-food-banks-cant-do-it-alone/.
GFN. 2020b. COVID-19 situation report. Food banking responses and best practices. Updated—13th April 2020. Accessed 14 April. https://www.foodbanking.org/wp-content/uploads/2020/04/0413_COVID-19-Update-Best-Practices-Trends-04-13-20_EN.pdf.
GFN. 2020c. Food bank response and best prectices. Accessed 24 April. https://www.foodbanking.org/wp-content/uploads/2020/04/COVID-19-Update-Best-Practices-Trends-04-21-20_EN.pdf.
GFN. 2020d. Food banks surge to meet demand as COVID-19 leaves communities reeling. Accessed 20 April. https://www.foodbanking.org/food-banks-surge-to-meet-demand-as-covid-19-leaves-communities-reeling/.
GFN. 2020e. The Global FoodBanking Network. Response to COVID-19. Accessed 1 September. https://www.foodbanking.org/covid19/.
GFN. 2020f. Message from the President & CEO—April 22, 2020. Accessed 23 June. https://mailchi.mp/foodbanking/food-banks-in-sub-saharan-africa-provide-aid-amidst-covid-19?e=8d71197c58.
GFN. 2020g. Open letter: The COVID-19 pandemic is deepening the hunger crisis. Food banks can't do it alone. Accessed 23 June. https://www.foodbanking.org/international-call-to-action-food-banks-cant-do-it-alone/.

GFN. 2020h. Powering communities for zero hunger. Accessed 18 September. https://www.foodbanking.org/.

GFN. 2020i. Press releases: Food banks surge to meet demand as COVID-19 leaves communities reeling. Accessed 13 April. https://www.foodbanking.org/food-banks-surge-to-meet-demand-as-covid-19-leaves-communities-reeling/.

Gibb, J. 2020. Many ask foodbanks for help. Accessed 17 April. https://www.odt.co.nz/news/dunedin/many-ask-foodbanks-help.

Gilbertson, G. 2020. Independent vegetable growers give produce to foodbanks amid Covid-19 pandemic. Stuffnz. Accessed 14 April. https://www.stuff.co.nz/business/farming/120771581/independent-vegetable-growers-give-produce-to-foodbanks-amid-covid19-pandemic.

Glover, Wiljeana J., Thanapol Poopunsri, and Robert Hurley. 2014. Applying lean to non-profit organizations: A food bank case study. In *IIE Annual Conference. Proceedings*, 274. Institute of Industrial and Systems Engineers (IISE).

Gregory, Christian A., and Alisha Coleman-Jensen. 2013. Do high food prices increase food insecurity in the United States? *Applied Economic Perspectives and Policy* 35: 679–707.

Hindle, Giles A., and Richard Vidgen. 2018. Developing a business analytics methodology: A case study in the foodbank sector. *European Journal of Operational Research* 268: 836–851.

Holling, Crawford S. 1973. Resilience and stability of ecological systems. *Annual Review of Ecology and Systematics* 4: 1–23.

IFPRI. 2020. Global food policy report 2020. Building inclusive food systems.

ILO. 2020. ILO Monitor: COVID-19 and the world of work. Fifth edition Updated estimates and analysis. Accessed 1 September. https://www.ilo.org/wcmsp5/groups/public/---dgreports/---dcomm/documents/briefingnote/wcms_749399.pdf.

IMF. 2020. Reopening from the great lockdown: Uneven and uncertain recovery', Accessed 5 September. https://blogs.imf.org/2020/06/24/reopening-from-the-great-lockdown-uneven-and-uncertain-recovery/.

Jia, Hongpeng, and Min Wu. 2020. Sustained research fund and dedicated research center for preparing next pandemic. *Precision Clinical Medicine*.

Lambie-Mumford, Hannah, and Tiina Silvasti. 2020. *The rise of food charity in Europe: The role of advocacy planning*. Policy Press.

Lang, T., and D. Barling. 2012. Food security and food sustainability: Reformulating the debate. *The Geographical Journal* 178: 313–326.

London Government. 2020. Coronavirus (COVID-19): Supporting foodbanks. Accessed 14 April. https://www.london.gov.uk/coronavirus/volunteer-and-donate/coronavirus-covid-19-supporting-foodbanks.

Loopstra, R. 2020. *Vulnerability to food insecurity since the COVID-19 lockdown*. London King's College.
Malan, Naudé. 2015. Urban farmers and urban agriculture in Johannesburg: Responding to the food resilience strategy. *Agrekon* 54: 51–75.
Martin-Neuninger, Rosemarie, and Matthew B. Ruby. 2020. What does food retail research tell us about the implications of Coronavirus (COVID-19) for grocery purchasing habits? *Frontiers in Psychology* 11.
Mayor of London. 2020. Coronavirus (COVID-19): Supporting foodbanks. Accessed 7 September. https://www.london.gov.uk/coronavirus/volunteer-and-donate/coronavirus-covid-19-supporting-foodbanks.
Ministry of Social Developement. 2020. Foodbanks, Food Rescue and Community Food Services. Accessed 12 April. https://www.msd.govt.nz/about-msd-and-our-work/newsroom/2020/covid-19/foodbanks-food-rescue-and-community-food-services.html.
NBC News. 2020. COVID-19 crisis heaps pressure on nation's food banks. Accessed 12 April. https://www.msd.govt.nz/about-msd-and-our-work/newsroom/2020/covid-19/foodbanks-food-rescue-and-community-food-services.html.
Net News. 2020. Food banks struggle to meet increased demand due to COVID-19. Accessed 14 April. http://netnebraska.org/article/news/1216625/food-banks-struggle-meet-increased-demand-due-covid-19.
Newshub. 2020. Coronavirus: Foodbank demand soars during COVID-19 pandemic. Accessed 14 April. https://www.newshub.co.nz/home/new-zealand/2020/04/coronavirus-foodbank-demand-soars-during-covid-19-pandemic.html.
Njagi, D. 2020. East Africa is seeing its worst swarms of locusts in many decades. How can these ravenous pests be stopped? *Future Planet*. Accessed 1 September. https://www.bbc.com/future/article/20200806-the-biblical-east-african-locust-plagues-of-2020.
Norberg-Hodge, Helena, Todd Merrifield, and Steven Gorelick. 2002. *Bringing the food economy home: Local alternatives to global agribusiness*. Zed Books.
nzherald. 2020. Covid 19 coronavirus: Auckland's Spark Arena becomes huge foodbank during lockdown. Accessed 13 April. https://www.nzherald.co.nz/nz/news/article.cfm?c_id=1&objectid=12323296.
OECD. 2020. Food security. Accessed 3 September. https://www.oecd.org/agriculture/topics/food-security/.
Patel, Raj. 2009. Food sovereignty. *The Journal of Peasant Studies* 36: 663–706.
Pollard, Christina M., and Sue Booth. 2019. Food insecurity and hunger in rich countries—It is time for action against inequality. *International Journal of Environmental Research and Public Health* 16: 1804.

Revie, E. 2020. Food isn't the answer to people needing food banks. The Trussel Trust. Accessed 13 September. https://www.trusselltrust.org/2020/06/05/food-not-the-answer/.

Robson, S. 2020. 'It's Christmas on steroids'—Foodbanks in huge demand across NZ. Accessed 22 April. https://www.rnz.co.nz/news/national/414809/it-s-christmas-on-steroids-foodbanks-in-huge-demand-across-nz.

Roser, M., and H. Ritchie. 2013. Hunger and undernourishment. Accessed 19 September. http://ourworldindata.org/.

Sanderson, T., G. Chapman, D. Walker, and P. Horne. 2020. *Food systems security, resilience and emerging risks in the Indo-Pacific in the context of COVID-19: A rapid assessment*. Canberra: Australian Centre for International Agricultural Research.

Stats NZ. 2020. Vegetable prices continue to grow. Accessed 17 October. https://www.stats.govt.nz/news/vegetable-prices-continue-to-grow.

Sterman, John D., and Gokhan Dogan. 2015. "I'm not hoarding, I'm just stocking up before the hoarders get here": Behavioral causes of phantom ordering in supply chains. *Journal of Operations Management* 39: 6–22.

Tendall, D.M., J. Joerin, B. Kopainsky, P. Edwards, A. Shreck, Q.B. Le, P. Krütli, M. Grant, and J. Six. 2015. Food system resilience: Defining the concept. *Global Food Security* 6: 17–23.

The Salvation Army. 2020. Online foodbank ramps up for Covid-19 response. Accessed 19 April. https://www.salvationarmy.org.nz/news/online-foodbank-ramps-covid-19-response.

The Trussell Trust. 2020. Tesco announces £15 million food donations to support food banks and local community groups. Accessed 17 April. https://www.trusselltrust.org/2020/04/01/tesco-announces-15-million-food-donations-support-food-banks-local-community-groups/.

The World Bank. 2020. Social protection and COVID-19 (Coronavirus). Accessed 22 April. https://www.worldbank.org/en/topic/socialprotection/brief/social-protection-and-covid-19.

Toth, Attila, Stacy Rendall, and Femke Reitsma. 2016. Resilient food systems: A qualitative tool for measuring food resilience. *Urban Ecosystems* 19: 19–43.

Trudeau, J. 2020. Prime Minister announces support for food banks and local food organizations. Accessed 17 April. https://pm.gc.ca/en/news/news-releases/2020/04/03/prime-minister-announces-support-food-banks-and-local-food.

UN. 2020. Policy brief: The impact of COVID-19 on food security and nutrition.

UNISEF. 2020. UNICEF: An additional 6.7 million children under 5 could suffer from wasting this year due to COVID-19.

WEF. 2020. How can we prevent a COVID-19 food crisis? Accessed 1 September. https://www.weforum.org/agenda/2020/05/preventing-a-covid-19-food-crisis/.

Wellington City Mission. 2020. Food bank demand increases by 400 per cent in 7 days. Accessed 8 April. https://wellingtoncitymission.org.nz/food-bank-demand-increases-by-400-per-cent-in-7-days/.

WFP. 2020a. COVID-19: Potential impact on the world's poorest people: A WFP analysis of the economic and food security implications of the pandemic.

WFP. 2020b. WFP global response to COVID-19: June 2020.

WFP. 2020c. World food programme to assist largest number of hungry people ever, as coronavirus devastates poor nations. Accessed 19 August. https://www.wfp.org/news/world-food-programme-assist-largest-number-hungry-people-ever-coronavirus-devastates-poor.

WHH. 2020. Hunger: Facts & figures. Accessed 4 September. https://www.welthungerhilfe.org/hunger/.

WHO. 2019. *Nutrition in universal health coverage*. World Health Organization.

WHO. 2020a. COVID-19 and food fafety: Guidance for food businesses: Interim guidance. Accessed 7 April. https://apps.who.int/iris/handle/10665/331705.

WHO. 2020b. Malnutrition. Accessed 7 September. https://www.who.int/news-room/fact-sheets/detail/malnutrition.

wtap. 2020. Kroger donates food, money to W.Va. food banks. Accessed 18 April. https://www.wtap.com/content/news/Kroger-donates-food-money-to-W-Va-food-banks-569731471.html.

CHAPTER 5

Young People, COVID-19 and Social Protection

Patrick Vakaoti

Introduction

On March 19, 2020, days after the World Health Organization (WHO) declared COVID-19 a pandemic, Antonio Guterres, the United Nations (UN) Secretary General, made the remark that the world is 'facing a global health crisis unlike any in the 75-year history of the United Nations–one that is spreading human suffering, infecting the global economy and upending people's lives' (Guterres 2020a, p. 2). From a health perspective, young people are not necessarily most at risk from COVID-19, but it is this invisibility that makes them a significant population to consider in any form of discussion about, and response to, the pandemic.

Whilst COVID-19 has had devastating health consequences, the impact on world economies has been equally severe. Many economies plummeted into a recession, with many experts regarding it the worst since the 1930s depression (Wearden and Jolly 2020). The pandemic

P. Vakaoti (✉)
University of Otago, Dunedin, New Zealand
e-mail: patrick.vakaoti@otago.ac.nz

S. Ratuva et al. (eds.), *COVID-19 and Social Protection*,
https://doi.org/10.1007/978-981-16-2948-8_5

is a significant generational moment for young people. It encapsulates their experiences and reactions embedded in the socio-cultural, political and material conditions of the pandemic (Wyn and Woodman 2007). In response to the pandemic, countries went into lockdown, and the world as young people knew it was transformed. Workplaces and entertainment precincts closed, and physical movement and social connections were restricted. Schools suspended classes, and universities moved teaching online. Whether they are defined according to the UN definition of 15–24 years of age or socio-culturally where in some societies this age definition is stretched to 35 years, the lives and experiences of young people will never be the same.

Since the pandemic, young people globally have been referred to as the 'lockdown generation'. This chapter is about this generation, how they experienced tertiary education, work and wellbeing during the pandemic and the place of social protection measures in this reality. It is inspired by the author's opinion piece, published online by The Big Q titled 'How are young tertiary students that work faring in the wake of COVID-19?' (Vakaoti 2020). Building on the opinion piece, the chapter draws extensively from secondary sources, particularly academic blog posts and rapid assessment reports by international agencies like the International Labour Organization (ILO) and the Asian Development Bank (ADB). Whilst the chapter offers a broad overview, detailed examples are drawn from New Zealand and the Pacific. This reflects the author's positionality: of Pacific heritage based in New Zealand. In addition, the two societies exist at different ends of the economic spectrum, New Zealand being a high-income country and Pacific countries falling into either low or upper-middle-income countries. This contrast allows us to explore the existence and/or absence of social protection measures as they pertain to young people. Finally, the chapter considers the response discourse of resilience and the need for young people to adjust to economies in flux. A critical view is warranted because the discourse of resilience places the responsibility on young people and undermines the immense contribution they currently make to their families and communities. This is particularly so in Pacific countries that rely heavily on the labour of their young populations. Social protection is about inclusivity and belonging, the burden of which needs to be shared collectively.

According to the International Labour Organization (ILO) (2017, p. xxix), 'social protection or social security is a human right and is defined as the set of policies and programmes designed to reduce and prevent poverty and vulnerability throughout the life cycle'. However, global social protection is still a far-fetched reality. ILO figures show that only about a third of the world's population benefits from universal social protection (ILO 2017, p. xxix). The majority of this population lives in high-income countries. In these countries, young people are well-protected, but growing inequality can mean that young people from deprived and marginal backgrounds are often most at risk. In lower and middle-income countries, the lack of social protection measures places the majority of young people at risk. The COVID-19 pandemic has further exacerbated this risk, creating economic, educational, health, social and wellbeing vulnerabilities for young people and other marginal groups.

Young People Pre-COVID-19

According to the UN (2018, p. 12), there are '1.2 billion young people, who currently make up 16 percent of the global population'. This number is even higher when one considers the socio-cultural definitions of youth that push the boundaries of chronological age in many indigenous communities. If we take the Sustainable Development Goals (SDGs) as the yardstick, the situation and experience of young people varies across regions and countries. For example, SDG4 refers to the promotion of inclusive and equitable education. The reality is far from ideal because at present '142 million youth of upper secondary age are out of school, and upper secondary enrolment rates average only 14 percent in low-income countries ... 30 percent of the poorest 12 to 14 year-olds have never attended school' (UN 2018, p. 1).

Low educational attainment has a direct relationship to poor employment outcomes. The United Nations estimates that about 71 million young people are unemployed, with millions more living in poverty even though they hold jobs (United Nations 2018). The situation in high and medium-income countries is no different: 'In 2019, 17.9 percent of rangatahi [young people] aged 15–19 years [in New Zealand] were unemployed, compared to an overall unemployment rate of 4.2 percent' (Ministry of Youth Development 2020). In Fiji, pre-COVID-19 youth unemployment was 14.8% (ADB and ILO 2020).

This reality is compounded by marginalisation, inequality and discrimination. As a result, young people become objects of concern, more so in societies where there is a youth bulge. The counter-narrative presents this youth cohort as an opportunity, as a demographic dividend. Young people are therefore acknowledged as major players in the realisation of the SDGs and in the attainment of a secure, inclusive and sustainable world (United Nations 2018). Young people as citizens become a formidable layer of protection for communities. In the wake of the COVID-19 pandemic, this role that young people play and the systems in place to support them have come under much stress. The situation of young people in tertiary education is one such example.

Tertiary Students

Tertiary education is touted as the preferred pathway for young people post high school. According to UNESCO and the International Institute for Educational Planning (IIEP) (2017, p. 1), 'between 2000 and 2014, the number of students in higher education institutions more than doubled, rising from 100 to 207 million'. However, enrolments are skewed towards Western countries and success and completion in favour of the privileged. In New Zealand, Māori and Pacific students 'show higher attrition rates, lower participation rates and are underrepresented in bachelor level programmes compared to non-Māori students' (Wikaire et al. 2017, p. 301). These students and others from less privileged backgrounds are adversely impacted by the pandemic. They have also been joined by other young people in general because the pandemic has indiscriminately affected everyone.

The response by tertiary institutions either to suspend or transition to online learning has equity and access implications. According to the ILO (2020b, p. 23), '44 percent of young students in low-income countries, 20 percent in lower middle-income countries and 4 percent in high-income countries reported not having received any courses'. Most affected are young people who come from backgrounds where either family and/or institutions have limited or no access to digital infrastructures and technologies (ADB and ILO 2020). In many cases, institutions have responded by providing learning devices to students, but these aren't enough to keep students engaged in learning. The University of the South Pacific reported that 'as of Sunday 31st May 2020, 861 students have withdrawn from 1332 courses. This is equivalent to 3.2 percent of Semester 1 students ... there are also students who have not logged into Moodle' since the beginning of the pandemic (USP 2020).

Suspending or transitioning learning caused disruptions for both academics and students. Students in particular had to contend with timetable and routine changes and varying experiences of this new online learning reality. Inequality of access was evident in cases where students had no internet connectivity or where access was intermittent, slow and expensive. Some students didn't have access to electronic devices. Anecdotal evidence reveals cases where siblings that attended university were sharing a single device at home. Many young tertiary students are also employed. The struggles of coping with online learning are compounded by the loss of work.

Young People and Work

Globally, precarious employment is a feature in the lives of young people. According to the ILO, young people between the ages of 15 and 24 years are three times more likely to be without work compared to those over the age of 25 years (ILO 2020b). Even young people in countries like Australia, with close to two decades of sustained economic growth, are not immune. Young people's work is characterised by casual, part-time and fixed-term contracts in retail, hospitality, events and other sectors (Chesters and Cuervo 2019). Before the pandemic, about 178 million young people were engaged in this work environment (ILO 2020b). These young people were amongst the earliest cohorts of people to lose employment during the pandemic. A recent ILO study found that about a quarter (23.1%) of young people aged 18–24 years reported having lost jobs during the pandemic (ILO 2020b). This includes tertiary students, most of whom work whilst studying.

Young tertiary students work for many reasons. This ranges from gaining work experience and earning an income to offset the cost of student loans, which in New Zealand averages about $NZD22,000. Prior to the pandemic and subsequent lockdown, many working tertiary students in New Zealand spoke of financial hardships; some became vegetarian whilst working in order to afford food and to pay for rent, whilst some dropped out of university completely (Woolf and Moore 2018). The pandemic has exacerbated these experiences because causal and part-time working tertiary students were the first to be without employment. In other sectors like supermarkets, young people were employed as 'essential' workers because older people were considered more vulnerable. This does not address young people's employment precarity nor their safety from COVID-19.

As future tertiary students, some high school students are leaving school, to work and support families. In September 2020, SBS News reported on how an 18-year-old Tongan in Melbourne, Australia left school to work and support his siblings and his sickly father (Dinham 2020). In New Zealand, the same has been observed with Pacific and Māori high school students dropping out of school to find work because adults are out of work. These students come from collective cultures where service and respect for elders is valued. This very act of working may decrease their chances of attending university and their earning capacity later in life (Quince 2020).

The COVID-19 pandemic is estimated to cause an increase in global unemployment of between 5.3 and 24.7 million people. Young people stand to be affected significantly as a cohort that are three times more likely to be unemployed than adults (ILO 2020b). Securing the future of the world post the COVID-19 pandemic means securing the future, livelihood and wellbeing of young people. Events like the Arab Spring, recent youth riots in French and British cities and the 2019 protests in Hong Kong demonstrate what youth discontent emanating from unemployment and restrictions on civil liberties can result in. In addition, these young people are easily drawn into or by other causes and events that magnify their existence. For example, at the height of the pandemic, protests were also breaking out in American cities over the police killing of George Floyd. Amidst genuine young protesters were looters. It would be irresponsible and damaging for countries to allow their young populations to descend in this way. Thereby setting them up to deal with long-term social and material deprivation and mental health and wellbeing issues.

Tertiary Students and Wellbeing

It is a known fact that young people in the contemporary world experience loneliness. COVID-19 has both accentuated and increased this reality. In New Zealand, youth loneliness 'increased from 5.8 percent before Covid-19 struck to 20.8 percent during the lockdown and remains high at 17 percent' (RNZ 2020). This group of young people includes tertiary students who have lost work, transitioned to online learning and are experiencing social isolation and uncertainties about the future of work.

As lockdown was enforced by governments across the globe, the transition to online learning became a necessity. This was experienced differently by students and was mediated to some extent by access to electronic devices, internet, home study environments and the continued availability of work for some. Whilst some students thrived, others felt isolated. The connectivity assumed of those belonging to Generation Z does not neatly transcend boundaries and experiences. This is because an online community is viewed as more fleeting than enduring. Students themselves express this sentiment and are critical of universities that make learning a priority over wellbeing. This was articulated by Isabella Lenihan-Ikin, National President of the New Zealand Union of Students' Associations (NZUSA), who said that 'shifting students away from lectures and campuses into the depths of their dark and cold flats, that they can't afford to heat, is not the solution' (Lenihan-Ikin 2020). Governments take charge of proposing and implementing solutions, many of which are economic in nature and not necessarily popular. International students are implicated in these decisions.

International students also comprise the cohort of tertiary students affected by, but who were largely invisible during, the pandemic. Governments appeared to be more concerned about the economic burden they confront with the decrease and uncertainty across the international student market. In New Zealand, international students contribute approximately $5 billion NZD dollars annually to the economy (Hipkins 2018). Government opposition argues that the country stands to lose $2 billion NZD should New Zealand's borders remain closed to international students (Collins 2020). These sentiments don't augur well in an environment where human despair is unprecedently high and where international students are very aware of their monetary value in comparison to domestic students. This was articulated by Belle Lim, the President of the Council of International Students Australia (CISA), who said that:

> in good times international students are part of the community–when we are spending loads of money and contributing to Australia's economy–but in bad times, when the pandemic hits, students [who have] lost their income have become a liability for the government. (Ross 2020)

Rights Denied

Government decisions to lock down countries for public health reasons are unprecedented in modern history and particularly in Western democracies. Lockdowns meant that only essential services remained open and movement was restricted to essential workers. Different countries managed this scenario differently. In New Zealand, for example, the government introduced four Alert Levels: Alert Level 4 meaning strict restrictions, with Alert Level 1 an almost 'normal' pre-COVID-19 scenario. Despite the well-intentioned health reasons, the lockdown was seen to infringe on people's rights. This has even been challenged in court in the case of Borrowdale v Director-General of Health–[2020] NZHC 2090. In its summary, the 'High Court [declared] the requirement that New Zealanders stay home for the 9 day period between 26 March and 3 April was justified, but unlawful' (Courts of New Zealand 2020).

As a vulnerable group, young people often find it challenging to enjoy their rights. This is more so the case for young people in marginal circumstances: the poor, unemployed, refugees and those with physical and mental impairments, to name a few. The pandemic has worsened this reality. The ILO (2020b) found that young people have reported increases in their inability to civically engage, practice their religion, access reliable information, afford decent accommodation and be guaranteed personal safety. In Fiji, the government introduced a nationwide curfew and related restrictions when the country recorded its first case of COVID-19 in March. The curfew is still in place (seven months later), and young people have accounted for the majority of breaches. Interestingly, some of the convictions have been overturned in court, including the very public case of a 19-year-old female who breached COVID-19 restrictions in April when she and her partner were found courting during the curfew (Talei 2020). A conviction would have impacted her future work prospects, including any international opportunities.

Tertiary students were also critical of university decisions to transition learning online, particularly in the medium to long term. The point of contention appears to be the absence or lack of consultation with students. Students feel that unilateral decision making reflects the traditional and oppressive pattern of adults making decisions about and for young people. In addition, students felt disadvantaged by inequitable access to online learning resources and the inability to experience value for money in programmes like medicine (Lenihan-Ikin 2020). They also felt exploited by some universities and student accommodation providers who continued charging rent during the lockdown (Tan 2020). Student dissatisfaction with the way they have been treated should be a significant consideration in any response to their learning, wellbeing and protection.

Social Protection Responses

Global responses to the pandemic have been mixed. Prosperous countries responded almost immediately by announcing stimulus packages, 3 trillion in the United States (BBC 2020), 130 billion in Australia (Karp 2020) and 12.1 billion in New Zealand (Robertson 2020). The bulk of this money was intended for wage subsidies and welfare support as—social protection. The ILO (2020a) found that young people, particularly those that stayed in jobs from middle and high-income countries, benefitted more from these responses. The intention of these responses was to try and keep as many people in employment as possible. The situation in low-income countries is less understood because of the absence of data. Data from low-income countries has been scant, thus the assumption that vulnerable citizens, including young people, are the worst affected. This is in part due to the absence of, or poorly developed, social protection strategies.

Some countries with adequate social protection strategies, however, have had to draw on schemes established for different purposes. For example, in Fiji, the government openly promoted the withdrawal of retirement funds from the Fiji National Provident Fund (FNPF) by citizens with adequate account balances and who have lost employment and are on reduced pay or reduced working hours. The government supported those with low FNPF balances with up to $1,100 FJD over a 10 week period. In May 2020, it was reported that 18,540 members of the FNPF had received government assistance (Reece 2020). The reliance on government assistance is worrying because about '69 percent of the 444,663 members have balances below $10,000' and '61,000 members have zero balances in their accounts' (Waqairadovu 2019). This is particularly concerning as the Fiji government has been accused of plundering the FNPF, rather than protecting the interests of its members (Iyer 2020). This speaks to the need for durable and sustainable social protection measures.

In New Zealand, the government announced a $130 million NZD student support package, allowing students to take out an additional

$1000 NZD for study-related expenses on their student loans. Universities established hardship funds. These strategies are acknowledged to be short-term in nature, with the government's support package criticised for putting students in more debt. However, the New Zealand government like other governments realises that recovering from COVID-19 will require a long-term plan. Tertiary students currently benefit from fees free (referred to as the fees free scheme) for the first year of their education. Perhaps this is the opportune time to extend the gesture into the second year of tertiary studies. This may also be a time to renew conversations on student debt repayment.

Government support for educational institutions is vital. Education has the potential to help people, particularly those from marginalised backgrounds, rebuild their lives after the pandemic. In New Zealand, initiatives like the $28.5 million Pacific Education Innovation Fund over four years to 'support new innovative practices that respond to the curriculum and wellbeing needs of Pacific learners which have emerged or been made worse by COVID-19' (Salesa 2020) could prove to be instrumental in the post-pandemic rebuild process.

Unemployment has been rife during the pandemic. Many families have found it difficult to afford food and provide for other necessities. As a result, demand for emergency food has increased to more than double the pre-COVID-19 demand. New demand is coming from those who have never had to seek assistance before. According to an Auckland Foodbank Manager, 'we're going to nicer houses, we're going to people who have been doing fine, who are now in a situation where they've lost their jobs' (Fanks 2020). Four months into the lockdown, The Salvation Army recorded supporting 11,242 first-time clients (The Salvation Army 2020). Non-governmental organisations have been a lifeline for many families during the pandemic.

In Fiji, the government made a decision not to provide lunches to students whose families have been impacted by COVID-19 (Cava 2020). Civil society organisations (CSOs) and faith-based groups instead took up the challenge. When schools in Fiji resumed on June 15, the TISI Sangam Foundation rolled out its free lunch programme to about 8000 students that attend their schools (Narayan 2020). Such initiatives are complemented by the Fiji CSO Alliance for COVID-19 Humanitarian Response. Known as the Alliance, this collective aims 'to improve access to information and to disseminate information from the different partners on the work that is happening on the ground … to ensure a more coordinated approach to the relief and recovery work of members' (Singh and Lockington 2020). The Foundation for Rural Integrated Enterprises and Development (FRIEND), a member of the Alliance, reported having processed 1000 assistance applications between August and September, 2020 (Krishant 2020). For countries like Fiji, which are heavily reliant on tourism, the impact of the pandemic is expected to persist.

According to the ILO (2020a), countries with social protection systems are better able to mitigate the impact of the pandemic compared to those without or with weak social protection systems. The Pacific is one such region with weak social protection systems and could benefit from the support of higher income countries like New Zealand. Whilst COVID-19 infections appear to be contained in the Pacific, border closures have had significant consequences for countries that heavily rely on tourism. In Fiji, about 150,000 people are either directly or indirectly involved in tourism. Young people who are part of this workforce are currently without work, and their situations are dire without social protection measures. Diplomacy could become a longer term social protection measure. As border restrictions are lifted and movement resumes, working holidays or an increased quota for seasonal workers from Fiji and other Pacific countries to New Zealand and Australia should be considered.

The United Nations (2020, p. 3) has suggested 'promoting the narrative of opportunity ... to learn how to engage youths in a work culture in flux'. This suggestion does little to deal with the issues of precarious employment. It returns young people to the politics of individualisation, making them responsible for secure work should they need it or taking initiative during this time of need. It neglects the reality that young people have been constantly adapting to the fluidity of the employment market.

Young people are a resilient cohort and can effectively mobilise during a crisis. In the days following the lockdown in New Zealand, the Student Volunteer Army (SVA) had activated its network, with members lending support to the elderly and childcare support to children of essential workers (Kenny and Guildford 2020). Similarly, 'in Colombia, Ghana, Iraq and several other countries, young peacebuilders and humanitarians are delivering supplies to frontline health workers and people in need' (Guterres 2020b).

In the Pacific, lockdowns, border closures and unemployment have seen a renewed interest in traditional and indigenous modes of subsistence and livelihood. In Fiji, social media barter systems have gained popularity. The Barter for Better Fiji Facebook group, which has close to

100,000 members has facilitated exchanges of food and services. Specifically, trades have included '100 dalo [taro] tops for a traditional voivoi [pandanus] mat, fresh coconuts for cans of RTD Woodstock, an entire infant clothing wardrobe for a pie ... a bag of food items and baby diapers for a puppy' (Williams 2020). Tuvalu is COVID-19 free, but precaution has led to border and school closures. The latter has seen many students returning home to the outer islands where they are learning traditional food production and preservation methods. Here, young people are actively responding and adapting to their changing reality. According to Kitara and Farbotko (2020), 'COVID-19 has opened the opportunity for Tuvaluan young people to think differently about important issues such as indigenous knowledge and values'.

Conclusion

The world is at a crossroad, a juncture beyond which life will never be the same. Young people are experiencing a generational moment. The pandemic will substantially influence immediate decisions and future outcomes. Even young people in tertiary education who hold jobs and young people in employment who have previously been buffered from economic shocks are not immune. Access to and the optimum experience of education, employment, health, and wellbeing will weigh heavily on their minds. Governments have the responsibility of allaying these fears. Well-resourced governments can do this and have the capacity to recognise and support youth-led innovation and creative initiatives. The challenge lies in low and middle-income countries where, for example, existing issues like sea level rise in low lying Pacific countries, the burden of infectious diseases in African countries and displacement in war-torn countries will be exacerbated. The reality for young people becomes dire.

To survive, citizens, including young people, particularly in states that have poorly developed social protection strategies, are discovering alternative ways of supporting individuals, families and communities. In the Pacific, many are returning to indigenous livelihood practices: subsistence farming and fishing, food preservation and bartering produce. Young people in particular are virtually connecting with each other, engaging about indigenous values and identity. Families and communities have become significant forms of support for young people. Whilst admirable, young people and their socio-cultural informal support systems should not be exploited nor should young people sacrifice themselves for causes that are larger than them. Our response to COVID-19 cannot, and must not, rely on young people's resilience to sustain them in the medium and long term. To do so places an immense burden on a group whose importance and susceptibility to risk and harm is often diminished and downplayed.

The pandemic and its impact are systemic in nature. Pandemic-related issues have demonstrated systemic gaps, particularly in communities with poorly developed social protection systems. A post-pandemic world requires a reimaging of a system where people, including young people, are placed at the centre. This is imperative because young people even those in employment do not often access social protection measures and social and health insurance (United Nations 2020). By actively considering young people and their diverse realities in our COVID-19 response, we have the opportunity to support a group that for so long has responded to events locally, regionally and internationally with resilience, a sense of community, sheer determination and creativity. As such, young people deserve a place in meaningfully contributing to the United Nations slogan of 'Building Back Better'.

References

Asia Development Bank (ADB) and International Labour Organization (ILO). 2020. Tackling the COVID-19 youth employment crisis in Asia and the Pacific. ILO, Bangkok & ADB, Manila. https://www.adb.org/sites/default/files/publication/626046/covid-19-youth-employment-crisis-asia-pacific.pdf. Accessed 27 October 2020.

BBC News. 2020. Coronavirus: Congress passes $484bn economic relief bill. https://www.bbc.com/news. Accessed 24 April 2020.

Cava, L. 2020. School lunches not on help list. *The Fiji Times*. https://www.fijitimes.com/school-lunches-not-on-help-list/. Accessed 8 July 2020.

Chesters, Jenny, and Hernan Cuervo. 2019. Adjusting to new employment landscapes: Consequences of precarious employment for young Australians. *The Economic and Labour Relations Review* 30 (2): 222–240. https://doi.org/10.1177/1035304619832740.

Collins, Simon. 2020. Covid19 coronavirus: International students look to NZ after Covid crushed. NZ Herald. https://www.nzherald.co.nz/nz/news/article.cfm?c_id=1&objectid=12339225. Accessed 13 June 2020.

Courts of New Zealand. 2020. Borrowdale v Director-General of Health–[2020] NZHC 2090. https://www.courtsofnz.govt.nz/cases/borrowdale-v-director-general-of-health-1-1. Accessed 19 August 2020.

Dinham, Abby. 2020. When coronavirus hit, Poasa wanted to quit school—But his community had other ideas. https://www.sbs.com.au/news/when-coronavirus-hit-poasa-wanted-to-quit-school-but-his-community-had-other-ideas?fbclid=IwAR2U-Kqs2Tx-PVarRxeWtHCwNSz6EtaJ6MIJZxotbLlCOCc-yqAp_LNu_70&cid=news:socialshare:twitter. Accessed 23 September 2020.

Fanks, Josephine. 2020. Coronavirus: Demand for food banks double pre-Covid levels, and still growing. *Stuff*. https://www.stuff.co.nz/national/122093506/coronavirus-demand-for-food-banks-double-precovid-levels-and-still-growing. Accessed 18 July 2020.

Guterres, Antonio. 2020a. COVID-19: A Call for Solidarity. https://www.un.org/. Accessed 19 March 2020.

Guterres, Antonio. 2020b. Secretary-General's remarks to virtual Security Council meeting on the Maintenance of International Peace and Security: Youth, Peace and Security. https://www.un.org/. Accessed 27 April 2020.

Hipkins, Chris. 2018. International education contributes $5.1 billion to New Zealand economy. https://www.beehive.govt.nz/release/international-education-contributes-51-billion-new-zealand-economy. Accessed 20 October 2020.

ILO. 2017. World Social Protection Report. Geneva, ILO. https://www.ilo.org/global/publications/books/WCMS_604882/lang--en/index.htm. Accessed 27 October 2020.

ILO. 2020a. Social protection responses to the COVID-19 crisis: Country responses and policy considerations. https://www.ilo.org/wcmsp5/groups/public/---ed_protect/---soc_sec/documents/publication/wcms_742337.pdf. Accessed 15 October 2020.

ILO. 2020b. *Youth and Covid-19: Impacts of Jobs, education rights and mental wellbeing*. Geneva: Switzerland. https://www.ilo.org/wcmsp5/groups/public/---ed_emp/documents/publication/wcms_753026.pdf. Accessed 25 September 2020.

Iyer, Kamal. 2020. FNPF—A social security scheme or a cash cow for government? NFP. https://www.nfpfiji.org/post/fnpf-a-social-security-scheme-or-a-cash-cow-for-government. Accessed 14 May 2020.

Karp, Paul. 2020. Australian economic stimulus package: How much government have committed to coronavirus crisis. *The Guardian*. https://www.theguardian.com/international. Accessed 31 March 2020.

Kenny, Jake, and Jonathan Guildford. 2020. Coronavirus: Student Volunteer Army rallies help with childcare and shopping. *Stuff*. https://www.stuff.co.nz/. Accessed 29 March 2020.

Kitara, Taukiei, and C. Carol Farbotko. 2020. Youth resilience to COVID-19: Indigenous knowledge in Tuvalu. DEVPOLICYBLOG. https://devpolicy.org/youth-resilience-to-covid-19-indigenous-knowledge-in-tuvalu-20200708/. Accessed 8 July 2020.

Krishant, Naveel. 2020. FRIEND FIJI has processed over 1000 applications for food rations. Fijivillage. https://www.fijivillage.com/news/FRIEND-FIJI-has-processed-over-1000-applications-for-food-rations-rx8f45/. Accessed 28 September 2020.

Lenihan-Ikin, Isabella. 2020. As universities go ever more online, students are getting left out in the cold. The Spinoff. https://thespinoff.co.nz/politics/28-06-2020/as-universities-go-ever-more-online-students-are-getting-left-out-in-the-cold/. Accessed 28 June 2020.

Ministry of Youth Development. 2020. Impact of COVID-19 on rangatahi. http://www.myd.govt.nz/young-people/youth-plan/impact-of-covid-19-on-rangatahi-youth-plan.html#Employmentandfinancialsecurity2. Accessed 27 October 2020.

Narayan, Vijay. 2020. TISI Sangam plans to give free lunches to 8,000 students when school resumes. Fijivillage. https://www.fijivillage.com/news/TISI-Sangam-plans-to-give-free-lunch-to-8000-students-when-school-resume-f8x r45/. Accessed 1 May 2020.

Otago Daily Times. 2020. Government's student assistance package decried. *Otago Daily Times*. https://www.odt.co.nz/. Accessed 15 April 2020.

Quince, Khylee. 2020. Coronavirus: Covid inequities are showing up in school leaver figures. *Stuff*. https://www.stuff.co.nz/national/education/122517 212/coronavirus-covid-inequities-are-showing-up-in-school-leaver-figures. Accessed 5 August 2020.

Reece, Lena. 2020. Second wave of FNPF assistance announced. FBC News. https://www.fbcnews.com.fj/news/covid-19/second-wave-of-fnpf-ass istance-announced/. Accessed 23 May 2020.

RNZ. 2020. Loneliness spikes among New Zealand Youth. https://www.rnz.co.nz/news/national/422553/loneliness-spikes-among-new-zealand-youth. Accessed 1 August 2020.

Robertson, Grant. 2020. $12.1 billion support for New Zealanders and business. https://www.beehive.govt.nz/release/121-billion-support-new-zea landers-and-business. Accessed 30 October 2020.

Ross, J. 2020. Neglect 'fuels perceptions of racism' against students in Australia. Times Higher Education. https://www.timeshighereducation.com/news/neglect-fuels-perceptions-racism-against-students-australia. Accessed 23 September 2020.

Salesa, Jenny. 2020. Support for innovative Pacific education responses to COVID-19 needs. New Zealand Government. https://www.beehive.govt.nz/release/support-innovative-pacific-education-responses-covid-19-needs. Accessed 23 September 2020.

Singh, Nalini, and Maryann Lockington. 2020. Fiji civil society solidarity driving the COVID-19 humanitarian response. DEVPOLICYBLOG. https://dev

policy.org/fiji-civil-society-solidarity-driving-the-covid-19-humanitarian-response-20200604-2/. Accessed 4 June 2020.

Talei, Fonua. 2020. Court quashes sentence and conviction of student caught dating during COVID-19 restrictions. Fiji Sun. https://fijisun.com.fj/2020/05/15/court-quashes-sentence-and-conviction-of-student-caught-dating-during-covid-19-restrictions/. Accessed 15 May 2020.

Tan, Lincoln. 2020. Covid 19 coronavirus: Students call for full rent reduction from university. NZ Herald. https://www.nzherald.co.nz/nz/news/article.cfm?c_id=1&objectid=12329409. Accessed 4 May 2020.

The Salvation Army. 2020. COVID-19 Social Impact Dashboard–Report 5. https://www.salvationarmy.org.nz/article/sppu-covid-19-social-impact-dashboard-report-5. Accessed 31 July 2020.

United Nations. 2018. Youth and the 2030 Agenda for Sustainable Development. https://www.un.org/development/desa/youth/wp-content/uploads/sites/21/2018/12/WorldYouthReport-2030Agenda.pdf. Accessed 15 October 2020.

United Nations. 2020. Special issue on COVID-19 and Youth. https://www.youthpower.org/resources/un-youth-flash-special-issue-covid-19-and-youth. Accessed 1 October 2020.

UNESCO and IIEP. 2017. Six ways to ensure higher education leaves no one behind. Policy Paper 30. https://unesdoc.unesco.org/home. Accessed 15 September 2020.

USP. 2020. University of the South Pacific's Response to COVID-19 Pandemic for Learning and Teaching. Fiji Sun Online. https://fijisun.com.fj/2020/06/08/university-of-the-south-pacifics-response-to-covid-19-pandemic-for-learning-and-teaching/. Accessed 8 June 2020.

Vakaoti, Patrick. 2020. How are young tertiary students that work faring in the wake of COVIC-19? The Big Q. https://www.thebigq.org/2020/06/03/how-are-young-tertiary-students-that-work-faring-in-the-wake-of-covid-19/. Accessed 10 November 2020.

Waqairadovu, Apenisa. 2019. 61,000 FNPF members have nil balances. FBC News. https://www.fbcnews.com.fj/news/12369000-fnpf-members-have-nil-balances/. Accessed 26 September 2020.

Wearden, Graeme, and Jasper Jolly. 2020. IMF: Global economy faces worst recession since the Great Depression-as it happened. *The Guardian*. https://www.theguardian.com/international. Accessed 14 April 2020.

Williams, Lisa. 2020. Facebook barter page grows cash-free trade in Fiji and beyond. RNZ. https://www.rnz.co.nz/international/pacific-news/415644/facebook-barter-page-grows-cash-free-trade-in-fiji-and-beyond. Accessed 2 May 2020.

Wikaire Erena, Elana Curtis, Donna Cormack, Yannan Jiang, Louise McMillan, Rob Loto, and Papaarangi. 2017. Predictors of academic success for Māori,

Pacific and non-Māori non-Pacific students in health professional education: a quantitative analysis. *Advances in Health Sciences Education* 22: 299–326. https://doi.org/10.1007/s10459-017-9763-4.

Woolf, Amber-Leigh, and Rebeca Moore. 2018. The new normal of students working jobs, on top of full time study. *Stuff*. https://www.stuff.co.nz/. Accessed 2 September 2020.

Wyn, Johanna, and Dan Woodman. 2007. Generation, youth and social change in Australia. *Journal of Youth Studies* 9 (5): 495–514. https://doi.org/doi.org/10.1080/13676260600805713.

CHAPTER 6

Rethinking Media and Communication in the COVID-19 Context

Tara Ross

Media are a key filter through which people understand and make sense of the world and, especially in the global COVID-19 pandemic, an important source of public health and safety information. However, critical issues of access and social justice beg a reassessment of the role media and communication channels might play in the COVID-19 response and recovery, particularly for marginalised and disadvantaged groups.

On the one hand, the COVID-19 pandemic has exacerbated a host of social inequalities, including the communication gaps between the haves and the have-nots (UNDP 2020) that can contribute to poorer health (Lupton 2014, p. 1353). Media paywalls, for instance, exclude poorer communities from getting the most accurate health-related news and information (Stroobant et al. 2019), potentially exacerbating their vulnerability to COVID-19, while the closure of hundreds of news media worldwide (Hare 2020; Meade 2020; Tracy 2020) has hit hardest

T. Ross (✉)
University of Canterbury, Christchurch, New Zealand
e-mail: tara.ross@canterbury.ac.nz

S. Ratuva et al. (eds.), *COVID-19 and Social Protection*,
https://doi.org/10.1007/978-981-16-2948-8_6

those media outlets serving disadvantaged, minority language and rural communities, further deepening communication inequalities.

On the other hand, the pandemic information campaigns deployed by different states, with varying degrees of success, highlight the need to look more closely at communities' communication infrastructures, both to overcome barriers to quality information and communication and to help amplify public health messaging into the communities that need it. For example, the universalised approach to public health messaging adopted by some states has often overlooked people's different communication capabilities or the distinctive ways in which information is shared and understood in different communities. Health information distributed through digital portals, for instance, will not reach people who lack access to the internet; contact tracing apps will not work for those who cannot afford a smartphone or the mobile data needed to run it; and information distributed through mainstream media is less likely to reach culturally and linguistically diverse communities (Ratnam et al. 2020; Ross 2016, 2017; Taylor 2020). Add to that, the high levels of government and media mistrust among marginalised communities, and it is clear that more needs to be done to support community-based and -led communication channels that can more accurately and effectively tailor information and provide the social protection that is needed to mitigate the worst effects of ongoing waves of COVID-19.

COVID-19 Exacerbates Inequalities and Disadvantage

Evidence shows that ethnic minority communities are at greater risk of serious health problems from COVID-19, partly as a result of a range of social health determinants such as being more likely to live in overcrowded and multi-generational households and being more likely to work in occupations that are more exposed to the virus, for example, service work in health care and social assistance industries (Ma'ia'i 2020; MBIE 2020). A report from the United Kingdom (Williamson et al. 2020) suggests that black and minority ethnic groups suffer death rates double those of white people, while in the United States, African-American and Pacific communities have been disproportionately affected (Steyn et al. 2020), with hospitalisation rates for Pacific groups 10 times those of other groups (Jackson 2020). In New Zealand, the risk of death from COVID-19 for Pacific peoples and indigenous Māori could be up to double that of European New Zealanders (Steyn et al. 2020), all of which makes a strong argument for prioritising marginalised groups in any pandemic response.

Notably, the socio-economic and health inequities that put ethnic minority groups at greater risk of COVID-19 transmission and complications are complex and multi-factorial (Steyn et al. 2020), and further exacerbated by the pandemic. For instance, as the health sector responded to the first wave of COVID-19, people were asked to switch to online or telehealth alternatives to face-to-face care, which posed challenges for ethnic minority groups, such as New Zealand's indigenous Māori and Pacific peoples, who are less likely to have internet access than other groups (Digital Inclusion Research Group 2017; Grimes and White 2019).

Indeed, as new media technologies become more pervasive, differences in internet and technology use between social groups becomes a more pressing issue. Already, the social inequalities that contribute to poorer health can be exacerbated, Lupton says (2014, p. 1353), by lack of access to or knowledge about digital technologies. When the internet and digital devices became people's main access to work, education and essential health information and services during COVID-19, those who lacked what they needed to be digitally included were at a serious disadvantage (Department of Internal Affairs 2020). Almost two-thirds (65%) of New Zealand GPs surveyed in a national study of general practice experience with COVID-19 reported they had patients who struggled with telehealth under raised alert levels (University of Auckland 2020). Best estimates in New Zealand are that one in five people lack at least one of the elements needed to be digitally included (Department of Internal Affairs 2020). In the United States, more than 21 million people lack the advanced broadband internet needed to access telehealth, so cannot socially distance when accessing health services (Merrefield 2020). They are also less likely to be able to work from home and more likely to have to work face to face (so at more risk of contracting COVID-19), and less likely to be able to access online education to keep up with classes (ibid.).

Indeed, when schools in 192 countries worldwide closed their doors at the height of the pandemic, sending home 1.6 billion students, UNICEF estimated at least a third were unable to access remote learning because of a lack of internet access, computers or mobile devices (UNICEF 2020). New Zealand government data (Ministry of Education, personal communication, September 29, 2020) reveals that when New Zealand went into

COVID-19 lockdown in April 2020, schools reported 95,000 of their students (11.3% of all learners) required a device to study remotely, with the need among Māori and Pacific students even higher, at 21.9 and 26.1%, respectively. Though the government moved quickly to despatch devices to those who did not have them, its response was not enough to make up for long-standing gaps in digital access: by 11 August, the government had distributed devices to 25,515 students, far short of the 95,000 students that schools had identified as needing a device for their remote learning. In addition, the government contracted with telecommunications companies to roll out internet connections to 53,000 households (Department of Internal Affairs 2020; Ministry of Education 2020) and, although 38,000 connections had been made or were in progress as of late August, and a further 14,200 connections were booked for installation, the data suggests there were significant delays in getting many students online. Moreover, as these connections were funded for only six months, it is unclear how this measure future-proofed students' education against subsequent waves of COVID-19 and lockdown.

Gaps such as these, even if felt only for a short time, can have a significant impact. A survey of young Māori students during lockdown found many faced problems with connectivity or access to the software needed for their learning (more than half had only an internet-enabled phone for remote learning), so fell back on less educationally challenging curricula (Hunia et al. 2020). Their reduced learning opportunities had a negative impact on mental health and resilience and, when coupled with their parents and caregivers' lower educational and literacy levels, exacerbated intergenerational disadvantage (ibid., p. 17). Indeed, experts warn the impacts of such exclusion may have long-term effects. UNICEF (2020) says that for the most marginalised, 'missing out on school–even if only for a few weeks–can lead to negative outcomes that last a lifetime', and has called on governments to scale up remote learning opportunities, especially for the most marginalised, to avoid disruption to learning.

Parallel problems have been raised in relation to people's increasing reliance on mobile phones to access the internet. United States data (Pew Research Center 2019a) shows an increasing share of Americans use smartphones as their primary means of online access at home, with roughly one in five American adults (especially younger adults, non-whites and those on lower incomes) now smartphone-only internet users. Humphry's (2019) research on digital use and homelessness suggests, however, that the rise of the mobile internet may be further stratifying access. For one, those who are dependent on smartphones and/or mobiles for internet access pay more for their data, which is a concern given more and more services, including government health and social support services, are moving online. New Zealand's government suspended mobile data charges for a handful of key health websites during the pandemic, after clear feedback from health providers that the cost of mobile data was preventing people from accessing key health information and services (Ministry of Health, personal communication, September 1, 2020). A survey in 11 emerging economies (Pew Research Center 2019b) suggests significant numbers of phone owners face similar cost barriers, with a median of 37% saying it could be a challenge to pay for their phone and 42% reporting frequently or occasionally avoiding activities on their phones because they used too much data. Clearly, the affordability of internet access is a key barrier for some, highlighting the need to include internet and data subsidies as part of social protection measures aimed at addressing digital inclusion and societal information gaps. Given the challenges, digitally excluded groups are likely to become more pronounced as the COVID-19 pandemic continues (Department of Internal Affairs 2020), it is imperative that barriers to reliable and affordable devices and internet connection are addressed as a matter of urgency.

Need for Tailored Communication Responses

As well as needing to account for people's access to communication tools, social protection measures and health interventions also a need to account for the distinctive characteristics of communities' communication networks, which are made up of varying mixes of interpersonal networks, community groups and community media, and larger scale agencies and media (Matsaganis and Golden 2015). For instance, traditional forms of networking (Amosa 2012) and informal information-sharing channels (Southwick et al. 2012) are important to consider when assessing where and how to effectively insert health interventions in a marginalised community. In the last large-scale study of internet use in New Zealand (Crothers et al. 2016), Pacific people stood out as valuing other people as information sources (more so than members of other groups), with 80% listing other people as 'very important' or 'important', giving peers a key role in Pacific communication networks, particularly on social and digital media. Thus, health communicators are likely to be more successful using peer-to-peer networks rather than a top-down, universal broadcast approach via mainstream media. Accordingly, when the New Zealand government launched a Pacific information campaign in response to the second wave of COVID-19 (which had hit Pacific communities hardest), it used 'Pacific influencers', well-known Pacific people, to share insights and key messages across social media accounts. Notably, it also targeted Pacific (rather mainstream) news media, and YouTube. With only 38% daily reach within the majority New Zealand European/Pākehā group, YouTube is, at first glance, an unlikely vehicle for universal health messaging, but as the media with the highest daily reach among Pacific peoples (65%) (NZ on Air 2020), it was an entirely appropriate medium for a targeted Pacific information campaign.

There are just as many examples, however, of how states failed to get the mix of measures right, particularly for the socio-economically disadvantaged groups most at risk of COVID-19. In New Zealand, for instance, the government's early COVID-19 communication response failed to account for Pacific groups. A daily press briefing held by the Prime Minister and Director General of Health quickly became a primary channel of information dissemination (it was the focal point of most news agendas across the country and its live stream drew tens of thousands of viewers [Walls 2020]), but it did not include key Pacific and other ethnic minority media. It was not until August, *after* the second wave of COVID-19 hit south Auckland, that a special press conference was held for Pacific media (Vaka'uta 2020). Similarly, the government's 'Sponsored Data' initiative—a partnership between the Ministry of Health and mobile network operators that defrayed the costs of using mobile networks to access 13 key health websites—not only came late in the pandemic response (after the country's almost five-week national lockdown), it also did not apply to key Pacific health sites, suggesting a lack of 'joined-up' thinking in the government's multi-agency response.

Other states similarly failed to take account of, and prioritise, vulnerable ethnic minority groups early in the pandemic. In Melbourne, Australia, the first wave of COVID-19 affected mostly wealthy returning travellers and their contacts, where the second wave hit the city's most culturally and linguistically diverse, and disadvantaged, communities (Taylor 2020). That required a shift in the government's communication strategy to target culturally diverse communities—by adopting simpler messaging for translation, employing more translators and interpreters, targeting key online and social media to reach specific communities (rather than relying on mainstream media), and using younger family members as trusted influencers to 're-narrate' and share public health messaging—yet those steps were not taken until more than two months into the second wave. Experts later said the government needed to have done more to consult culturally diverse communities in the early days of the virus' spread to ensure that public health messaging reached the communities that needed it (ibid.).

That these failures occurred suggests lessons are not being learned from previous pandemics or research that provides plenty of evidence of the need to tailor health and social protection interventions to different community networks. Research from the 2009 H1N1 or swine flu pandemic suggests that different population groups have different levels of access to accurate and up-to-date information during a health crisis, and communication efforts should focus on particular at-risk groups, such as the young, the less educated and the indigent (Lin et al. 2014). Research also demonstrates a need to tailor and improve health communication and collaboration with racial and ethnic minority communities, who tend to have a higher disease risk, with Lin et al.'s (2014) review of the literature on communication inequalities during the H1N1 pandemic highlighting the need to partner and collaborate with community leaders and community groups, ideally, long before any evidence of an impending pandemic (Plough et al. 2011). Research also suggests that, to be effective, communication should be culturally competent and pitched at lower literacy levels (to reduce communication inequalities), and provided through multiple trusted channels, including ethnic minority media (Hutchins et al. 2009; Lin et al. 2014).

In addition, health promoters and government agencies could do more to understand different communities' public spheres in terms of their structure and information flows and how they are used, the language and meanings that circulate, and the network of key influencers and connectors within and across different channels and media platforms. In this era of interactive and increasingly social media, wherein audiences and consumers can engage with and create content on their own terms, it is important that social protection agencies understand the power of ordinary people to shape health/social service messaging and communication flows. Saha et al.'s (2019) study of social media sharing of mental health campaigns, for instance, found community influencers and information networks may be more influential for health communication than external health experts, indicating a vital role for social media-based peer support. Their study's finding that personal tips and inspiration were the most widely shared social media content further suggests that effective campaigns need to find the right people (bridgers, influencers and high-profile community members, as well as ordinary people with lived experience) to increase the impact of social media for health promotion. Interestingly, their finding that favourited posts perform better than retweets (2019, p. 1204), demonstrates, too, that endorsement and acknowledgement behaviours (as characterised by favourites) can spread information more effectively than the information-broadcasting behaviours (characterised by retweets) that are often the first resort of health promoters and information campaigns.

Need for Trustworthy Information

Getting ahead of COVID-19 also requires accurate, trustworthy and consistent information that people can understand and act on to keep themselves safe (Garrett 2020; Aslani 2020), yet missteps in early media reports have demonstrated the potential for harm through the reporting of misleading or inaccurate information. In New Zealand, live coverage of panic-buying at supermarkets was questioned for potentially undermining public messaging about the security of food supplies (Peacock 2020), while, Cinelli et al. (2020, p. 2) note how CNN's publication of rumours of a possible lockdown in Italy's Lombardy region, hours before the official lockdown announcement, contributed to people overcrowding trains and airports to escape the region before the lockdown—thereby undermining containment measures and potentially increasing the virus' spread. Studies on the COVID-19 outbreak thus far have largely focused on its clinical aspects (La et al. 2020), so research on the media's role and impact in this pandemic is patchy, but earlier research and pandemic experience gives some guide to how the media's coverage of COVID-19 might impact on people's perceptions and behaviour. For instance, Hopman et al.'s work (2020) noted the media's negative effect in the West-African (2014–2016) and Democratic Republic of the Congo (2019–2020) Ebola response, when coverage led to suspicion of infection protection and control measures and the stigmatisation of patients.

There is evidence to suggest that in this pandemic the rise of rumours and misinformation online arguably presents a bigger challenge, whether by preventing key health messages and information from getting through to the communities that need them or by promoting false prevention measures or cures that potentially harm the public's health (WHO 2020).

New Zealand GPs have reported concerns about patients presenting with conspiracy theories who were failing to protect themselves or others through mask-wearing and lockdown measures (University of Auckland 2020). Rumours and conspiracy theories that blame and 'other' ethnic minority groups or incite xenophobic violence have also proved problematic, with New Zealand Health Minister Chris Hipkins forced to issue a call for people to stop spreading a rumour that targeted and blamed Pacific and Māori communities amid concerns that it would discourage them from getting a COVID-19 test (Coughlan 2020).

As First Draft's Claire Wardle (2020) warns, however, knowing when and how to tackle falsehoods or COVID-19 conspiracies (such as those linking the virus to 5G networks) is difficult. Debunking a rumour or falsehood can give it legitimacy and, through repetition, help fix the misinformation in people's memories or lead to increased interest in conspiracy-like content (Zollo et al. 2017). Studies such as Swire and Ecker (2018) have shown that, unless a correction is done appropriately, people are actually more likely to remember the falsehood. An analysis by Brennan et al. (2020) of a sample of COVID-19 misinformation published in English between January and the end of March 2020 and drawn from a collection of fact-checks maintained by First Draft, raises a further tricky issue for communicators. Paralleling research that points to the information-sharing potential of key 'influencers', Brennan et al. (2020) found that prominent public figures, such as politicians and celebrities, played a disproportionate role in spreading misinformation about COVID-19. While accounting for only 20% of the misinformation claims in the study sample, public figures accounted for 69% of total social media engagement. In addition, Stephens' (2020) mapping of COVID-19 conspiracy theories on Twitter found tweets were concentrated in places where politicians and news media echoed or amplified online conspiracies, such as in the United States or Brazil, where posts shared by Brazilian President Jair Bolsonaro were removed by the social media platforms Twitter, Facebook and YouTube because they included COVID-19 misinformation.

In New Zealand, Soar et al. (2020) found a shift in the nature of the 'infodemic' over time, from mostly unreliable information related to the origins of the virus or potential cures in the early days of the pandemic, to narratives reflecting United States-based disinformation and conspiracies related to state control and individual rights. This shift in the social and mainstream media discourse is concerning, the researchers warned, as the multi-faceted science and public health communication approaches that were successful earlier in the pandemic could no longer be relied on to counter the new narratives. Instead, 'a wide-ranging response to the increasing discussion of unreliable sources, untrustworthy narrators, and conspiracy narratives in media, political, and civil society discourses is required' (Soar et al. 2020, p. 14).[1] For the ethnic minority communities who often lack trust in governments and mainstream media (especially in the context of colonisation, systemic racism and state failures) and who are among the most at risk of COVID-19, even more work is needed to develop the relational networks and culturally competent practices necessary to develop effective counter-narratives and trustworthy communication (Soar et al. 2020; Taylor 2020).

Rethinking Effective Communication

These compounding factors necessitate a broader response to protecting and improving people's health and wellbeing; health systems alone cannot achieve what is needed to address these communication issues (CSDH 2008). For one, it may require re-looking at government supports for news media to fulfil an effective communication role. The sharp downturn in business (and, thus, advertising) during the COVID-19 pandemic has had a severe impact on media: thousands of workers at news media globally have been laid off, furloughed or had their pay cut, and many media outlets, particularly those that relied on ad revenue, have shut down. This puts at risk not just the independent and critical work of the media that is necessary for combating mis- and disinformation, but also media plurality and the breadth of media voices that are needed to speak on behalf of diverse and disadvantaged groups. In New Zealand, for instance, the government offered a financial support package for news media to help them weather a national lockdown, but there was little in the package for the smaller outlets that served ethnic minority communities, such as the *Samoa Times*, the longest-serving and last remaining

[1] Such a trust-building project will also need to address people's mistrust of new media technologies which, through their ability to generate vast amounts of data about users' activities, raise all sorts of questions about privacy, surveillance and the ownership of content that further complicate people's relationship with and trust in media (Lupton 2014).

Samoan-language newspaper in New Zealand, which did not survive the lockdown and has since closed down.

In addition, public communication researcher Jess Berentson-Shaw (2020) says, because exposure to false information is such a danger to people's wellbeing, governments need to adopt multi-level policies aimed at improving information quality, through setting information standards, monitoring and evidence-based interventions that develop and uphold quality. Cinelli et al.'s (2020) analysis of the spread of COVID-19 rumours and misinformation on social media also suggests more work is needed to understand wider social patterns in relation to content consumption and social media, so that government and non-government agencies can design more efficient epidemic models, which better account for social behaviour, and to implement more efficient communication strategies in times of crisis (ibid., p. 9).

A broader view of the socially protective role of communication might also help to accelerate work to address digital exclusion—and extend it beyond a focus on simply providing devices to also providing affordable connectivity (such as increased access to free Wifi) and education to increase digital literacy and confidence (Department of Internal Affairs 2020; Citizens Advice Bureau New Zealand 2020). As the Digital Council of Aotearoa/New Zealand says, it is not enough just to supply devices:

> supplying a device should not be categorised as digital inclusion any more than supplying a car to an unlicensed teenager would be seen as providing transport. Digital inclusion requires a coherent, sustainable response that addresses connectivity, training and support, and this requires significantly more effort. (Digital Council for Aotearoa New Zealand 2020)

In their report on digital exclusion, the community support organisation Citizens Advice Bureau New Zealand (2020) says measures must also avoid a narrow focus on being 'digital first', and instead prioritise putting people first. It pointed to clients who needed the organisation's help with tax returns, applying for citizenship and immigration applications, because those services had moved online where these clients could not access them, thus demonstrating how the people who are already negatively impacted by social inequality are at risk of being further disadvantaged when the digitisation of government services outstrips efforts to address digital exclusion.

Finally, a broader approach to communication is also more likely to enable the inclusive and culturally competent communication models that are needed to work with and within the marginalised and ethnic minority communities most at risk of COVID-19. As noted above, states need to anticipate the unique communication characteristics of diverse communities and establish the relational networks required for effective communication long before a pandemic occurs (indeed, states need to undertake that work as a matter of urgency to avoid being caught flat-footed in subsequent waves of the coronavirus pandemic). Key to this is understanding the fractured nature of audiences (and their different social behaviours) across multiple platforms and media, and, thus, the need for more targeted communication strategies. Developing frameworks and ways for government and non-government organisations to engage with, and between, diverse communities (Ratnam et al. 2020) has to be a communication priority in the COVID-19 response and recovery, particularly for marginalised and disadvantaged groups.

References

Amosa, Desmond. 2012. *Social policies in Samoa*, vol. 6. Commonwealth Secretariat.

Aslani, Parisa. 2020. What are our health expectations in a pandemic? *Health Expectations* 23 (2): 257–258. https://doi.org/10.1111/hex.13052.

Berentson-Shaw, Jess. 2020. Tackling the digital threat to health and wellbeing. *Newsroom*, September 17.

Brennan, J. Scott, Felix Simon, Philip Howard, and Rasmus Klaus Nielsen. 2020. *Types, sources and claims of COVID-19 misinformation*. Reuters Institute. https://reutersinstitute.politics.ox.ac.uk/types-sources-and-claims-covid-19-misinformation. Accessed 15 May 2020.

Cinelli, Matteo, Walter Quattrociocchi, Alessandro Galeazzi, Carlo Michele Valensise, Emanuele Brugnoli, Ana Lucia Schmidt, Paola Zola, Fabiana Zollo, and Antonio Scala. 2020. The covid-19 social media infodemic. *arXiv preprint* arXiv:2003.05004.

Citizens Advice Bureau New Zealand. 2020. *Face to face with digital exclusion: A CAB spotlight report into the impacts of digital public services on inclusion and wellbeing*. Wellington: Citizens Advice Bureau New Zealand.

Coughlan, Thomas. 2020. Coronavirus: Chris Hipkins and Ashley Bloomfield slam spreading of 'vile' rumours about latest Covid-19 cluster. *Stuff*, August 16.

Crothers, Charles, Phillippa Smith, Poutasi Urale, and Allan Bell. 2016. *The Internet in New Zealand 2015*. Auckland: Auckland University of Technology.

CSDH. 2008. Closing the gap in a generation: Health equity through action on the social determinants of health. Final report of the Commission on Social Determinants of Health. www.who.int/social_determinants/final_report/csdh_finalreport_2008.pdf. Accessed 15 September 2020.

Department of Internal Affairs. 2020. Digital inclusion action plan 2020–2021. https://www.digital.govt.nz/dmsdocument/174~digital-inclusion-action-plan-20202021/html#emerging-issues-and-opportunities. Accessed 1 August 2020.

Digital Council for Aotearoa New Zealand. 2020. Aotearoa's digital landscape beyond the Covid-19 response. https://www.slideshare.net/JacquiGibson1/beyond-covid19-our-advice-to-ministers. Accessed 15 September 2020.

Digital Inclusion Research Group. 2017. Digital New Zealanders: The pulse of our nation. https://www.mbie.govt.nz/dmsdocument/3228-digital-new-zealanders-the-pulse-of-our-nation-pdf. Accessed 1 February 2020.

Garrett, Laurie. 2020. The art of medicine. COVID-19: The medium is the message. *Lancet* 395 (10228): 942–943.

Grimes, Arthur, and Dominic White. 2019. *Digital inclusion and wellbeing in New Zealand*. Wellington: Motu Economic and Public Policy Research.

Hare, Kristen. 2020. The coronavirus has closed more than 50 local newsrooms across America. And counting. *Poynter*, September 14.

Hopman, Joost, Benedetta Allegranzi, and Shaheen Mehtar. 2020. Managing COVID-19 in low- and middle-income countries. *JAMA* 323 (16): 1549–1550. https://doi.org/10.1001/jama.2020.4169.

Humphry, Justine. 2019. 'Digital First': Homelessness and data use in an online service environment. *Communication Research and Practice* 5 (2): 172–187.

Hunia, Rangimarie, Shazeaa Salim, Stuart McNaughton, Rochelle Menzies, Peter Gluckman, and Anne Bardsley. 2020. *Addressing rangatahi education: Challenges after COVID-19*. Auckland: Ngāti Whātua Ōrākei and Koi Tū: The Centre for Informed Futures.

Hutchins, Sonja, Kevin Fiscella, Robert S. Levine, Danielle C. Ompad, and Marian McDonald. 2009. Protection of racial/ethnic minority populations during an influenza pandemic. *American Journal of Public Health* 99 (S2): S261–S270.

Jackson, Lagipoiva C. 2020. Pacific Islanders in US hospitalised with Covid-19 at up to 10 times the rate of other groups. *The Guardian*, July 26.

La, Viet-Phuong, Thanh-Hang Pham, Manh-Toan Ho, Minh-Hoang Nguyen, Khanh-Linh P. Nguyen, Thu-Trang Vuong, Trung Tran, Quy Khuc, Manh-Tung Ho, and Quan-Hoang Vuong. 2020. Policy response, social media and science journalism for the sustainability of the public health system amid the COVID-19 outbreak: The Vietnam lessons. *Sustainability* 12 (7): 2931. https://doi.org/10.3390/su12072931.

Lin, Leesa, Elena Savoia, Foluso Agboola, and Kasisomayajula Viswanath. 2014. What have we learned about communication inequalities during the H1N1 pandemic: A systematic review of the literature. *BMC Public Health* 14 (1): 484.

Lupton, Deborah. 2014. Critical perspectives on digital health technologies. *Sociology Compass* 8 (12): 1344–1359. https://doi.org/10.1111/soc4.12226.

Ma'ia'i, Leni. 2020. 'Devastating impact': South Auckland's Pasifika bear brunt of new Covid-19 outbreak. *The Guardian*, August 18.

Matsaganis, Matthew, and Annis Golden. 2015. Interventions to address reproductive health disparities among African-American women in a small urban community: The communicative construction of a "field of health action." *Journal of Applied Communication Research* 43 (2): 163–184. https://doi.org/10.1080/00909882.2015.1019546.

Meade, Amanda. 2020. More than 150 Australian newsrooms shut since January 2019 as COVID-19 deepens media crisis. *The Guardian*, May 18.

Merrefield, Clark. 2020. Rural broadband in the time of coronavirus. *Journalist's Resource*, March 30.

Ministry of Business, Innovation and Employment (MBIE). 2020. Pacific peoples in the labour market—December 2019 Year. https://www.mbie.govt.nz/dmsdocument/11268-pacific-peoples-in-the-labour-market-december-2019. Accessed 1 July 2020.

Ministry of Education. 2020. Distance learning. https://www.education.govt.nz/covid-19/distance-learning/. Accessed 1 August 2020.

Ministry of Health. 2020. *Ola Manuia: Pacific health and wellbeing action plan 2020–2025*. Wellington: Ministry of Health.

NZ on Air. 2020. Where are the audiences? 2020. https://www.nzonair.govt.nz/research/where-are-audiences-2020/. Accessed 1 September 2020.

Peacock, Colin. 2020. Media strive to adapt to 'the new normal'. *RNZ*, March 22.

Pew Research Center. 2019a. Mobile fact sheet. https://www.pewresearch.org/internet/fact-sheet/mobile/. Accessed 15 September 2020.

Pew Research Center. 2019b. Mobile divides in emerging economies. https://www.pewresearch.org/internet/2019/11/20/mobile-divides-in-emerging-economies/. Accessed 1 September 2020.

Plough, Alonzo, Benjamin Bristow, Jonathan Fielding, Stephanie Caldwell, and Sinan Khan. 2011. Pandemics and health equity: Lessons learned from the H1N1 response in Los Angeles County. *Journal of Public Health Management and Practice* 17 (1): 20–27. https://doi.org/10.1097/PHH.0b013e3181ff2ad7.

Ratnam, Charisma, Rebecca Wickes, Rebecca Powell, and Chloe Keel. 2020. Towards active engagement: Understanding how organisations are using technology to connect with diverse groups during COVID-19. *Monash University*. https://doi.org/10.26180/5f50413fc219c.

Ross, Tara. 2016. Rethinking journalism and culture. *Journalism Studies* 18 (12): 1559–1575. https://doi.org/10.1080/1461670X.2016.1146626.

Ross, Tara. 2017. Locating ourselves: An analysis and theoretical account of strategic practices of identity and connection in Aotearoa/New Zealand's Pacific news media. Unpublished PhD thesis, University of Canterbury.

Saha, Koustuv, John Torous, Sindhu Kiranmai Emala, Conor Rizuto, Amanda Stafford, and Munmun De Choudhury. 2019. A computational study of mental health awareness campaigns on social media. *Translational Behavioral Medicine* 9: 1197–1207. https://doi.org/10.1093/tbm/ibz028.

Soar, Max, Victoria Smith, M.R.X Dentith, Daniel Barnett, Kate Hannah, Giulio Dalla Riva, and Andrew Sporle. 2020. Evaluating the infodemic: assessing the prevalence and nature of COVID-19 unreliable and untrustworthy information in Aotearoa New Zealand's social media, January–August 2020. Te Pūnaha Matatini pre-print. https://www.tepunahamatatini.ac.nz/2020/09/06/covid-19_disinformation-in-aotearoa-new-zealand-social-media/. Accessed 10 September 2020.

Southwick, Margaret, Timothy Kenealy, and Debbie Ryan. 2012. *Primary care for pacific people: A Pacific and health systems approach*. Wellington: Pacific Perspectives.

Stephens, Monica. 2020. A geospatial infodemic: Mapping Twitter conspiracy theories of COVID-19. *Dialogues in Human Geography*. https://doi.org/10.1177/2043820620935683.

Steyn, Nicholas, Rachelle Binny, Kate Hannah, et al. 2020. *Estimated inequities in COVID-19 infection fatality by ethnicity for Aotearoa New Zealand*. Te Pūnaha Matatini. https://www.tepunahamatatini.ac.nz/2020/04/17/estimated-inequities-in-covid-19-infection-fatality-rates-by-ethnicity-for-aotearoa-new-zealand/. Accessed 1 July 2020.

Stroobant, Joyce, Sarah Van den Bogaert, and Karin Raeymaeckers. 2019. When medicine meets media: How health news is co-produced between health and media professionals. *Journalism Studies* 20 (13): 1828–1845. https://doi.org/10.1080/1461670X.2018.1539344.

Swire, Briony, and Ullrich Ecker. 2018. Misinformation and its correction: Cognitive mechanisms and recommendations for mass communication. In *Misinformation and mass audiences*, ed. Brian Southwell, Emily Thorson, and Laura Sheble, 195–211. University of Texas Press.

Taylor, Josh. 2020. How a trust breakdown left Melbourne's minority communities hardest hit by Covid second wave. *The Guardian*, August 29.

Tracy, Mark. 2020. News media outlets have been ravaged by the pandemic. *New York Times*, May 1.

Vaka'uta, Koro [@The_KorOcle]. 2020. PM & Dir of Health held specific press conference for Pacific Media due to lack of access for such media at daily briefings…[Tweet]. Twitter, August 21. https://twitter.com/The_KorOcle/status/1296698759250759681.

UNDP. 2020. Covid-19 and human development: Assessing the crisis, envisioning the recovery. http://hdr.undp.org/sites/default/files/covid-19_and_human_development_0.pdf. Accessed 1 July 2020.

UNICEF. 2020. UNICEF Executive Director Henrietta Fore remarks at a press conference on new updated guidance on school-related public health measures in the context of COVID-19. https://www.unicef.org/press-releases/unicef-executive-director-henrietta-fore-remarks-press-conference-new-updated. Accessed 16 September 2020.

University of Auckland. 2020. Executive summary for Series 6 (September): 3–11. https://covid-19-pc.auckland.ac.nz/results/series-6-executive-summary/. Accessed 18 September 2020.

Walls, Jason. 2020. Covid-19 coronavirus: Inside NZ's favourite reality TV show—The 1pm press conference. *New Zealand Herald*, April 23.

Wardle, Clare. 2020. What role should newsrooms play in debunking COVID-19 misinformation? *NiemanReports*, May 15.

World Health Organisation (WHO). 2020. 2019 novel coronavirus (2019-nCoV): Strategic preparedness and response plan. https://www.who.int/docs/default-source/coronaviruse/srp-04022020.pdf. Accessed 1 September 2020.

Williamson, Elizabeth, Alex Walker, Khrisnan Bhaskaran, et al. 2020. Factors associated with COVID-19-related death using OpenSAFELY. *Nature* 584: 430–436. https://doi.org/10.1038/s41586-020-2521-4.

Zollo, Fabiana, Alessandro Bessi, Michela Del Vicario, Antonio Scala, Guido Caldarelli, Louis Shekhtman, Shlomo Havlin, and Walter Quattrociocchi. 2017. Debunking in a world of tribes. *PLoS ONE* 12 (7): e0181821. https://doi.org/10.1371/journal.pone.0181821.

CHAPTER 7

COVID-19 and Its Impact on Indigenous Community Resilience and Schooling in New Zealand, the United States of America and Canada: Some Recurring Messages for Consideration

Teena M. Henderson, Joseph Martin, Lori Whiteman, Richard F. Manning, Jon Reyhner, and Larry Steeves

Introduction

This chapter provides the following autoethnographic accounts of the impact of COVID-19 upon Indigenous schooling and related community resilience initiatives from New Zealand, the United States of America (USA) and Canada:

T. M. Henderson · R. F. Manning (✉)
University of Canterbury, Christchurch, New Zealand
e-mail: richard.manning@canterbury.ac.nz

J. Martin · J. Reyhner
Northern Arizona University, Flagstaff, AZ, USA

S. Ratuva et al. (eds.), *COVID-19 and Social Protection*,
https://doi.org/10.1007/978-981-16-2948-8_7

(i) Teena Henderson: Ngāti Waewae (West Coast of New Zealand's South Island);
(ii) Dr Joseph (Joe) Martin: Navajo Nation (Arizona; Utah; New Mexico, USA);
(iii) Lori Whiteman: Treaty 4 area (Saskatchewan, Canada).

First, we discuss the autoethnographic method central to the research underpinning this chapter. Our presentation of the three autoethnographies next provides accounts of the three writers' lived experiences observing the COVID-19 pandemic's impact upon their respective Indigenous communities and schooling systems. While we acknowledge that differences do exist between the three autoethnographies, and are worthy of future research for a range of socio-cultural reasons, this would be beyond the scope of this chapter. The final passage, alternatively, focuses on providing a thematic analysis of the four recurring messages, or key themes, arising from these autoethnographies. Each of the four themes help us to highlight shared challenges facing Indigenous communities globally—particularly those located in rural/remote settings.

Methodology

Our research team came together motivated by a common concern—to record the impact of the COVID-19 pandemic upon Indigenous communities and schools. Two of the Indigenous team members (Teena Henderson, Joe Martin) are full-time academics. Lori Whiteman, meanwhile, is an Executive Director of the Treaty Education Alliance (Treaty 4). Our team reflects a blend of Indigenous education leaders and their respective (non-Indigenous) academic colleagues/friends (Dr Richard Manning, New Zealand; Dr Jon Reyhner, USA; Dr Larry Steeves, Canada). Inspired by Harrison et al. (2020), we embraced two forms of

L. Whiteman
Treaty Education Alliance (Treaty 4, Saskatchewan), Fort Qu'appelle, SK, Canada

L. Steeves
University of Regina, Regina, SK, Canada

autoethnography (evocative and analytic) to identify recurring challenges facing Indigenous communities in our three countries, each supported by a brief commentary to illuminate emerging themes during the autoethnographies and thematic analysis (Allen-Collinson 2013; Jones 2016). Our autoethnographies offer an "evocative form of autoethnography in that they provide stories that are value-centred rather than pretending to be value free" (Ellis et al. 2011, p. 274). They seek to sketch modes of generating thoughtful, understandable and evocative research founded in lived experience, or research that would alert readers to recurring questions facing Indigenous community leaders, school administrators and teachers of Indigenous learners amidst the trauma of the COVID-19 pandemic. Ellis et al. (2011, p. 275) add that evocative autoethnographies "acknowledge and accommodate subjectivity, emotionality, and the multitude of ways of speaking, writing, valuing and believing".

While an evocative methodology is clear within our autoethnographies, they each reflect the analytic autoethnographic method evident within the collaborative analysis and presentation of our qualitative data findings (Snow et al. 2003). An analytic autoethnographic approach mirrors what Anderson (2006, p. 373) described as "research in which the researcher is (1) a full member in the research group or setting, (2) visible as such a member in published texts, and (3) committed to developing theoretical understandings of broader social phenomena." To facilitate our data collection, analysis, ethics and writing, we used Zoom conferencing to meet online. This allowed us to give value to the Māori concept of kanohi kitea (the seen face) and trial our ability to conduct further research together (O'Carroll 2013). The adoption of Zoom, moreover, allowed us to overcome COVID-19 travel restrictions, share personal perspectives grounded in Indigenous peoples' senses of place and to co-write in a way that "does more than recount events, it recounts events in a way that renders them [more] intelligible, thus conveying not just [quantitative] information but also understanding" (Vellerman 2003, p. 1).

Autoethnographies

Autoethnography #1: Teena Henderson (Ngāti Waewae, New Zealand)

Although the New Zealand Government asked us to maintain social distancing to limit the spread of the virus, we ensured our tribal interactions continued—but in a safe manner to ensure the survival of our most vulnerable people. The traditional whakataukī (proverb) “waiho i te toipoto, kaua i te toiroa”, after all, exhorts us to be close together and not far apart. New Zealand’s first COVID-19 death was that of an elderly Pākehā (non-Māori) woman residing in our tribal territory (Te Tai Poutini). Her death prompted us to reflect upon the traditional values inherent within our whakataukī and to draw closer together and collectively support our most vulnerable tribal members. With support from our wider tribal grouping (Ngāi Tahu) and Crown agencies, Ngāti Waewae initiated a programme of manaakitanga (care and support) for the elderly and other vulnerable community members (Peters 2020) during the national lockdown in April and May of 2020.

First, our kaumātua (elders) and other vulnerable community members were asked (via survey) to identify what they needed to enhance their hauora (wellbeing). Next, a person from the hapū, outside their immediate whānau (family) would begin to: (i) do shopping for them (with free hygiene and food packages also provided), (ii) pick up medical prescriptions, or (iii) just chat on the phone to maintain social contact. With schools and early childhood centres also closed across New Zealand during that lockdown, our tamariki (children) and rangatahi (youth/s) also faced challenges of isolation. Our whānau (families) were, therefore, encouraged to support their learning by accessing official online learning support programmes put in place by schools and our Treaty partner—the New Zealand Ministry of Education (Radio New Zealand 2020).

Hence, we did not encounter the same scale of a digital divide–experienced by my co-authors Joe and Lori in Arizona and Saskatchewan. On a broader scale, various hapū of Ngāi Tahu (like other Māori communities) have become accustomed to supporting the wider public during civil emergencies over the last decade. Our iwi, like other tribes, was praised by media, politicians and public commentators for generously applying traditional cultural values during civil emergencies (Harris 2020).

This was evident following the Christchurch earthquakes of 2010–2011 when Ngāi Tahu received much credit for supporting quake victims and investing extensively in the economic recovery process (Carter and Kenney 2018). Our iwi was also involved in the development of legislative frameworks, which placed our tribal rūnanga (council) on an equal footing with the Christchurch City Council (Kenney and Phibbs 2015). Among other things, this led to the establishment of the Matapopore Charitable Trust (2020), which ensured the aspirations and narratives of the local hapū (Ngāi Tūāhuriri) inform the city’s regeneration projects.

The design of the Christchurch Central Business District landscape no longer creates a sense of place that marginalizes the mana whenua (customary authority) of Ngāi Tūāhuriri. The experience of other Ngāi Tahu hapū in the wake of the 7.8 magnitude Kaikōura earthquake of 2016, however, has not been so positive.

This is what concerns me the most as we move forward. The local (Ngāti Kuri) hapū of Kaikōura generously supported trapped tourists and many residents of Kaikōura. Yet, this did not translate into a greater voice in local community policy-making decisions (Carter and Kenney 2018). Unlike Ngāi Tūāhuriri, Ngāti Kuri were not included as a statutory partner in the subsequent *Hurunui/Kaikōura Earthquakes Recovery Act 2016* (Nation 2017). It is imperative, therefore, that Ngāti Waewae and other hapū/iwi around Aotearoa (New Zealand) are alert to the risk of providing manaakitanga (hospitality) to our neighbours with little reciprocity displayed by the Crown/New Zealand Government. Now is not the time to marginalize Māori voices from decision-making processes. Yet, Simon Bridges (former leader of the Government's opposition National Party) was criticised for the under-representation of Māori voices on the New Zealand Government's Epidemic Response Committee—which he chairs (Hurihanganui 2020a).

Although he said it was important more Māori voices be heard, Bridges blamed a busy agenda for preventing that from happening (Hurihanganui 2020a). While events like earthquakes and pandemics hold opportunities for Ngāti Waewae to draw upon our traditional values to thrive, Māori communities in general must learn from the aftermath of the 2010–2011 Christchurch quakes and the 2016 Kaikōura quakes, especially when moving forward our Treaty relationship with the Crown during this COVID-19 pandemic. Our iwi (Ngāi Tahu) has after all, demonstrated expertise in disaster management and mobilisation, resilience and recovery initiatives. Our Indigenous knowledge (including crisis management expertise) should not be undervalued, especially when robust policies are required to develop resilient Māori communities and schools across Aotearoa/New Zealand. Our voices must be heard at the decision-making table if Māori communities are to continue to follow our Prime Minister Jacinda Ardern's advice to be kind to each other so New Zealanders can all move forward as a team of 5 million people (Television New Zealand 2020). To conclude, now is not the time for Ngāti Waewae and Crown agencies/entities (including schools and public health providers) to stand far apart, but to draw close together.

Autoethnography #2: Joseph [Joe] Martin (Navajo Nation, USA)

The National Congress of American Indians suggests the disparate impact of COVID-19 in tribal communities around the United States is the result of historical and current systemic racism that has long ignored American Indian Nations and/or prevented them from making the most of resources made available by the Federal Government (Sharp 2020). The pandemic has hit Indian Country disproportionately hard, particularly in terms of tribal government shutdowns, school closures, and infection and death rates. Among some 500 Indian tribes and 318 reservations recorded in the United States, the Navajo Nation covers 69,930 square kilometres, occupying portions of northeastern Arizona, southeastern Utah, and northwestern New Mexico (Navajo Tourism Department, n.d.).

By area, the Navajo Nation is larger than ten US States. It is the largest land area in the United States retained by an Indigenous tribe, with a population of 332,129 of which 156,823 live within the Nation's boundaries (Navajo Tourism Department, n.d.). Hence, Navajo Health officials have emphasized that for families living in the remote areas, the ongoing pandemic has interrupted the delivery of food and health supplies and made the provision of support services more complicated. In normal times, many remote communities need to drive, mostly on unpaved roads, to purchase supplies at grocery stores that are an hour or more away. My sources suggest this is problematic because as Dr Henry Fowler, a member of the Navajo Nation Board of Education, advised me: "when pandemic panic buying started, stores and gas stations soon closed" (Dr Henry Fowler, telephone interview, July 23, 2020). Cecil Hubbell—President of the Wide Ruins Chapter (Navajo Chapters are local divisions of Navajo government, similar to counties)—shared related concerns when he advised: You're driving two hours to get to a place where there's only bare and empty shelves ... You also have, due to the COVID situation, higher prices (Cecil Hubbell, telephone interview, July 6, 2020).

Gilbert Yazzie, Supervisor of the Fort Defiance Food Distribution Program at the Navajo Nation's Division of Public Health Services, added "We've seen increased reliance on the federal nutrition programs across the Nation of about 30 percent, but in some areas, the increase is more like 50 percent" (Gilbert Yazzie, telephone interview, August 5, 2020). The pandemic hit the Navajo Nation disproportionately hard, both in terms of unemployment, plus growing infection and death rates (Nez and Lizer 2020). Navajo Council member Daniel Tso feels the COVID-19 crisis "hasn't broken anything ... It just revealed what was already broken" (Daniel Tso, telephone interview, August 11, 2020).

The pandemic crisis facing the Nation is further compounded by poverty-related factors. For example, Kevin Allis, Chief Executive Officer for the National Congress of American Indians, reports that within the general (USA) population, about 11 to 14% of Americans are food insecure (NCAI COVID-19 Situation Summary IHS Area Data 2020). Within the Navajo Nation, that rate is three to four times higher (Pardilla et al. 2013). With regard to the impact of COVID-19 on schools and students across the Navajo Nation, Percy Deal (a former tribal leader, now community activist), described his concerns in a telephone interview:

> No one in the world knows what the outcome of the lockdowns will be, nor does anyone know how and when the virus will end. What I do know about education is our ancestors were entrepreneurs; we were a community of doers. We must instill these same values in our children with perseverance and drive like no other. We were a nation that respects Navajo culture and values, puts others before ourselves. I remember my grandfather telling me if you have a sack of corn left in your house and a stranger knocks on your door asking for food, give the corn to them. Are our schools so weak that we cannot get a handle on this virus? Maybe it does not matter what I have to say. What matters is we need to create ethical leaders and to look after those who do not have a voice. I believe the Navajo community that will emerge the strongest are those that have the sturdiest people, being doers and working together. (Percy Deal, telephone interview, August 24, 2020)

In another telephone interview, Patricia Gonnie, Interim Superintendent for the Navajo Tribe's Department of Diné [Navajo] Education, described challenges facing schools now required to deliver virtual learning:

> Most students have had some disruptions to their traditional education. COVID-19 has caused a large majority of students to miss important learning that would have occurred during the last few months of school. Specifically, [in] schools in remote locations operated by the Bureau of Indian Affairs and the State Departments of Education (Arizona, New Mexico, and Utah), teachers and students were unprepared to teach and learn online. In some of the schools, technology access is a problem. The

> schools had to purchase new laptops for students and provide a source of internet to those who needed it—this caused inequities between students who already had technology and those who did not.
>
> … The achievement gap will widen as students have different access to technology and resources. Added to this [digital divide], instruction has been uneven during the pandemic. Some students have been able to participate fully in online learning while others have faced obstacles. The States and the Bureau of Indian Education have put out guidelines and mandates for schools to handle re-opening of campuses and balancing of in-person and remote learning. The states have allowed for some level of leeway given to individual schools and mandates to put together for health and safety practices within their unique contexts. Unfortunately, the Bureau of Indian Education was adamant to prepare their schools strictly for an in-person set-up. (Patricia Gonnie, telephone interview, September 11, 2020)

In addition to the devastating physical illness and education threats posed by COVID-19, some tribal and non-tribal leaders are concerned COVID-19 will create a huge amount of trauma among Navajo people, particularly younger members of the Nation. Daniel Press, of The Roundtable for Trauma Informed Training based within Washington D.C., told me:

> COVID-19 will create a huge amount of trauma among our people, particularly among the younger generation whose brains are still developing and are most vulnerable to the effects of trauma. When piled on top of the historical trauma Navajo people have already suffered, it has the potential to harm our younger generation. A program is needed to enable the students to meet the immediate problems COVID-19 triggered trauma will unload on them when the schools reopen. Otherwise, there will be a surge in students' acting out their trauma, getting suspended or expelled, and an increase in teacher-turnover, as their classrooms become unmanageable. (Daniel Press, personal communication, July 13, 2020)

Autoethnography #3: Lori Whiteman (Treaty Education Alliance, Saskatchewan)

COVID-19 was declared a pandemic on March 11, 2020 (Ghebreyesus 2020) as I was travelling to the Treaty 8 territory with my colleagues from the Treaty Education Alliance. We were excited to attend the annual Think Indigenous Education Conference together. We arrived in

Edmonton, Alberta on the evening of March 10, but less than 48 hours later we were huddled in the lobby of the hotel—making the decision to return home early. The conference was called off a few hours later. The drive home to Treaty 4 territory was sombre and the chatter muted. The full reality of what was happening across the globe had yet to settle into our understanding. That weekend, I spent hours on the phone with Chiefs, leaders and colleagues enacting our emergency response teams. All around us, the world was closing, and we needed to organize ourselves quickly to make sound decisions. First, we needed to determine what was happening in the First Nations' schools we worked with (Treaty Education Alliance 2020). Powered by adrenaline, we re-directed our focus and responded to the situation at hand.

The information flow was lighter back in March and April. As people settled into their new quarantined, virtual states of being, the information began to grow in volume and content. The bulletins and updates, briefings, research papers, articles and statistics came at me from every direction. Internally, our Critical Planning Team met twice weekly to manage and synthesize information and to organize and focus our teams. A "saving grace" for our organization was the time we invested, pre-pandemic, in technologies and digital literacy development. Working with First Nations has shaped my leadership skills to adapt to the lived realities of communities where high mortality rates are now so common (Feir and Akee 2019) that one of the Chiefs I work with calls himself "The Funeral Chief". This is owing to the endless, needless deaths he experiences in his Nation (Chief George Cote, personal communication, September 25, 2020). The educational leadership challenge I was facing was new, but in reality, it was also a continuation of what First Nations leaders have been struggling against since the onset of colonization.

In moments of quiet reflection—between intensive bursts of virtual meetings—I took to social media to see how other educational leaders, students and educators were managing. The posts about fear, sadness, anxiety and strain were everywhere, but they were also dotted with posts of creative generosity designed to lift spirits and bring about hope. As the world and those around me settle into the reality of the global pandemic, the hopeful posts have diminished. As conversations shift to the re-opening of schools, I hear the anxiety and fear in the voices of the school principals, teachers and families. As I try to sleep, some nights my mind fills with the following anxious thoughts: *We are sending our children back into unknown danger. We are returning to a professional life we love, but fear. How can we possibly reassure ourselves that everything will be ok?*

As the weeks and months have gone by, conversations have shifted to discussions about what the potential mental health impacts of COVID-19 will be, on Indigenous children in particular. In our workplace, staff share what they are hearing from the communities: the lack of technology infrastructure, the deep worry for Elders and for many people living on reserves with compromised immune systems (Giroux et al. 2020). As First Nations communities prepare for the re-opening of their on-reserve schools, there is concern about the potential long-term impacts of COVID-19, including how the pandemic shutdowns will emotionally affect principals, teachers, students and their families (Cameron et al. 2020). As an Indigenous educational leader, I am faced with questions about how under-resourced organizations, like mine, and the schools we serve will manage (Blackstock and Day 2020). How will our children and youth express what they are feeling in the midst of this pandemic? Do administrators and staff in schools have the resources to support students' mental wellness, given they may be struggling to manage their own mental health challenges? How can we, as an Indigenous organization, best provide supports?

In the 1970s, Dr Pauline Boss pioneered the term "ambiguous loss" and reshaped the field of psychology. In doing so, Dr Boss named the emotional turmoil of facing loss with little or no hope for closure (Boss 1999). Like so many others across Canada who were part of the child welfare abductions now known as the "Sixties Scoops" (Kestler-D'Amours 2017), I grew up struggling with my self-identity as a daughter of a missing Indigenous woman and as a child who was part of the "Sixties Scoops". Learning about ambiguous loss helped me frame and name the abiding feelings of confusion, loss and grief, of feeling frozen in time without answers. As someone who has lived the experience of separation from family and culture and who witnesses the impacts of colonization on the Indigenous Peoples of this land, I am determined to forge healing pathways for future generations.

It will, however, take every bit of our courage and energy to welcome these children and young people back to school with the confidence that they will be safe. The Indigenous People in the nations I work with are truly beautiful and resilient, and likewise the educators and support personnel. The pandemic presents unique challenges, but when cast in the context of the long trail of inequality and injustice, I am humbled and inspired at how much our people have overcome. When I am feeling exhausted, I have to remind myself: *that's what our ancestors did, that's why we are still here pushing forward despite all odds. After all, this isn't our first pandemic.* To quote Ray Petit:

> We're given a way of life for a reason. For example, when we [our ancestors] hunted, we never left anything laying around. We have tipis that were much different long ago. The way they were set up with liners on the walls and ground was for air flow. (Ray Petit, personal communication, August 28, 2020)

There are many clues and guideposts in our tribes' historical journeys of survival in the stories of our past. These can help us in the current uncertainty we face!

Thematic Analysis

While recurring themes emerged across the three autoethnographies, it is important to acknowledge that differences also arose. Ultimately, where we sit in the world does shape what we see, and it is obvious that differing cultural, historical and geographical experiences inevitably shaped differences in the narratives presented above. While these differences are interesting (and worthy of further research), they sit beyond the narrow scope of this chapter/passage. Here, we focus upon the similar experiences of Indigenous communities on the international stage and identify how any recurring themes relate to international literature. We found the following four themes arose, and these will be related to the literature as follows:

(i) Protection of elders and children: Preservation of traditional knowledge/cultural values;
(ii) Learning from the historical resilience of the ancestors/elders to move forward;
(iii) Intersections between poverty, the digital divide, historical trauma and the potential of place and land-based learning;
(iv) The need for inclusion in decision-making processes.

Theme #1: Protection of Elders and Children: Preservation of Traditional Knowledge/Cultural Values

Our research suggests the theme of protecting elders and children was the most pressing concern for the three autobiographers because they are custodians of Indigenous knowledges and most vulnerable to COVID-19. Children, in turn, are vital as recipients of elders' knowledge and so vital in the survival of Indigenous nations. This finding also appears to be a common concern for Indigenous communities worldwide. The United Nations Department of Economic and Social Affairs (UN DESA) advises the function of elders in Indigenous communities is acutely important as they play a major part in preserving and transmitting Indigenous traditional knowledge and culture and "practices that can contribute to the health, well-being and recovery of their own and wider communities" (UN DESA 2020a, p. 1). Garrison et al. (2020) add further weight to this argument:

> Indigenous peoples across Latin America are cutting off their communities from the outside world, worried that the coronavirus could pose a grave threat to their culture by putting at risk tribal elders, the keepers of their heritage. Latin America is home to 42 million Indigenous people, making up about 8% of the population, according to World Bank data, yet their way of life is already threatened by rapid development in mining, oil extraction and deforestation. The virus represents a new, and potentially catastrophic, risk. The elderly—the group most vulnerable to complications from COVID-19—are the guardians of many traditions and languages threatened with extinction.

When comparing and contrasting the three autoethnographies with community resilience responses emerging in Latin American countries, we also found it interesting to observe the Global Environment Facility (2020) report, which describes how:

> In times of crisis, it is typically rural areas that are most vulnerable to adversity and it is often big cities that send humanitarian aid to the countryside. With the COVID-19 crisis, however, the situation has reversed. The pandemic's mobility restrictions are disrupting food supply chains and hindering access to traditional and nutritious food in urban areas. Family farmers, belonging to several Indigenous communities in rural parts of Peru, are sending help to their relatives in the cities, reviving the tradition

> of Apachicuy–help the loved ones in the Quechua language–an ancestral Indigenous practice which ensures that whatever the hardship, family, friends and community get the support they need. Thanks to the Apachicuy initiative, 2,856 families in major Peruvian cities such as Lima, Nazca, Pisco, Ica, Cañete, Tacna, Moquegua, and Arequipa have already received sustainable and nutritious food shipments. (Global Environment Facility, August 7, 2020)

Learning from the resilience of one's ancestors was another recurring theme to emerge from the three autethnographies that resonated with the international literature.

Theme #2: Learning from the Historical Resilience of the Ancestors/elders to Move Forward

During our team's second Zoom meeting (September 7, 2020), where we identified emerging themes from our autoethnographic data, we discussed various historical precedents with Lori and Joe concluding, with dark humour, that this pandemic "is not our first [metaphorical] rodeo". Teena appreciated the bleak metaphorical humour of her North American colleagues–agreeing that, "this is not the first time we [Māori] have experienced a pandemic either". This is historically significant because the UN DESA (2020c) elsewhere cautions:

> Indigenous peoples in many regions have a long history of devastation from epidemics brought by colonizers, from the arrival of the first Europeans in the Americas, who brought smallpox and influenza to a measles outbreak among the Yanomami of Brazil and Southern Venezuela in the 1950s/60s that nearly decimated the tribe. COVID-19 presents a new threat to the health and survival of Indigenous peoples. Indigenous peoples in nearly all countries fall into the most vulnerable health category ... Contributing factors that increase the potential for high mortality rates caused by COVID-19 in Indigenous communities include mal-and under-nutrition, poor access to sanitation, lack of clean water, and inadequate medical services. Additionally, Indigenous peoples often experience widespread stigma and discrimination in healthcare settings such as stereotyping and a lack of quality in the care provided, thus compromising standards of care and discouraging them from accessing health care, if and when available. (UN DESA 2020c, p. 1)

It was not surprising, therefore, to find the UN DESA also observing that globally Indigenous communities are drawing upon historical experiences to find their own answers to this pandemic. They are initiating social actions and "using traditional knowledges and practices such as voluntary isolation, and sealing-off their territories, as well as preventive measures—in their own language" (UN DESA 2020b, p. 1). Likewise, it was not surprising to learn that elsewhere in North America, Indigenous communities are very cognizant of the risks of ambiguous loss and intergenerational trauma, and that they (like Māori) are adapting their ancestors' wisdom and experiences to develop new solutions. The Suicide Prevention Resource Centre, for example, reports:

> Indigenous communities are being disproportionately affected by the COVID-19 pandemic. Data from the United States and Canada show Native communities have higher rates of severe illness and death than the general population. The pandemic also may be having an outsized mental health impact, with data from Canada showing increased mental health concerns among some First Nations people. According to experts, COVID-19 has worsened pre-existing disparities linked to factors such as intergenerational trauma and limited access to resources. In response, Indigenous leaders and organizations are offering coping strategies, such as staying connected with family and friends through phone or video.
>
> The Native Wellness Institute in Oregon is hosting a virtual Power Hour, a forum for storytelling, comedy, and workshops. At the national level, the National Indian Health Board's COVID-19 Tribal Resource Center and Centers for Disease Control and Prevention's COVID-19 Tribal Communities webpage offer relevant tools and guidance. Glorinda Segay of the Navajo Department of Health recommends exercising self-compassion. People need to consider being more gentle with themselves through reassurance and prayers and forgive themselves for making mistakes while adjusting to the new norm. (Suicide Prevention Resource Centre, July 17, 2020)

Theme #3: Intersections Between Poverty, the Digital Divide, Historical Trauma and the Potential of Place and Land-Based Learning

The three autoethnographies propose that access to digital technology is a basic human right and a necessity for those Indigenous people who are isolated or geographically distant. For remote/rural Indigenous communities to participate in meaningful policy changes, they must be enabled to engage with that (digital) world. Yet, many Indigenous children and youth, in New Zealand and North America alike, cannot learn during this COVID-19 pandemic. This is because they have no access to electricity, let alone the internet (Groetzinger 2020; Hurihanganui 2020b). This scenario, therefore, highlights the need for governments to recognize and validate Indigenous communities' ongoing design and research of culturally responsive curriculum/pedagogical practices that have emerged before and during this pandemic. From a Canadian perspective, Last (2020) explains that:

> Even before a pandemic forced schools to close, interest in outdoor education was climbing. Across Canada and around the World, public school systems are integrating on-the-land learning as benefits for students become increasingly clear. In Scotland, authorities began encouraging outdoor Forest schools years ago, in response to a growing body of evidence showing both academic performance and childhood development benefit from time outdoors. Closer to home, public schools in Saskatchewan have begun to incorporate on-the-land programming piloted in Indigenous communities and hailed as a tangible form of reconciliation. This is our way of learning, this has always been our way of learning, said Etua Snowball, the director of educational services for the Kativik Regional School Board in Northern Quebec. Like other school boards across the [Canadian] North, when the pandemic forced classrooms closed, Snowball said he encouraged parents to spend more time teaching their children how to hunt, fish, and be safe on the land. (Last 2020, pp. 2–3)

Theme #4: The Need for Inclusion in Decision-Making Processes

As Joe Martin suggested to our team, a recurring message from the three autoethnographies is "the need for Governments to work with, and through, Indigenous communities rather than doing things to them". This final theme is entirely consistent with the recommendations of the UN DESA (2020a), which when acknowledging the provisions of the *United Nations Declaration on the Rights of Indigenous Peoples* (United Nations 2007), argued governments and representative institutions "should consider recognizing Indigenous peoples" representative institutions, authorities and governments as the legitimate representatives of Indigenous peoples" (UN DESA 2020a, p. 1). Among many other recommendations, the UN DESA (2020a) suggested governments:

- Include Indigenous peoples' representatives, leaders, and traditional authorities in emergency and health entities in their communities, overseeing responses to the COVID-19 pandemic. Indigenous people should be included in both responses to the pandemic as well as to its repercussions;
- Respect the right of Indigenous people to self-determination, including the right to be or remain in voluntary isolation. Adhere to and support Indigenous peoples' that have imposed lockdowns or limitations to stop the spread of the COVID-19 virus in their communities;
- Respect the right of Indigenous peoples' free, prior and informed consent in the prevention, development, implementation and monitoring of measures to address COVID-19;
- Engage in effective cooperation with neighbouring states where Indigenous peoples live in cross border areas, ensuring that good practices are exercised by all actors in close cooperation with the affected Indigenous peoples;
- Consider establishing post COVID-19 reconstruction funds and public resources specifically aimed at Indigenous peoples' needs to support and re-establish their traditional livelihoods, economies, and sustain their communities;
- Ensure access to education for Indigenous children and youth by providing necessary tools for remote learning, in close cooperation with teachers and authorities of Indigenous peoples. Support Indigenous people's own education initiatives. (UN DESA 2020a, pp. 1–3).

While there are more than 476 million Indigenous peoples in the world, the UN DESA (2020a) suggests these people are probably three times more likely to be existing in severe poverty then non-Indigenous people. They constitute nearly 19% of the planet's extreme poor, notwithstanding their region or residence in rural or urban areas (UN DESA 2020a). Where they live often transcends international borders—historically imposed upon them without consent—by foreign surveyors and cartographers.

Conclusion

As the three autoethnographies suggest, Indigenous peoples in New Zealand, the United States of America and Canada are, like their Indigenous counterparts elsewhere, "custodians of a wealth of traditional knowledge and practices, languages and culture, which includes time tested responses to crises" (UN DESA 2020a, p. 1). Yet globally, many Indigenous peoples live in "extreme poverty and often reside in isolated or remote communities, where health-care services are difficult to reach and have limited capacity, or do not exist" (UN DESA 2020a, p. 1). As the autoethnographies and international literature also suggest, the function of elders in Indigenous communities is especially noteworthy as they play a key role in the inter-generational preservation and transfer of Indigenous knowledge, culture and practices that underpin the wellbeing and potential recovery of their own and broader Indigenous communities (local, national and global).

The *United Nations Declaration on the Rights of Indigenous Peoples* (UN DESA 2007), however, provides a structure for policy action on COVID-19 founded on the rights of Indigenous peoples to enjoy the utmost achievable standard of physical and mental health and to access, without prejudice, social and health services (Cultural Survival 2020). The past influences of colonization, supplemented by continued underfunding and the absence of satisfactory social services in Indigenous communities, worldwide, becomes more evident in the face of a pandemic such as this (UN DESA 2020a, b, c; Cultural Survival 2020). It is vital, therefore, that Indigenous peoples, frequently among the most vulnerable members of society, are not left lagging behind the rest of society (UNDESA 2007, 2020a, b, c).

This inevitably necessitates the sharing of accurate information in Indigenous languages, an adequate distribution of medical necessities and services, emergency sanitation supplies and, where necessary, emergency food and cash aid (UNDESA 2020a). It is also our view that COVID-19 policies affecting Indigenous peoples should be determined and implemented following full consultation/engagement with and agreement from Indigenous leaders. This approach appears most likely to ensure support is provided with the full involvement of the Indigenous peoples themselves (by enabling them to interact with policy decision-makers at the local [provincial/state] and national levels of government). Such collaborations must, furthermore, reflect culturally responsive processes of consultation and engagement directly relevant to each of the Indigenous communities concerned (UN DESA 2007, 2020a, b, c; Cultural Survival 2020; Grantham-Philips 2020; Groetzinger 2020; Hurihanganui 2020a, b; Nelson 2020; Last 2020).

References

Allen-Collinson, Jacquelyn. 2013. Autoethnography as the engagement of self/other, self/culture, self/politics, and selves/futures. In *Handbook of autoethnography*, ed. S. Holman Jones, T.E. Adams, and C. Ellis, 281–299. Walnut Creek, CA: Left Coast Press.

Anderson, Leon. 2006. Analytic autoethnography. *Journal of Contemporary Ethnography* 35 (4): 373–395. https://doi.org/10.1177/0891241605280449.

Blackstock, Cindy, and Isadore Day. 2020. History will repeat itself if first nations remain underfunded in the fight against COVID-19. *The Globe and Mail*, April 8. https://www.theglobeandmail.com/opinion/article-history-will-repeat-itself-if-first-nations-remain-underfunded-in-the/. Accessed 2 October 2020.

Boss, Pauline. 1999. *Ambiguous loss: Learning to live with unresolved grief*. Boston: Harvard University Press.

Cameron, J. Kevin, Marleen Won, William Pollack, and Patrick G. Rivard. 2020. *Guidelines for re-entry into the school setting during the pandemic: Managing the social-emotional and traumatic impact (School Version)*. Lethbridge: North American Center for Threat Assessment and Trauma Support.

Carter, Lucy H., and Christine M. Kenney. 2018. A tale of two communities: B-race-ing disaster responses in the media following the Canterbury and Kaikōura Earthquakes. *International Journal of Disaster Risk Reduction* 28: 731–738. https://www.sciencedirect.com/science/article/pii/S2212420918301225. Accessed 20 October 2020.

Cultural Survival. 2020. UN expert mechanism on the rights of indigenous peoples releases statement on COVID-19, April 14. https://www.culturalsurvival.org/news/un-expert-mechanism-rights-indigenous-peoples-releases-statement-covid-19. Accessed 25 October 2020.

Ellis, Carolyn, Tony E. Adams, and Arthur P. Bochner. 2011. Autoethnography: An overview. *Historical Social Research* 36 (4): 273–290. https://doi.org/10.17169/fqs-12.1.1589.

Feir, Donna, and Randall Akee. 2019. First peoples lost: Determining the state of status first nations mortality in Canada using administrative data. *Canadian Journal of Economics* 52 (2): 490–525. https://doi.org/10.1111/caje.12387.

Garrison, Cassandra, Marina Lammertyn, and Anthony Boadle. 2020. Latin America's indigenous shield elderly 'cultural guardians' from Cronavirus. *Reuters: Healthcare and Pharma*, May 11. https://www.reuters.com/article/us-health-coronavirus-latam-Indigenous-f-idUSKBN22N1BO. Accessed 21 October 2020.

Ghebreyesus, Tedros Adhanom. 2020. WHO Director-General's Opening Remarks at the Media Briefing on COVID-19, March 11. https://www.who.int/director-general/speeches/detail/who-director-general-s-opening-remarks-at-the-media-briefing-on-covid-19---11-march-2020. Accessed 25 October 2020.

Giroux, Ryan, Cindy Blackstock, Radha Jetty, Susan Bennett, and Sarah Gander. 2020. COVID-19 and indigenous children in Canada: What can paediatricians do? Canadian Paediatric Society, May 28. https://www.cps.ca/en/blog-blogue/covid-19-Indigenous-children-in-canada-what-can-paediatricans-do. Accessed 20 October 2020.

Global Environment Facility. 2020. *Indigenous peoples and COVID-19: Response and resilience*. Global Environment Facility, August 7. https://www.thegef.org/blog/Indigenous-peoples-and-covid-19-response-and-resilience. Accessed 26 October 2020.

Grantham-Phillips, Wyatte. 2020. On the Navajo Nation, COVID-19 death toll is higher than any US State. Here's how you can support community relief. *USA Today*, October 24. https://www.usatoday.com/story/news/nation/2020/10/24/covid-native-americans-how-to-help-navajo-nation/3652816001/. Accessed 26 October 2020.

Groetzinger, Kate. 2020. Navajo families without Internet struggle to home-school without internet. NPR. April 22. https://www.npr.org/2020/04/22/839948923/navajo-families-without-internet-struggle-to-homeschool-during-covid-19-pandemic. Accessed 15 September 2020.

Harris, Aroha. 2020. Māori mobilisation in a crisis: A proud history. *The Spinoff*, May 7. https://thespinoff.co.nz/atea/07-05-2020/maori-mobilisation-in-a-crisis-a-proud-history/. Accessed 21 September 2020.

Harrison, Neil, Sue Stanton, Richard Manning, and Wally Penetito. 2020. Teaching in the name of justice: Empathy and vulnerability as a basis for understanding difficult histories. *Pedagogy, Culture & Society*, 1–16. https://doi.org/10.1080/14681366.2020.1845786

Hurihanganui, Te Aniwa. 2020a. Simon bridges ignored proposals for Māori at epidemic response committee. *Radio New Zealand Politics/Te Ao Māori*, May 6. https://www.rnz.co.nz/news/te-manu-korihi/415943/simon-bridges-ignored-proposals-for-maori-at-epidemic-response-committee-mp-says. Accessed 20 October 2020.

Hurihanganui, Te Aniwa. 2020b. COVID-19: Māori education providers tackle students' internet connectivity. *Radio New Zealand: Te Ao Māori/COVID-19*,

April 15. https://www.rnz.co.nz/news/te-manu-korihi/414273/covid-19-maori-education-providers-tackle-students-internet-connectivity. Accessed 20 October 2020.

Jones, Stacy Holman. 2016. Living bodies of thought: The 'critical' in critical autoethnography. *Qualitative Inquiry* 22 (4): 228–237. https://doi.org/10.1177/1077800415622509.20October2020.

Kenney, Christine M., and Suzanne Phibbs. 2015. A Māori love story: Community-led disaster management in response to the Ōtautahi (Christchurch) earthquakes as a framework for action. *International Journal of Disaster Risk Reduction* 14 (1): 46–55. https://doi.org/10.1016/j.ijdrr.2014.12.010. Accessed 29 September 2020.

Kestler-D'Amours, Jillian. 2017. Mixed feelings over Canada's '60's scoop settlement. *Al Jazeera*, October 11. https://www.aljazeera.com/features/2017/10/11/mixed-feelings-over-canadas-60s-scoop-settlement/. Accessed 2 October 2020.

Last, John. 2020. Why on the land educators see opportunity in a global pandemic. *CBC News*, May 19. https://www.cbc.ca/news/canada/north/on-the-land-education-covid-19-1.5571602. Accessed 19 October 2020.

Matapopore Charitable Trust. 2020. Matapopore. https://matapopore.co.nz/. Accessed 20 October 2020.

Nation, Deborah. 2017. One year on. *Te Karaka* 87, December 19. https://ngaitahu.iwi.nz/our_stories/one-year-on-tk76/. Accessed 29 September 2020.

Navajo Department of Health: Epidemiology and Health Command Operations Centers. 2020. COVID-19 Cases Reported—23 September 2020. Reference for Fig. 2. Retrieved from Indianz.com: https://www.indianz.com/covid19/2020/09/05/navajo-nation-arizona-new-mexico-utah-221/. Accessed 26 August 2020.

Navajo Tourism Department. n.d. Fact Sheet. https://www.discovernavajo.com/fact-sheet.aspx. Accessed 26 August 2020.

Nelson, Cody. 2020. Covid Ravages Navajo Nation as Trump Makes Election Play for Area. *The Guardian*, October 8. https://www.theguardian.com/us-news/2020/oct/08/navajo-nation-coronavirus-pandemic. Accessed 5 October 2020.

Nez, Jonathan, and Myron Lizer. 2020. Jonathan Nez, President of the Navajo Nation and Vice-President Myron Lizer, Digital Town Hall Meeting, April 29. https://www.facebook.com/watch/live/?v=350017432625413&ref=watch_permalink. Accessed 15 August 2020.

Ngāi Tahu. 2013. Big Ups for Canterbury Marae. *Te Karaka*, October 8. https://ngaitahu.iwi.nz/our_stories/big-ups-canterbury-marae/. Accessed 20 September 2020.

Ngaī Tahu Property. 2020. Who Are We. Ngāi Tahu Property. https://ngaitahuproperty.co.nz/about-us/who/. Accessed 21 October 2020.

O'Carroll, Acushla Deanne. 2013. Kanohi ki te kanohi—A thing of the past? Examining the Notion of 'Virtual': Ahikā and the Implications for Kanohi ki te Kanohi. *Pimatisiwin: A Journal of Aboriginal and Indigenous Community Health* 11 (3): 441–455.

Pardilla, Marla, Divya Prasad, Snali Suratkar, and Joel Gittelsohn. 2013. High levels of household food insecurity on the Navajo Nation. *Public Health Nutrition* 17 (1): 58–65. https://doi.org/10.1017/S1368980012005630.

Peters, Kayne N. 2020. Iwi throw support behind those in need. *Newsroom*, April 1. https://www.newsroom.co.nz/1104395/iwi-do-their-thing-helping-those-in-need. Accessed 20 October 2020.

Pinterest. 2020. West Coast of the South Island (Reference for Fig. 1). Retrieved from: https://www.pinterest.com.au/pin/142426406938132207/. Accessed 25 August 2020.

Radio New Zealand. 2020. COVID-19: Ministry Reveals Support Plans for Distance Learning. *Radio New Zealand*, April 8. https://www.rnz.co.nz/news/national/413763/covid-19-ministry-of-education-reveals-support-plans-for-distance-learning. Accessed 16 October 2020.

Sharp, Fawn. 2020. U.S. Commission on Civil Rights Hearing on COVID-19 in Indian Country: The Impact of Federal Broken Promises on Native Americans, Written Testimony of President Fawn Sharp, National Congress of American Indians, July 17. https://www.ncai.org/attachments/Testimonial_DZsioKxiANtlqzyGvRcGDaWpLsbZjlzhnmJpREpHubPVEyMOlYO_NCAI-Written-Testimony-USCCR%207_17_20-Hearing.pdf. Accessed 17 November 2020.

Snow, David, Calvin Morrill, and Leon Anderson. 2003. Elaborating analytic ethnography: Linking fieldwork and Theory. *Ethnography* 4 (2): 181–200. https://www.jstor.org/stable/24047808?seq=1#metadata_info_tab_contents. Accessed 17 November 2020.

Television New Zealand. 2020. 'We're a Team of Five Million'–Lockdown Timeline Depends on Kiwis' Behaviour, Ardern Says. *Television New Zealand 1 News*, April 21. https://www.tvnz.co.nz/one-news/new-zealand/were-team-five-million-lockdown-timeline-depends-kiwis-behaviour-ardern-says. Accessed 1 October 2020.

Treaty Education Alliance. 2020. Treaty Education Alliance–Returning to the Classroom. https://educationalliance.ca/. Accessed 3 October 2020.

United Nations Department of Economic and Social Affairs [UN DESA]. 2007. The United Nations Declaration on the Rights of Indigenous Peoples. https://www.un.org/development/desa/indigenouspeoples/wp-content/uploads/sites/19/2018/11/UNDRIP_E_web.pdf. Accessed 16 October 2020.

United Nations Department of Economic and Social Affairs [UN DESA]. 2020a. Indigenous Peoples and the COVID-19 PANDEMIC: Considerations. https://www.un.org/development/desa/Indigenouspeoples/wp-content/uploads/sites/19/2020/04/COVID19_IP_considerations.pdf. Accessed 21 October 2020.

United Nations Department of Economic and Social Affairs [UN DESA]. 2020b. COVID-19 and Indigenous Peoples. https://www.un.org/development/desa/Indigenouspeoples/covid-19.html. Accessed 26 October 2020.

United Nations Department of Economic and Social Affairs [UN DESA]. 2020c. *The Impact of COVID-19 and Indigenous Peoples*. UN DESA, Policy Brief, No. 70. https://www.un.org/development/desa/dpad/wp-content/uploads/sites/45/publication/PB_70.pdf. Accessed 24 October 2020.

Vellerman, J. David. 2003. Narrative explanation. *The Philosophical Review* 112: 1–25. https://philarchive.org/rec/VELNE. 17 November 2020. https://doi.org/10.1215/00318108-112-1-1.

CHAPTER 8

Ageing, Vulnerability and COVID-19

Nii-K Plange

Introduction

The sudden arrival, spread and pandemic nature of COVID-19 has had, and continues to have, a destructive impact on the global economy and society. The pandemic's effects have resonated deep into the fabric of society, with differential consequences and suffering for categories of national populations. Globally, lives continue to be taken with frightening speed, and there is an increasingly upward trajectory of fatality rates even in the developed countries (United Nations 2020) with advanced and sophisticated health systems, access to a wide breadth of health and medical specialists and strong economies. In the developing countries, the effects are of special and worrying significance, as they will undermine already weak economies, constrain efforts at attaining the Sustainable Development Goals and threaten already fragile social protection systems. Certainly, the impact, and the capacity for effective response, differs in societies and across age, gender and class lines. Among older people, or ageing populations, those with pre-existing vulnerabilities either in health and illness or minimum to no access to the means of livelihood and those

N.-K. Plange (✉)
National University of Fiji, Suva, Fiji
e-mail: nii-k.plange@fnu.ac.fj

S. Ratuva et al. (eds.), *COVID-19 and Social Protection*,
https://doi.org/10.1007/978-981-16-2948-8_8

dependent on either the state, charities or family and kin will be the most affected.

A recent overview of the global situation of the pandemic notes that the fatality rates for older people, especially those aged over 80 years, is five times the global average (United Nations 2020). The review further notes that critical areas of impact of COVID-19 on older people in developing countries include economic well-being, especially as "less than 20% of older persons in developing countries have access to pensions" (United Nations 2020, p. 3). The review also cautioned that "as the virus spreads rapidly to developing countries, likely overwhelming health and social protection systems, the mortality rate for older persons could climb even higher". These together constitute a significant challenge to continuing global efforts, of more than five decades ago, to ameliorate the crisis of old age, some of which are captured in the World Bank commissioned work "Averting the Old Age Crisis" (1999).

Over the past three decades, the World Health Organization has drawn attention to the critical issues relating to healthy ageing, including poverty (WHO 2003, 2012), and in 2003 the Madrid Plan of Action on Ageing (United Nations 2003) articulated the global concerns with the greying of the world population, with an outline of global action. Other and continuing studies have also underlined deep gender variations and gaps in ageing, such as higher life expectancy, economic vulnerability and the higher propensity of women to poverty at old age (Arber and Ginn 1991). Existential situations of growing old have become more concerning in developing countries, with their weaker and dependent economies, health systems and formal social protection schemes (Soneja 1999; Adamchack and Wilson 1999; Seniloli and Tawake 2014, 2015) and the diminishing returns from traditional and familial relations of care and support, as the global economy continues its relentless assault (Barrientos et al. 2003).

Within the global economy itself, older peoples' livelihoods have been severely affected by changes in the nature of work, especially the practice of pension and retirement as a time of withdrawal from formal employment, on the assumption that one must have accumulated enough resources to prevent a return to work. The specific age of retirement has, however, continued to vary since the Bismarckian era and appears increasingly unrelated to the ability to work. The risk of limited resources for life and livelihood at old age has prevailed to underscore Bismarck's initiative and the rise of labour unions to press the state towards "settlements" to avoid poverty at old age (Esping-Andersen 1998, p. 24).

Against this background, it is perhaps safe to state that old age and associated resources for livelihood is a function, primarily, of the nature of the economy, with other factors as contributory (Seeman and Crimmins 2001).

While welfare and protection schemes have developed and expanded in the developed countries (Esping-Andersen 1998, 2002), developing countries continue to struggle with the legacy of colonial welfare systems, with their notable under-investments in social policies with welfare outcomes. Efforts to revamp these systems and address acute situations of poverty have been constrained by "growth"—informed development strategies underscored by programmes of structural adjustment, with austerity measures which limit the capacity of the state to provide needed assistance through universal schemes of protection (Jenson 2014). Nevertheless, governments in developing countries continue to introduce few assistance programmes to vulnerable groups as "social protection" schemes (ILO 2006a, b; Handayani 2010), while charity associations and family contribute their bit to constitute a welfare matrix.

COVID-19 and Society

It is within this context that COVID-19 made its unexpected arrival in the world, and then Fiji, in early March. With recourse to the existing Public Health Act and its inherent dangers of infringement on individual liberties, prevention strategies have been implemented by governments across the global community, albeit with differences.

The logic of the prevention methods is derived from the elusive, and at times asymptomatic, nature of the virus and its subtle means of transmission. These include social distancing and face-masking to avoid the potential, of transmitting/inhaling the virus through conversation; regular hand-washing and personal hygiene to eliminate any potential of infection through touching one's face; and quarantine, in cases of suspected or real infection, to avoid onward and multiple transmissions and the dreaded community transmission. In certain circumstances, the state throws in a night curfew to curb mobility. Additionally, there is the option of international border closures to prevent the arrival of potential and real "diseased bodies" who will transmit and infect national populations.

These health strictures look innocuous. However, translated into practice, they embrace a swathe of unprecedented economic and social actions, with significant impacts on national productivity, life and livelihood and threats to social liberties, in a democratic dispensation, including especially the freedoms of movement and association. The economic practices include industrial shutdown, or reduction, of manufacturing, production and service facilities, with their immediate ripple effects on workers and wages as labour is terminated or reduced to minimal hours of work. Social measures have included lockdowns or the de-concentration of public spaces. This means closure of public facilities, such as schools and entertainment centres, limited movement and confinement to home space or "sheltering in place", and in some cases introduction of large-scale testing to reduce community transmission. Supermarkets, the post-modern garden of international produce, food supplies and miscellaneous household items, are kept open but with face-masking required.

Thus, governments have responded to avert an otherwise veritable economic and social crisis with unforeseen consequences. Such responses have included the provision of financial benefits to workers in lieu of lost wages and salaries and stimulus packages of huge financial allocations to business enterprises to avoid collapse. Highly developed economies in Europe and North America have been liberal with their economic support, stimulus packages and protection packages, the significant challenges notwithstanding. Predictably, many developing countries have struggled to produce such stimulus and economic protection schemes from deficit-ridden economies. The situation is exacerbated by the abrupt shutdown of economic lifelines of production, transport and communications networks in the developed countries. Significantly, the preventive strategy of COVID-19 has exposed the inherent weaknesses of existing social protection schemes in the developing countries, as governments sought to stimulate economies and provide assistance to un/underemployed workers and the vulnerable communities.

This chapter explores the vulnerability of older persons in Fiji to COVID-19, as the country struggles to implement a response strategy to forestall devastating effects on the economy.

Fiji: Aspects of Society and Economy

Fiji is an archipelago in the South Pacific, with a multi-ethnic population of predominantly indigenous or I'taukei and Indo-Fijians who make up about 57 and 37%, respectively, of the national population (Fiji Bureau of

Statistics 2017). Other ethnic groups include Chinese, Pacific Islanders, and Europeans. The country covers a total area of about 18,272 kilometres and spreads over 300 islands, of which about a hundred are inhabited. Current Fiji's total population is 898,315. A cultural value and practice of extended family relations, reciprocity, and communal care of the needy, including children, older people and the disabled, is predominant among the I'taukei, with variations of this within the Indo-Fijian community. This despite over a century of British colonialism. The deep roots of this value and practice exist within the former ethnic group and the vocabulary of the Vanua is enlisted to express its enduring binding nature. The ramifications of this for social behaviour and relations have been articulated in the works of Ratuva (2007) and Koya-Vaka'uta (2017).

Recently, the Tourism industry has dislodged sugar from its primacy of place in the economy as "the key driver of economic development" with high visitor arrivals. Together with the service industry as a whole, tourism provides direct and indirect employment to over 100,000 people (Lockington 2020) and commands an almost 71% share of GDP. Fiji's tourism is dominated by resorts which straddle the western coastline while others are on exclusive remote islands. Primary resort employees are mostly from villages and as main breadwinners. Additionally, there is commercial agriculture, fisheries, hardwood, gold mining and remittances, with the latter providing an average of 300 million dollars a year. There is also manufacturing on a small scale for consumer items, as well as garments and textile (ILO 2016). Major exports currently include bottled water, textiles, precious stones, spirits, fish and vegetables.

The slow demise of the sugar industry, from the late 1990s, has been due partly to the end of European Union preferential prices, persistent uncertainties with land leases and the departure of second- and third-generation sugar cane family offspring to white collar jobs, including the professions. It also triggered an urban ward migration by youthful farmhands in search of unavailable jobs, thus swelling the ranks of the unemployed and depleting the resources of many intergenerational rural households (Fiji Bureau of Statistics 2017).

Fiji's rate of unemployment, prior to COVID-19, was at about 6.2% and higher at 18.2% among the 15–24 age category (ILO 2016). Informal employment remains high at 60% and varies between male and female at 57 and 65%, respectively (ILO 2016). The economy is currently in free fall and has contracted about 4.3% (Gounder 2020) resulting in about 10% fall in GDP. There is endemic poverty in the country, with the current national poverty rate at 28% (Fiji Bureau of Statistics 2017), in response to which government has declared its intentions to lower the poverty rate to 25% by 2021 and 20 per cent by 2026. Poverty is exacerbated by low and increasingly stagnant (between 2009 and 2016) wages, 20% devaluation of the Fiji dollar in 2009 and consequent 38% rise in basic food items and a fluctuating (between 17 and 12%) value-added tax (Barr 2017).

Life expectancy as of 2013 figures at 67.6 and 69.9 for males and females, respectively. The country continues to witness rapid urbanization, with 60% of the national population residing in cities and towns and sprawling squatter settlements within and on the fringes of the city and major towns. The geographical location of the country makes it susceptible to hurricanes, sometimes with destructive effects, especially on housing and to the economy as a whole. The recent Cyclone Winston's effect on agriculture, housing and the economy as a whole persists, with research also indicating severe multiple effects of climate change (Pacific Community 2016);

From the mid-1980s, a neo-liberal development framework informed by the IMF and the World Bank (now with offices in Fiji), with emphasis on growth, has continued to influence the development strategies. In the latter part of the 1990s, faced with increasing poverty and strident protests from civil society, government implemented the World Bank growth-driven Poverty Alleviation Program (Akram-Lodhi 1992). This was grafted onto an existing non-contributory and targeted Family Assistance Programme, which provided some respite to older people but only after an assessment of household welfare status together with a (supervisory) home visit (World Bank 2011). This has since continued but unpacked into specific social protection schemes. These include the Poverty Benefit Scheme, the Care and Protection Allowance and the Social Pension Scheme for people aged 65 years and above with no sources of income.

Population Ageing in Fiji: Poverty and Livelihood

Issues relating to population ageing have remained part of Fiji's development and demographic changes. From about 5% in the early 1980s (Andrews et al. 1986; Plange 1987), the current elderly population, that is those aged 60 years and over, is 9% or a little over 80,000 of the total population (Fiji Bureau of Statistics 2017), with a projected increase to

17% in 2050. Currently, the female component of the population aged 60 years and over is 52.4% and expected to increase to 55.1 in 2025. With a higher life expectancy of women, there are currently more widows in the ageing population than widowers (Plange 1987; Ministry of Social Welfare 2011). This marks the onset of the feminization of population ageing in Fiji; a global trend.

Critical issues relating to health, livelihood and well-being of older people in Fiji have been given, and continue to be given, attention in Fiji (Plange 1987, 1990a, 2006, and more recently Seniloli and Tawake 2014, 2015; UNESCAP 2016). Central to these concerns are the threat of poverty and livelihood, health, including disabilities and chronic diseases (Plange 1991; Seniloli and Tawake 2014). These conditions of living are exacerbated by the enduring poverty in Fiji and acutely limited options for employment of older people (Plange 1990a, b) leading to threats of income security. Gender disparities, including in education and employment, informed partly by patriarchal values of the two key ethnic categories, underline the differences in health, poverty and employment of older men and women in Fiji.

Income security, as a major means of sustaining a livelihood for older people, is limited to receipts from the National Provident Fund and a high percentage of population 60+ are not covered. Nor are the rest covered by any other employment-related superannuation scheme. For these, the available options include continuing work, especially in the informal sector and semi-subsistence farming in rural areas, post-retirement employment, family and kin support, including in some cases remittances, or a combination of aspects of all of these, and since 2013 a non-contributory and targeted state assistance known as the Social Pension Scheme. This provides FJD$100 per month to older people aged 65 years and above. Those deemed undeserving by the criteria remain the responsibility of family and kin and the charity organizations. That there is a crisis of poverty and livelihood in old age is underscored by a deeper analysis of the data. The Social Pension Scheme covers a total of 47,000 older people. This is over 50% of the total elderly population (80,000) and an equivalent percentage of the total coverage of the expansive government social protection programme.

But the Provident Fund itself is limiting as income security as a large percentage of "members a balance of FJD 50,000 or less, well below the threshold required to sustain them during old age". The average monthly pension is about FJD$350.00 a little above the basic poverty line and chances of augmenting this are limited due to lack of opportunities for post-retirement employment especially in the formal sector (Plange 1990a, b)

The pathways to poverty at old age include pre-pension social withdrawal, leaving a reduced sum for annuity calculations; the practice of lump-sum withdrawal of accumulated contributions by retiring workers, only to have this spent within a short time, and then recourse to family and kin for support; low wages and thus a meagre total contribution to the Provident Fund; a large informal sector, mostly women, without Provident Fund coverage (Bolabola 2019); and limited opportunities for employment of older people (Plange 1990a, b).

These together place the burden of care and provision of livelihood on family, kin and community or the "traditional solidarity". However, research has shown (Plange 1987), and continues to show (Seniloli and Tawake 2014), that traditional solidarity itself is under threat as able-bodied younger generations of youth and adults continue to face challenges of unemployment in a sluggish economy, with severe impacts on resources in intergenerational households of children and grandchildren. Seniloli and Tawake (2014) found that older people with an income of FJD$15,000 or less are more likely to live in intergenerational households and especially "in urban areas (and) this is a response to increasing housing and food costs" (p. 147). Meanwhile, there is also a decrease of family size with diminishing resources. For example, in 1984 about 60% of older people in Fiji lived with others, including their children (Plange 1987). This has shrunk to about 30% in 2017 (Seniloli and Tawake 2014). An analytical work on poverty trends in Fiji (World Bank 2011), the results of which underlined the state Poverty Alleviation Programmes, found that "households with children and elderly are much more likely to be poor," and that "households with both elderly and children are the poorest with a poverty head count of 52 percent" (UNICEF 2011, p. 16).

Health is a core component of livelihood. The absence of disease and ailments has been constantly identified as constituting the wealth of old age. In Fiji, the national disease burden is driven by non-communicable diseases and the prevalence of risk factors including smoking, alcohol use and over-nutrition. Health conditions of older persons in Fiji include diabetes, hypertension, heart disease and cerebra-vascular diseases (Ministry of Health 2014). There has been a steady increase in diabetes (T2DM) prevalence in the population aged 60 years and over in the past two decades; from 17% in 1980 to 36.8 in 2011. Obesity and cardiovascular diseases have also recorded similar increases (Morrell et al. 2016). A recent study (Seniloli and Tawake 2015) noted that "... the older population is more likely to be sick, infirm or disabled than ... middle aged"; and the typical elderly "is the one who is not mobile and has some form of disability or other serious medical ailments that need constant medical attention and health care" (Seniloli and Tawake 2015, 140ff). These health conditions are also characterized by gender differences, as was found by Panapasa and Maharaja (2002). Their study noted the tendency in Fiji for older widows to be susceptible to disabilities due to poverty and unmet health needs. Notably, government has intervened with credible efforts at assistance through a non-contributory service of free prescription drugs to older people.

In the Eye of the Storm: Older People in Fiji and the COVID-19 Pandemic

In mid-March, the government declared COVID-19 as the country's "Enemy number one". Forthwith, it pulled out of the arsenal of state power the dictates of COVID-19 prevention underlined by colonial public health regulations periodically amended to fit modern times (Fiji Public Health (COVID-19 Response) (Amendment)Act, 2020). Lest public-spirited libertines, or the press, raise a voice, a senior military officer remarked menacingly that "Government would be justified to 'stifle criticism' of its policies by the press" (Guardian Australian 2020). This notwithstanding, government's prevention strategies have followed the international blueprint without much of any overbearing regulations. Social distancing, face-masking and at-border quarantine of incoming travellers, and a ban on internal and international air travel were the early regulations, with a more recent night curfew thrown into curb nocturnal activities, especially of popular entertainment, a fertile ground for viral transmission. Shutdown of schools and limitations on numbers at places, spaces and sites was initially limited to 30 and later extended to 50. All this with stringent policing, which resulted in arrests and prosecutions in court, some of which exposed the ineffectiveness/incompetence of case presentation and management by the police. The country appears to have benefited from limited COVID-19 infections/transmissions and fatalities. However, this limited transmission and fatality belie the wounding social and economic impact on the country, especially as the effects trickle down to households and then on to older persons, many of whom are already facing livelihood challenges (Seniloli and Tawake 2015).

The major devastation on the economy was the abrupt end to international travel, with a damaging impact on the national tourism industry. Over 100,000 tourism and allied tourism workers were laid off or had reduced working hours. The national airlines immediately terminated over 400 of its flight attendants to the protestation of the unions. Tourism sector earning declined suddenly by 20%, with the gloomy forecast that recovery is not in immediate sight (Reserve Bank of Fiji May 2020). Reeling from the devastating impact, key sectors of the economy, including construction and government's own capital projects, stalled with predictable and additional job losses amidst chronic issues with government tax collection and revenue. Indeed, while police were busy arresting curfew trespassers in the night, the country woke up to daily job losses.

In response, a COVID-19-influenced budget was introduced by government. It contained the usual stimulus package for business, including the tourism industry and consumer item importers, tax reduction here and there and rebooting of the existing social protection scheme but without any effort to add other categories within the population or change any of the criteria for accession to a recipient of the different schemes. For workers with the Provident Fund, guarantees were made to them by government, only for withdrawals, of their accumulating pensions savings ostensibly as a government "give away". The foreboding consequence of this withdrawal for poverty in later or post-retirement life has been articulated by many. This is especially the case for those, nearing or at, retirement. For a large number of workers, including older people and especially women, in the informal sector at the market, the roadside and in the sugar, cane farms, the budget was mute. The consequent reduction in the workforce of over 120,000 and the reduced hours of work meant an abrupt and acute diminishing of household resources, with dire consequences for household members. Additionally, a schoo l lunches for children programme ostensibly to ease family's cost of food, was removed, with a later announcement of its uncertain future, if at all. (Minister of Education; *Fiji Times* 2020).

In spite of the enduring belief and perception of family care for older people, recent research has provided deep insight into the dynamics of care. Seniloli and Tawake (2015) found that intergenerational households' expenditure choices do not give priority of place to older people.

Indeed, as the research noted "working children look after the welfare of both younger and older family members. For the majority, the priority is to look after the welfare of the family as a whole by providing food and basic necessities; and minor priority is given to health and welfare of the elderly" (p. 143). "For many" they continued "daily survival of all members of the household is more important than anything else—so putting food on the table is priority" (p. 143). This scenario apparently changes if the elderly members of the household do earn. But evidence from the Provident Fund, and the government Social Pension and Poverty Benefit Schemes, show that majority of older Fiji citizens face a crisis of income security and that only a minority do have the means for independent living and authority to influence household livelihood decisions (Seniloli and Tawake 2015). Evidence of the vulnerability of older people was visibly demonstrated by the numbers that recently thronged the Social Welfare Department in dire need of the monthly allowance, which has been delayed, and is facing the probability of being terminated, due to either late deposit into respective bank accounts or incomplete verification forms.

In the face of this apparent crisis, family care, informal assistance, charities and non-governmental organizations continue to provide needed assistance to provide some respite for vulnerable households. Included in this is the traditional barter system (Polanyi 2001, p. 71) or the "moral economy" (Bowles 2019). It has returned. Not to encourage and enhance trade. On the contrary to engender social relations through "traditional forms" of exchange of garden produce, food items, and services, not with money as the medium of exchange but other items in need. This is a traditional economic dynamic that sustained livelihood, established and maintained relations, which has, apparently, stood the test of time and against the onslaught, and indeed as the shock absorber, of structural adjustment programmes characteristic of dependent economies. Increasingly, media reports are replete with these services outside, and supplanting, the weak state structures and systems of care and protection. Charity organizations such as the Sabha Dharma Pratinidi, the Foundation for Rural Integrated Enterprise and the Fiji Council of Social Services are providing food rations to households to assist in maintaining their livelihood and providing for older persons (*Fiji Times* 2020). Recently, a COVID-19 Humanitarian Response Centre has opened in Nadi "to respond faster or better to older persons and households in need".

COVID-19-related vulnerability of older people has not been related only to food as only one component of livelihood. Indeed, the most challenging is access to medications for chronic ailments, with older women the most vulnerable (Panapasa 2002). Plange (1991) enlisted the phrase "social disability" to express the existential condition of chronic disease and ailments of older people in Fiji leading, in some situations, to the inability to undertake the basic activities of daily living with associated gender difference to the disfavour of older women Later, Panapasa and Maharaj (2002) found hypertension and stroke as health problems of older people in Fiji, with associated chronic disabilities, especially of older women (Panapasa 2002).

Other studies by Seniloli and Tawake (2015) have confirmed the challenging health status of older people in both urban and rural settings and noted that "still a significant proportion, 35 percent of rural elderly are unhealthy" (2015, p. 12). Additionally, recent community-based data collected by student nurses of the College of Medicine, Nursing and the Health Sciences of the Fiji National University, also noted the prevalence of Non-Communicable Disease among elderly members of families in one province (Fiji School of Nursing 2017).

The issue with health and health care almost inevitably translates into cost for either prevention, treatment or both. Government's own policy document of 2011 noted unequivocally that "the high cost associated with providing health care for the elderly persons arises largely from the fact that older people are more likely to suffer from chronic non-communicable diseases that are expensive to treat" (Ministry of Women 2011, p. 12). The policy response was, and now is, a Free Medicine Scheme (specific medications identified by government and provided at specific pharmacies in the country). The success of the scheme received a laudable endorsement from older people surveyed a few years ago (Plange 2015). However, shortages and the cost of medications outside the state archive of free medicines have remained the main concern of older people.

It is such pre-existing conditions of health and well-being, together with the epidemiologically established higher rates of COVID-19 mortality of older people (United Nations 2020), that also underlines the vulnerability of older people in Fiji. This has been exacerbated with the abrupt shutdown of commercial supply lines in Fiji, with a consequent shortage of relevant medications. In this is an important and popularly prescribed medication for hypertension in Fiji; Enalapril and others such as Atacand-Plus. In the midst of this apparent health crisis, government responded that "Enalapril (is) out of stock but alternative blood pressure meds are available ... and that it is fighting tooth and nail to bring ordered and pre-ordered meds through freight flights, ships and global connections" (Minister of Health 2020). The Minister continued that "for those who have high blood pressure and cannot get medication like Enalapril, they can get guidance from specialists and senior doctors". But this could come with a cost, and an inevitable impact on household budgets already in crisis. For the other medications in the free medicine archive, the Minister commented that "They are also strategizing on the best delivery of the Free Medicine Scheme and looking at corporate pharmacies. This will result in people not just relying on government pharmacies".

Beyond the medications, COVID-19 has also created social conditions that make older people in Fiji vulnerable to mental health and physical health conditions. Physical and social distancing which, in Fiji, entails restrictions on familial visits, close interaction, and sometimes, play with grandchildren; participation in social, especially religious gatherings and, among indigenous Fijians, the perennial Vanua gatherings for deliberations, will have significant consequences for older Fijians as it limits mobility and social interaction. The United Nations (2020) has cautioned that efforts are now, more than before, needed to ensure economic well-being of older persons and strengthen their social inclusion and networks in order to "strengthen health and rights through collective action" (p. 1) and maintain the "value of respect for older persons that are deeply ingrained in societies" (p. 4).

Conclusion

Pre-existing conditions of vulnerability of older persons in Fiji underscored by critical issues with income security, diminishing household size and systemic poverty and challenging health conditions was the context within which COVID-19 made a landing in Fiji. The impact of prevention measures which, primarily, included the shutdown of major economic lifelines of the country affected household resources, with consequent effects on older people, many of whom are dependent on traditional family values of care. The impact also exposed weaknesses in government's social protection schemes. The unfunded National Provident Fund became the government's main support mechanism but only for workers and the minority of older people who are members. For others, the charities and civil society organizations, together with a resurrected "moral economy" of traditional barter, appear to be the prevailing sources of assistance. Fiji is yet to experience a second wave, with an apparent ambiguity of what care and protection will be for older persons.

References

Arber, S., and J. Ginn. 1991. *Gender and later life*. London, Newbury Park, New Delhi: Sage.

Adamchak, Donald J., and Adrain O. Wilson. 1999. The situation of older people in Zimbabwe. In *The ageing & development report: Povert, independence & the world's older people*, chapter 14. HelpAge International. London: Earthscan Publications.

Akram-Lodhi, A. 1992. Structural adjustment in Fiji under the Interim Government, 1987-1992. *The Contemporary Pacific* 18 (2) (Fall): 259–290. 1996.

Akram-Lodhi, A.H. 1996. Structural adjustment in Fiji under the interim government, 1987-1992. *The Contemporary Pacific* 8 (2): 259–290.

Andrews, G., et al. 1986. Aging in the Western Pacific: A four country study. Western Pacific Reports and Studies No. 1. World Health Organization Regional Office of the Western Pacific.

Barr, K. 2017. Address delivered at the Fiji Labor Party Convention. Suva, November 15.

Barrientos, A., M. Gorman, and A. Heslop. 2003. Old age in developing countries: Contribution and dependence in later life. *World Development* 31 (3): 555–570.

Bolabola, C. 2019. Comments on the state of informal workers. NGO Alliance Workshop, Suva, Fiji.

Bowles. S. 2019. Why good incentives are no substitutes for good citizens. University of Carlifornia. Youtube Lecture series.

Esping-Andersen, C. 1998. *The three worlds of welfare capitalism*. Princeton, NJ: Princeton University Press.

Esping-Andersen, C. 2002. *Why we need a new welfare state*. Oxford: Oxford Univbersity Press.

Fiji Bureau of Statistics. 2017. Fiji Bureau of Statistics, Government of Fiji, Suva, Fiji.

Fiji School of Nursing. 2017. Fiji School of Nursing, College of Medicine, Nursing and the Health Sciences, Fiji National University.

Fiji Times. 2020. CSOs: Increase in demand for NCD Medications, August 16.

Gounder, Neelesh. 2020. Fiji's economic free fall and government response. Development Blog, April.

Government of Fiji. 2011. National strategic human resource plan, 2011-2015. Ministry of Strategic Planning, National Development & Statistics.

Guardian Australian (On-Line). 2020. April 27.

Handayani, Sri Wening. 2010. Enhancing social protection in the Asia and Pacific. Proceedings of a Regional Workshop.
Help Age International. 2000/2001. Action on ageing. Annual Review. Help Age International.
International Labour Organization. 2006a. Social protection for all men and women project: -RAS/04/59/NET (RAS/04/SP11/N-RAM) Sub regional Initiative on Social Security in Pacific Island Countries.
International Labour Organization. 2006b. Extension of social protection. International Labour Organization, Geneva, Switzerland.
International Labour Organization. 2016. Fiji labour market update. ILO Office for Pacific Island Countries, April.
Jenson, Jane. 2014. Diffusing ideas for after neo-liberalism: The social investment perspective in Europe and Latin America. In *The welfare state reader*, ed. Christopher Pierson, Francis G. Castles, and Ingela K. Nauman, 3rd ed. Cambridge: Polity.
Koya-Vaka'uta, F. 2017. Rethinking research as relational spaces in the Pacific: Pedagogy and Praxis. In *Relational hermeneutics: Decolonizing the mindset and the Pacific Itulagi*, ed. Upolu Luma Vaai and Aisake Casimira, 65–84. Suva: University of the South Pacific.
Lockington, F. 2020. Comments on the tourism industry in Fiji. Fiji Village News, September 7.
Panapasa, S.V., and J. Maharaj. 2002. Burden of stroke among Fiji older persons. Paper presented at 2002 IUSSP Regional; Population Conference, Bangkok, Thailand.
Minister of Health, Fiji. 2020. Enalapril out of stock but alternative High blood pressure meds available: Fiji Village, August 13.
Ministry of Health. 2014. Strategic plan 2013-2020. Ministry of Health, Suva, Fiji.
Ministry of Women, Social Welfare and Poverty Alleviation. 2011. National Policy on Ageing (2011-2015). Fiji ministry of Women.
Morrell, S., et al. 2016. Diabetes incidence and projections from prevalence survey in Fiji. *Population Health Metrics*. https://doi.org/10.1186/s12963-016-0114-0.
Pacific Community. 2016. Climate change impact in Ra and Kadavu Provinces. Pacific Community.
Panapasa, S. V. 2002. Disability among older women in Fiji: Concerns for the future. PSC Research Report No.02-501. Population Studies Centre. Institute for Social Research, University of Michigan.
Plange, Nii-K. 1987. Aspect of ageing in Fiji. Fiji Ageing Research, School of Social and Economic Development, University of the South Pacific.

Plange, Nii-K. 1990a. Longevity with chronic disability: Health problems of Fiji's elderly. *Fiji Medical Journal* 16 (3) (July–September). Fiji Medical Association, Suva, Fiji.
Plange, Nii-K. 1990b. Older workers in a developing economy: An overview of Fiji's older workers and current policies. In *Rethinking life options for older persons*, ed. J. Habib and C. Nusberg, 99ff. Washington, DC: International Federation on Ageing.
Plange, Nii-K. 1991. Longevity and increasing social disability. Paper presented at the International Symposium, WHO Collaboration Centre for Well-being on Ageing, Tohuk University of Medicine, Sendai, Japan.
Plange, Nii-K. 2006. *Integrating poverty and gender in health programmes: (Initial draft)*. World Health Organization. Regional Office for the Western Pacific.
Plange, Nii-K. 2015. Assessment of customer satisfaction of Fiji National Provident Fund Services. Fiji National Provident Fund, Suva, Fiji.
Polyani, K. 2001. *The great transformation. The political origins of our time.* Boston: Beacon Press.
Ratuva, S. 2007. Na kilaka vaka-Viti kei na veikabula: Indigenous knowledge and Fijian cosmos; Implications on bio-prospecting. In *Pacific genes and life patents. Pacific indigenous experience & analysis of commodification & ownership of life*, 1st ed., ed. A.T.P. Mead and S. Ratuva, 90–101. Wellington: Call of Earth Llamado Terra and the United Nations University of Advanced Studies.
Reserve Bank of Fiji. 2020. The Reserve Bank, Suva, Fiji.
Seeman, T.E., and E. Crimmins. 2001. Social environmental effects on health and aging: Interpreting epidemiologic and demographic approaches and perspectives. In *Population health and aging: Strengthening the dialogues between epidemiology and demography*, ed. Weinstein, et al., 88ff. New York: New York Academy of Sciences.
Seniloli, K., and R. Tawake. 2014. Living arrangements of the elderly in Fiji. *Journal of Pacific Studies* 34 (2): 129–152.
Seniloli, K., and R. Tawake. 2015. The health status of the silver generation. *Journal of Pacific Studies* 35 (3): 168–187.
Soneja, Shubha. 1999. The situation of older people in rural and urban India. In *The ageing & development report: Poverty, independence & the world's older people*, chapter 11. HelpAge International. London: Earthscan Publications.
The World Bank. 1999. Averting the old age crisis: Policies to protect the old and promote growth. Policy Research Working Papers. World Bank.
The World Bank. 2011. Republic of Fiji. Poverty trends, profiles and small area estimation (poverty maps) in Republic of Fiji (2003–2009).
UNESCAP. 2016. Income security for older persons in Fiji. United Nations UNESCAP.

United Nations. 2003. The political declaration and Madrid plan of action. New York.

United Nations. 2020. Policy brief: The impact of COVID -19 on older persons, May. United Nations.

United Nations Children's Education Fund (UNICEF). (2011) Atlas.

United Nations Fund for Population Activities. 2012. *Ageing in the twenty-first century: A celebration and a challenge*. New York: UNFPA.

World Health Organization. 1986. Growing older-staying well: Ageing and physical activity in everyday life. WHO/HPR.AHE/98.1.

World Health Organization. 2003. Gender, health and ageing. November, WHO, Geneva, Switzerland.

World Health Organization. 2012. Good health adds life to years: Global brief for World Health Day, Geneva.

CHAPTER 9

Protecting the Poor in Extraordinary Times: *Covid-19 Pandemic and Social Protection Architecture in the Philippines*

Jovanie Camacho Espesor

Introduction

The Philippines, like any country in the world, is facing the biggest health crisis owing to the outbreak of the SARS-CoV2 virus, which caused the Covid-19 disease. Based on the Covid-19 case tracker of the Department of Health (DOH), the Philippines has a total of 264,588 cases of infection and 4,371 deaths as of September 13, 2020 (Philippines 2020a). With that figure, it is taking the lead in the ASEAN Region, with the highest number of people infected by the deadly virus. Next to the Philippines are Indonesia and Singapore (Center for Strategic and International Studies 2020). As an immediate action to combat the pandemic, President Rodrigo Duterte put the national capital region under strict community quarantine in March 2020. Different regional and local government organisations implemented the same measure to prevent the spread of

J. C. Espesor (✉)
Mindanao State University, General Santos, Philippines
e-mail: jovanie.espesor@msugensan.edu.ph

S. Ratuva et al. (eds.), *COVID-19 and Social Protection*,
https://doi.org/10.1007/978-981-16-2948-8_9

infection in localities in the countryside. The imposition of lockdowns and community quarantine has consequently led to the suspension of key social and economic activities in the country. Public transportation was suspended, school classes were terminated and millions of people, especially in the private sector, lost their jobs due to permanent and temporary closure of business establishments.

The Covid-19 crisis has undeniably generated major economic repercussions that gravely affected the disadvantaged and vulnerable population, particularly the ordinary workers and overseas Filipino workers (OFW). In a survey of the Social Weather Station in July 2020, 45.5% or about 27.3 million Filipinos were jobless (Lopez 2020). Meanwhile, according to the forecast of the Department of Labour and Employment (DOLE), the Covid-19 pandemic will likely displace 10 million workers this year (Yumol 2020). In a study of the Philippine Institute for Development Studies, the adverse impact of the pandemic on the economy could lead 1.5 million Filipinos into poverty (Abad 2020). According to Senate President Vicente Sotto III, the Covid-19 crisis is no longer a health nor a labour concern, rather the continuous spread of the virus is a threat to national security (Gregorio 2020a). To respond to this national security threat, the Philippine government has taken pro-poor measures that provide social protection to vulnerable groups.

There is an emphasis in the development policy literature on the affirmative utility and transformative potential of social protection in promoting human development as an intergenerational pathway for the poor out poverty. Development scholars (Devereux and Sabates-Wheeler 2007; Merrien 2013; Barrientos and Hulme 2008; Ulriksen 2012; Voipio 2007) have put forward an argument that social protection can serve as a functional framework to attain bigger development objectives, such as even economic growth and the Millennium Development Goals (now Sustainable Development Goals) (Devereux and Sabates-Wheeler 2007). Moreover, it can facilitate pro-poor growth of the economy (Voipio 2007), and when combined effectively with sound economic strategies, can likely result in equitable development (Ulriksen 2012). Social protection is also deeply embedded in the development cooperation policies for developing economies of many international development organisations, especially the World Bank, International Labour Organisation and Asian Development Bank (World Bank 2001; Merrien 2013; Barrientos and Hulme 2008; Schelzig 2015), including donor countries (Voipio 2007). Areas and components of social protection include social insurance, social assistance and labour market regulation. Some scholars (Kabeer 2004; Munro 2008) have argued that the provision of social security guarantees is a matter of right rather than charity or discretion of political leaders. As the primary social security framework to combat poverty, the Conditional Cash Transfer (CCT) has become the cornerstone of the social protection floor in many developing countries (Schubert 2008; de Britto 2008; Schubert and Slater 2006).

The threat brought about by the virus is particularly detrimental to the welfare of poor Filipinos. The poor are particularly vulnerable to the adverse impacts of the pandemic, as they have limited agency to absorb livelihood and other economic shocks in this extraordinary time. Because of the dismal situation of the poor, the Philippine government has turned to social protection to help them mitigate detrimental consequences of the Covid-19 disease to their welfare. Based on Philippines context, the Development Academy of the Philippines describes:

> social protection as consists of policies and programmes that seek to reduce poverty and vulnerability to risks and enhance the social status and rights of the marginalised by promoting and protecting livelihood and employment, protecting against hazards and sudden loss of income, and improving people's capacity to manage risks. (cited in Ofreneo 2012, p. 6)

The aim of this chapter is to explain the nature of vertical engagements of the national and subnational governments in the provision of social protection for the poor in the Philippines. In this chapter, I will outline key social protection programmes of the national and local governments in the Philippines that are designed to manage and mitigate the detrimental socio-economic impacts of the Covid-19 pandemic. The information that I utilised to support the argument presented in this chapter are from secondary sources, such as news reports from media organisations, as well as reports and advisories from key agencies of the Philippine government. I also reviewed pertinent laws and policies that provide legal bases for the implementation of a universal social protection floor (USPF) in the Philippines, especially during pandemics.

This chapter is structured into three parts. The first part tackles the state of social protection in the country before the outbreak of the pandemic. The second part explains the array of social safety nets taken by the Philippine national government to fight the Covid-19 pandemic. The third part discusses briefly the complementary role of subnational governments in managing the pandemic in their respective domains. It is the conclusion of this chapter that the pandemic has induced the Philippine government to reinforce its existing universal social protection floor through the establishment of additional social security guarantees, especially for the poor.

Social Protection in the Philippines Prior to the Pandemic

Universal social protection is evident in the development policy track of the Philippine government, even before the outbreak of the pandemic. It is the prominent feature of the government's anti-poverty investments that aim to provide social safety nets to poor Filipinos, especially those living below the poverty line. In fact, institutions and programmes are well-placed within the bureaucracy to carry out the USPF that guarantees basic social security to the poor and vulnerable groups in the Philippines. Some examples of these institutions are the Government Service Insurance System and Social Security System that provide social security benefits to workers in the public and private sector respectively, the Home Development Mutual Fund that offers affordable housing, the Philippine Health Insurance Corporation (PhilHealth) that provides affordable health insurance coverage to all Filipinos and the Overseas Workers Welfare Administration that extends assistance to Filipinos working abroad (Orbeta 2012). The Philippine Development Plan 2017–2022 clearly states that:

> A universal and transformative social protection will be provided to all, to empower the people and make them capable of preventing, responding to, and recovering from various risks (i.e., economic, governance, and political risks, risks from natural hazards and individuals' inherent vulnerabilities). (Philippines 2020i, p. 26)

It can be noted that alleviating the plight of poor Filipinos is at the forefront of policy attention of the Philippine government. The multi-pillar social safety nets mentioned by Holzmann and Hinz (2005) in a publication of the World Bank are all present in the Philippines (see Orbeta 2012; World Bank 2018).

Some of the notable social protection milestones in the Philippines that focus on the welfare of the poor are the Pantawid Pamilyang Pilipino

Programme (4Ps), free basic education, free tuition for tertiary students, food subsidies and employment assistance. 4Ps is the CCT programme of the Philippines that started in 2008. To date, the CCT programme has served 5,084,797 poor Filipino families in 17 regions of the country (Philippines 2020j). According to the Asian Development Bank, 4Ps "has become a cornerstone of social protection in the Philippines" by aiding poor families in ensuring the health and education well-being of their children (Schelzig 2015). In the education sector, students in elementary and high school are entitled to free education pursuant to the Governance of Basic Education Act (Philippines 2001), while students enrolled in state universities and colleges and technical-vocational education and training programmes are exempted from paying tuition fees because of the Universal Access to Quality Tertiary Education Act (Philippines 2016). Moreover, the National Food Authority provides food subsidies to the poor, while the Metro Manila Development Authority, Philippine National Police and Department of Public Works and Highways provide emergency employment on a seasonal basis (Ofreneo 2012). To some extent, the coverage and variety of social safety nets in the Philippines is broad and comprehensive, particularly in terms of CCT, a state-financed health insurance scheme, and social pensions for the elderly. Nevertheless, according to Social Watch Philippines, "social protection remains fragmented, inaccessible and unreachable to many Filipinos" (2017).

Social Protection Policies: Philippine Government's Approaches to Mitigate Crisis

On top of constitutional provisions, there is an abundance of legal instruments that empower the President of the Philippines to respond to and abate public health emergencies like the Covid-19 pandemic. Months before the outbreak of the 2019 novel coronavirus in January 2020, President Rodrigo Duterte signed into law the Republic Act No. 11332 or the *Mandatory Reporting of Notifiable Diseases and Health Events of Public Concern Act* on April 26, 2019. The said law stipulates that the Philippine state "recognises the epidemics and other public health emergencies as threats to public health and national security" that may produce harsh social, economic and political impacts to the country. Moreover, the law grants power to the President to "declare a state of public health emergency and mobilise government and nongovernment agencies to respond to the threat." It is apparent that the Philippines is ready to face complex health emergencies like the pandemic in terms of legislation.

On January 31, 2020, the Duterte government ordered the temporary ban of travellers from Wuhan in the Hubei Province of China, which was the epicentre of the 2019 coronavirus (CNN Philippines 2020a). The presidential order was issued following the report of the DOH of the first case of Covid-19 infection in the Philippines on January 30, 2020 (Gregorio 2020b). In a public statement released on February 13, 2020, Duterte said that despite the presence of the threat due to three confirmed cases in the country, the public should not worry because no Filipinos have been infected by the virus (CNN Philippines 2020b). It took the President until March 8, 2020, to declare a public health emergency due to confirmed local transmission and outbreak of the coronavirus in the country (Peralta et al. 2020) through Presidential Proclamation No. 922, series of 2020. The said proclamation mandated all government agencies and local government units in the Philippines "to render full assistance and cooperation and mobilise the necessary resources to undertake critical, urgent and appropriate response and measures in a timely manner to curtail and eliminate the Covid-19 threat". Nevertheless, the President refused to put Metro Manila under lockdown despite increasing cases of Covid-19 infection in the capital region (Nakpil 2020). On March 15, 2020, President Duterte ordered the implementation of quarantine measures in Metro Manila until April 13 (CNN Philippines 2020c). Two days after, the entire island of Luzon was placed under enhanced community quarantine. The government assured the public it would provide some social safety nets, such as food aid and early release of workers cash benefits to those affected by quarantine measures (Gregorio 2020a). To manage the threat posed by Covid-19, the Congress of the Philippines granted additional powers to President Duterte on March 24, 2020. These extra emergency powers vested to the President were enshrined in Republic Act No. 11469, which is popularly known as the Bayanihan to Heal as One Act. This law provides a wide range of state-sponsored affirmative actions that are designed to install immediate layers of social protection for poor Filipinos. The following are the major social safety nets undertaken by the Philippine government during this extraordinary time of pandemic.

Cash Assistance to Individuals in Crisis Situations

The landmark feature of the Bayanihan to Heal as One Act is the provision of an emergency cash aid to around 18 million low-income families in the Philippines. According to this law, eligible households may receive a cash subsidy from the government amounting to between PHP 5000 and 8000 (USD 103-165) a month for two months. The computation of the emergency cash subsidy is based on prevailing regional minimum wage rates. Hence, poor families in Metro Manila are entitled to receive the maximum amount of PHP 8000 due to higher cost of living standard there, unlike those in the provinces outside the capital region. To implement this social safety net, the government created the Social Amelioration Programme (SAP) to grant cash assistance to poor Filipinos who are affected by the imposition of community quarantine. Under SAP, the government designed the Emergency Subsidy Programme (ESP) to help three categories of poor families: the recipients of 4Ps, low-income families, and indigent families and other vulnerable groups. The second group includes different sub-categories of the poor, such as directly hired or occasional workers, sub-contracted workers, home-workers, house helpers, public transportation drivers, micro-entrepreneurs and producers, family enterprise owners, sub-minimum wage earners, farmers, fisherfolks and stranded workers. Meanwhile, the third group comprises indigent indigenous peoples, underprivileged and homeless individuals and overseas Filipinos in distress and other vulnerable groups, particularly the elderly, persons with disabilities and lactating and pregnant women (Philippines 2020c). It is apparent that the inclusion criteria of defining the poor who are qualified to receive cash assistance are broad and comprehensive.

The imposition of lockdown and community quarantine measures, particularly the immediate closure of schools, prevent 4Ps beneficiaries to meet conditions set forth by law. Consequently, the Philippine government suspended conditions related to attendance of children in school and visits to health facilities from February to May 2020. The 1.3 million 4Ps beneficiaries are given cash subsidy of PHP 3,650 to 6,650 (USD 72-132) every month (International Labour Organization, henceforth ILO 2020; *Philippines News Gazette* 2020). Such flexibility in the implementation of the conditional cash transfer programme constitutes an immediate layer of protection to the poorest of the poor to mitigate the adverse economic impact of the crisis.

Another set of vulnerable groups affected by the pandemic are the OFWs and public utility vehicle (PUV) drivers. According to DOLE, 336,806 OFWs deployed in different countries requested financial assistance from the Philippine government. However, only 85,849 qualified to receive a one-time payment of PHP 10,000 or USD 200, as they are displaced from their jobs owing to the imposition of lockdowns in their host countries. Some of these qualified beneficiaries are repatriated workers or those OFWs who returned to the Philippines because of the Covid-19 pandemic. OFWs who have been infected by the virus are also entitled to receive cash aid from the government (Philippines 2020f). Meanwhile, 40,000 PUV drivers who lost their means of livelihood due to lockdowns are also given cash aid under the SAP (Esmael 2020).

Emergency Employment and Aid for Displaced and Stranded Workers

The stoppage of work in almost all industries has led to a widespread displacement of workers who are vulnerable to economic shocks brought about by the pandemic. To aid displaced, underemployed and seasonal workers, DOLE implemented the Tulong Panghanapbuhay sa Ating Disadvantaged/Displaced Workers (TUPAD) or employment emergency programme for displaced workers. Under TUPAD, DOLE created employment for displaced workers for 10 days, but not to exceed 30 days. These displaced workers are assigned to do work in social, economic and agro-forestry community development projects of the government. They are also required to undergo safety orientation and disinfect their houses and immediate vicinity (Philippines 2020d; ILO 2020) Moreover, beneficiaries of TUPAD may avail of skills development training under the Training for Work Scholarship Programme of the Technical Education and Skills Development Authority (Philippines 2020d).

DOLE earmarked PHP 2 billion to fund the emergency employment programme, which provided financial assistance to workers who have been affected by travel restrictions and community lockdowns, particularly in Metro Manila. DOLE Undersecretary Benjo Benevidez said "workers may take a leave or go absent from factories while Metro Manila is under quarantine. If they have already consumed their leaves, DOLE can step in and extend financial assistance" (CNN Philippines 2020d). According to the report of the ILO (2020), 220,320 displaced workers have benefited from the emergency employment programme of the Philippine government.

The imposition of lockdown in Metro Manila has led to massive job loss of workers, especially Filipinos from the countryside who went to Manila for employment. A major dilemma caused by the outbreak of the pandemic in the capital region is the displacement of workers from the provinces who do not have the financial means to stay in Manila. Consequently, these workers have become locally stranded individuals (LSI) because they cannot go back to their respective provinces due to the suspension of land, sea and air travels. OFWs who recently arrived in the country and were quarantined in Manila, tourists, and students are also categorised as LSIs. Poor LSIs, especially construction workers and domestic helpers, were forced to stay and seek shelter for days outside the airport, stadiums and under the overpass without observing basic health protocols like social distancing, while waiting for homebound flights and bus rides (Manuel 2020). Apparently, they have to grapple with such a dismal situation and face the greater risk of being infected of the coronavirus disease. In fact, a stranded mother named Michelle Silvertino, age 33, died at the footbridge in Pasay while waiting for a bus ride to Camarines Sur for over five days (Marquez 2020). The unfortunate death of Silvertino shows that the poor stranded workers in Metro Manila were not immediately provided with basic social protection, particularly decent temporary shelter, to keep them safe from illnesses like the Covid-19 disease.

Major affirmative actions of the Philippine government that seek to afford protection to LSIs include the Balik Probinsya, Bagong Pag-asa (BP2) Programme, and the Hatid Tulong Programme. The BP2 Programme is designed to decongest the capital region by urging "people, especially informal settlers to return to their home provinces and assist them in this transition with support and incentives in transportation, family, livelihood, housing, subsistence and education" (Philippines 2020e). The Hatid Tulong Programme, on the other hand, is an initiative to provide transportation assistance to LSIs affected by lockdown in Metro Manila to go back to their respective provinces (ABS-CBN News 2020). Under these programmes, thousands of LSIs were able to travel back to their home provinces. Ships of the Philippine Coast Guard, Bureau of Fisheries and Philippine Navy were utilised to ferry LSIs to different parts of the country (Kabagani 2020; Philippine Navy

2020). Private transportation companies have joined the government also in implementing the said programmes to aid LSIs, especially poor and distressed workers (Kabagani 2020). Moreover, some LSIs received sanitary and sleeping kits from the government (GMA News 2020d), while those who are qualified were given cash aid of PHP 2000 (USD 41) (Kabagani 2020).

Health Emergency Measures

An important objective of the Bayanihan to Heal as One Act is the immediate provision of healthcare, along with medical tests and treatments, to persons infected by the Covid-19 disease, as well as persons under investigation or persons under monitoring. The law mandated PhilHealth under its National Health Insurance Programme to shoulder the full cost of treatment of all Covid-19 patients. Moreover, the law specifies social safety nets for medical front-liners who are at risk of contracting the coronavirus because of the nature of their work. These medical workers in public and private healthcare institutions are assured that PhilHealth will pay for all medical expenses in case of exposure to Covid-19 or any work-related injury or ailment for the duration of the pandemic (Philippines 2020b). Nevertheless, in an advisory from the President and Chief Operating Officer of PhilHealth, retired Brigadier General Ricardo C. Morales said that the insurance firm will shoulder the full cost of treatment for all Covid-19 cases until April 14, 2020, only. Hence, after that date, PhilHealth can no longer guarantee to pay for the full costs of treatment of patients infected by the virus. Health workers are exempted from this advisory (Philippines 2020g).

The outbreak of the pandemic reveals vulnerabilities in the health sector, particularly the weakness of the public health facilities in detecting and diagnosing the SARS-CoV2 virus. During the start of the pandemic in February 2020, the Research Institute for Tropical Medicine (RITM) of the DOH was the lone accredited laboratory that had the capacity and needed expertise to detect the virus. In March 2020, RITM was assisted by five subnational laboratories, namely, the Baguio General Hospital and Medical Center, San Lazaro Hospital, Lung Center of the Philippines, Vicente Sotto Memorial Center and the Southern Philippines Medical Center (Philippines 2020h). The Bayanihan to Heal as One Act mandated for the immediate accreditation of testing kits by the DOH, public and private health institutions are enjoined to carry out prompt testing of persons under investigation and persons under monitoring. Patients who tested positive for the virus should be isolated and treated immediately (Philippines 2020b). Secretary Carlito Galvez, the chief implementer of the government's response in fighting the Covid-19 pandemic, reported that as of September 5, 2020, there are 117 Covid-19 laboratories across the country. The increase in the number of testing laboratories in the Philippines is seen as an initial success of the government in combating the pandemic (Bajo 2020). The presence of more accredited laboratories does not only intensify the testing capacity of health institutions, but it is also beneficial to people in the provinces outside the capital region because they are no longer required to send swab samples to RITM. Moreover, according to DOH Secretary Francisco Duque, the testing for the Covid-19 disease is free, as the cost will be shouldered by PhilHealth. This social safety net is particularly favourable to the poor because each coronavirus test kit costs around PHP 8,000 (USD 165), which is apparently not affordable for poor patients or those suspected to have been infected by the virus (CNN Philippines 2020e). The cost of testing in the Philippines is beyond the financial capacity of poor individuals, especially those who lost their jobs and means of livelihood because of lockdown and community quarantine.

Food Aid to Mitigate Hunger

Aside from cash transfer, creation of emergency employment and installation of additional health measures, the Bayanihan to Heal as One Act mandated for the urgent mobilisation of aid and delivery of basic necessities to Filipinos affected by the community quarantine, particularly those poor and indigent families (Philippines 2020b). When the entire Luzon Island was placed into enhanced community quarantine in March 2020, the Department of Social Welfare and Development (DSWD) distributed food to affected residents (Gregorio 2020a). The food packs are usually comprised of rice, canned goods and instant noodles, which are distributed to every household in villages under lockdown. Moreover, the Department of Education has carried out a feeding programme in schools, while the DSWD provided a supplemental feeding programme for children in day care (Philippines 2020b).

The distribution of emergency relief goods, especially food, and feeding activities for children are beneficial to the poor and indigent families because many of them do not have the means to earn a living, while others lost or were suspended from their jobs because of the pandemic. Poor individuals cannot simply go to the market to buy food because public transportation is suspended, unlike those Filipinos who are relatively well-off, have the economic means to purchase food, and are in possession of private vehicles to go to supermarkets.

Educating Students in the Midst of the Pandemic

The education sector in the Philippines, like anywhere else, in the world, has been significantly affected by the outbreak of the pandemic. Classes in public and private schools, colleges and universities in the country were terminated and their operations halted as early as March 2020, when the rate of Covid-19 infection started to rise and led to the imposition of lockdowns in most places in the Philippines. Due to lockdowns and strict community quarantines, students in all levels (kindergarten, elementary, secondary and tertiary) were not required to undertake major assessments. Moreover, instead of August, the academic year 2020–2021 in public schools officially starts on October 5, 2020, as decreed by President Duterte. The postponement is necessary to give time to the Department of Education to recalibrate its learning modalities under the "new normal" (Santos 2020a).

The adverse impact of the pandemic on education is particularly detrimental to the welfare of poor Filipinos. According to the Department of Education, the complex health emergency brought about by the Covid-19 disease will likely result in the increase of out-of-school youth and out-of-school children, as four million learners are gravely hit by this health crisis. The enrolment rate as of August 11, 2020 is "around 83.1% of the last year's figure of 27.7 million" (CNN Philippines 2020f). It is apparent that the pandemic has led to marginalisation of children to access education due to a wide array of limitations posed by the crisis. Low-income families and those living below the poverty line are no longer capable of sending their children to school because of loss of income and very limited livelihood opportunities. It is a glaring reality in the Philippines that poor children are not ready to participate in the new learning environment created by the Department of Education in this extraordinary time. Children from poor families do not have access to internet and means to buy equipment like computers and smartphones to undertake and join online classes. Another major challenge confronting poor children to access education in times of crisis is that they are not allowed to go out of their homes or to go to places where there are internet signals for mobile data. Further, not everyone in the Philippines has wifi connectivity at home. The introduction of online classes is designed to ensure access to education for children in the midst of the pandemic. Nonetheless, it is clear that online modes of learning have a marginalising impact on children from poor families. To address this dilemma in the education sector, the Department of Education has set up some affirmative actions or policies that, to some extent, grant social protection to the poor. Examples of these affirmative actions are the introduction of offline learning environments in which schools will produce modules and send them to learners who do have to means or are not willing to participate in online classes, and the Education Department allows the transfer of 380,000 students in private schools from kindergarten to senior high schools to public educational institutions (CNN Philippines 2020f).

Social Protection at the Subnational Government Level

In the preceding section, I have outlined major social protection programmes spearheaded by the Philippine national government in managing and responding to the threats brought about by the Covid-19 pandemic and designed to lessen its adverse impacts on the social and economic well-being of poor Filipinos. Although the national government is taking the lead in combating this health crisis, it is worth noting that subnational government organisations or local government units (LGUs) in the Philippines are playing a crucial role in the fight against Covid-19. As provided in the Local Government Code of 1991, LGUs composed of provincial, city, municipal and barangay (the basic political unit) governments are granted with political autonomy, particularly in the area of healthcare, social welfare and development, environment, disaster management, public works and agriculture. Fiscal autonomy is also granted to LGUs that entitles them to receive a share of wealth from the national government in the form of internal revenue allotment (IRA) (Philippines 1991). Moreover, the Philippine Disaster Risk Reduction and Management Act of 2010 authorised LGUs to allocate and utilise 5% of their IRA for the management of man-made and natural disasters within their respective jurisdictions. 30% of this fund may be used by LGUs for quick response (Philippines 2010). It means that LGUs may disburse a portion of the disaster management fund, such as purchase rice, noodles, canned foods and other relief goods, in anticipation of impending disasters like an outbreak of war and flash floods. Because of the pandemic, the Bayanihan to Heal as One Act lifted the 30% ceiling on the disaster management fund to boost LGUs' capacity in the provision of emergency aid to constituents, especially the poor (Philippines 2020b). Hence, it is clear that LGUs have sufficient political and financial power, as well as agency to aid the national government in combating the Covid-19 crisis and providing additional safety nets for the poor.

The pandemic forced LGUs to roll out their respective Covid-19 action plans and strategies. It can be noticed that their initiatives are designed to reinforce social protection programmes of the national government, with some modifications depending on their financial capacity and current situations vis-à-vis the rate of infection in their area. Most LGUs have concentrated their assistance to their poor constituents in safety net areas, such as food security, cash transfer and health. There is an abundance of innovation and best practices of LGUs when it comes to combating the current health crisis. These innovative initiatives are documented in the website LGUvsCOVIDPH in cooperation with the Department of the Interior and Local Government with support from The Asia Foundation and funded by the Australian Government.

An interesting case in point is the city of Manila that had a comprehensive social protection programme in place as early as March 2020 to fight the pandemic. The city of Manila implemented the Code Red Covid-19 Action Plan: Contain and Delay, which is the primary blueprint for the city in curtailing the spread of the disease within its domain. The action plan focuses on the provision of food and water, medicines and procurement of medical equipment. A specific affirmative action of the city government that is worth noting is the preferential treatment extended to the elderly population. According to Manila Mayor Isko Moreno, vitamins are given to the elderly folks of the city because they are the most vulnerable to the deadly coronavirus. In addition, the city of Manila allocated hundreds of millions of pesos to provide food aid to affected families and purchase medical equipment to upgrade the Manila Infectious Disease Control Center, which is now qualified to treat Covid-19 patients (GMA News 2020a).

Other cities in Metro Manila are also recognised for their innovative Covid-19 programmes, such as the "Stay Safe", which is a mobile application used by Makati for contact tracing (Santos 2020b); the "Race to Zero" campaign of Quezon City that grants cash incentives to *barangay*

LGUs with effective programmes against Covid-19 (Ornedo 2020); the PHP 1 billion (USD 20 million) worth of cash aid for poor families in Pasig City (Punzalan 2020); and the rice distribution programme for shoemakers of Marikina City, which is known for its thriving shoemaking industry (GMA News 2020b). Meanwhile, LGUs outside the capital region are also hailed for their innovation and best practices not only in combating the dreadful virus but also in granting social protection to vulnerable groups. The Municipality of Cainta, Rizal focused on aiding the elderly by giving them free vitamins to boost their immune system (Cepeda 2020), while the City of Batangas in partnership with the Philippine National Police created employment for prisoners involved in illicit drugs to provide express delivery services to residents of the city in buying essential needs like food and medicines (LGUvsCOVIDPH 2020). The Province of Maguindanao in the war-torn Bangsamoro Autonomous Region in Muslim Mindanao purchased vegetables produced by women farmers and distributed these vegetables as food aid to poor people (Medenilla 2020), while the city of Iloilo provided cash aid to 250 members of the LGBT (lesbian, gay, bisexual and transgender) community, who are displaced from the entertainment industry due to imposition of lockdown (Pineda 2020).

Those cited examples of LGUs' sterling initiatives in designing innovation in this extraordinary time are perhaps anecdotal. Those various programmes and policies formulated at the subnational government level are demonstrative of LGUs' agency to reinforce social protection apparatus of the national government, especially in aiding the poor and the vulnerable groups during complex a health emergency. The provision of political and fiscal autonomy warrants LGU to initiate quick responses and formulate initiatives that are aptly suited to their needs and current circumstances in the midst of the pandemic. Nonetheless, not all LGUs like those cited above are stalwarts of innovation and led by politicians who have the political will to implement swift responses against the dreadful virus and give priority in promoting the welfare of the poor. Local governments have varying capacities in terms of wealth to finance social protection programmes and expertise, especially in the area of health, to manage and contain the outbreak of the Covid-19 disease in their own domain. LGUs in rural communities are not as affluent as highly urbanised cities like those in Metro Manila, particularly in terms of IRA and local income to finance social safety nets for the poor.

At the time of writing, LGUs are facing their own battle, as pockets of Covid-19 crisis loom in the provinces. For instance, the city of General Santos in the southern Philippines declared the presence of local transmission of coronavirus on August 31, 2020 only. Consequently, several *barangays* in the city were placed in targeted lockdowns for medical frontliners to conduct contact tracing and contain the spread of the virus (Gubalani 2020). The city and regional Inter-agency Task Force for the Management of Emerging Infectious Diseases (IATF-MEID) requested the national IATF-MEID that is chaired by Defense Secretary Delfin Lorenzana to place the entire city under general community quarantine from modified general community quarantine status on September 13 to 27, 2020 due to the recent spike of Covid-19 infection (Jubelag 2020). The setback in the performance of the city LGU to fight the virus is expected to yield additional challenges in its capacity to extend social protection to affected families, particularly the poor. It can be noted that General Santos has spent hundreds of millions of pesos to provide food relief aid consisting of rice, canned goods, noodles, meat, fish and vegetables to its residents for two months (Mindanews 2020). In addition, public and private hospitals in General Santos are also catering Covid-19 patients from neighbouring towns and provinces because of the lack of health facilities there. Hence, the growing cases of Covid-19 infection entail an additional burden to the city LGU to allocate more funds and mobilise its heath professional and medical experts in managing and containing the spread of the virus. The case of General Santos is just an illustration of how the pandemic impacts the performance of LGUs in the Philippines in providing social protection to its poor constituents. Other key cities outside Metro Manila like Cebu are also faced with the same dilemma (GMA News 2020c).

Conclusion

The Philippines case demonstrates that the universal social protection floor is at the forefront of the anti-poverty investment of the Philippine government. Although not devoid of flaws and imperfections, comprehensive and multi-pillar social security guarantees in the form of social insurance, social assistance and labour market regulations are well in place in the social service delivery system of the Philippines. These social safety nets and affirmative actions have been established primarily to reduce poverty and vulnerability to risks of destitute people, minorities and marginalised groups in the country. Major social security programmes, particularly conditional cash transfer, universal health care and free education, are designed to ameliorate the plight of poor Filipinos and promote equitable development, even before the outbreak of the dreaded coronavirus. Hence, the poor are at the centre of policy attention in the Philippines.

The imposition of lockdown and community quarantine in different regions, accompanied by the closure of some business establishments has resulted in the surge of poverty, deprivation, unemployment and other unprecedented economic shocks, which have adverse and direct impacts on the welfare of destitute people in the country. The outbreak of the Covid-19 pandemic has reinforced the imperative for the Philippine government to create additional social protection mechanisms and safety nets to address vulnerabilities and mitigate economic repercussions confronting the poor. This wide range of social protection measures focuses on the area of food aid and food security, health care, education, emergency employment and cash transfer. This array of social security guarantees was immediately installed in the Philippines social protection architecture because of the emergency powers vested by Congress to President Duterte to take swift measures and allocate billions of pesos to finance social protection in this extraordinary time. To some extent, the Covid-19 pandemic has catalysed reinforcement in the social protection arsenal of the Philippine government on top of existing pro-poor programmes that were already established prior to the outbreak of the pandemic. Moreover, the provision of autonomy has allowed subnational government organisations to complement the efforts of the national government in the delivery of social protection programmes. The amount of political and fiscal autonomy extended to local governments enabled vertical engagements at the national and subnational levels in fighting the pandemic. Although the pandemic has revealed different and varying capacities of local governments to address the crisis and protect their poor constituents, some of them have turned out to be repositories and producers of innovation and best practices when it comes to the management of a complex health emergency. Nevertheless, the Philippine government is faced with the imperative to design innovative and well-thought action plans, including raising more revenues, to sustain its social protection architecture because, at the time of writing, the rate of Covid-19 infection has no sign of abating.

References

Abad, Michelle. 2020. Pandemic could push 1.5 million Filipinos into poverty—study. *Rappler Philippines*, August 10. https://rappler.com/nation/coronavirus-pandemic-push-million-filipinos-poverty-pids-study. Accessed 14 September 2020.

ABS-CBN News. 2020. 54 K stranded individuals assisted by Hatid Tulong program, 13 K more await help, June 26. https://news.abs-cbn.com/news/06/26/20/54k-stranded-individuals-assisted-by-hatid-tulong-program-13k-more-await-help. Accessed 13 September 2020.

Bajo, Anna Felicia. 2020. Philippines now has 117 accredited labs for Covid-19 testing, Galvez says. *GMA News Online*, September 7. https://www.gmanetwork.com/news/news/nation/754549/philippines-now-has-117-accredited-labs-for-covid-19-testing-galvez-says/story/. Accessed 10 September 2020.

Bautista, Dessy, and Melissa Luz Lopez. 2020. Timeline: How the Philippines is handling COVID-19. *CNN Philippines*, April 21. https://cnnphilippines.com/news/2020/4/21/interactive-timeline-PH-handling-COVID-19.html. Accessed 4 September 2020.

Barrientos, Armando, and David Hulme (eds.). 2008. *Social protection for the poor and poorest: Concepts, policies and politics*. Basingstoke: Palgrave Macmillan.

Center for Strategic and International Studies. 2020. Southeast Asia Covid-19 tracker. https://www.csis.org/programs/southeast-asia-program/southeast-asia-covid-19-tracker-0. Accessed 13 September 2020.

Cepeda, Mara. 2020. Cainta under quarantine starting March 15 due to coronavirus cases. *Rappler Philippines*, March 13. https://rappler.com/nation/mayor-nieto-place-cainta-quarantine-coronavirus. Accessed 12 September 2020.

CNN Philippines. 2020a. Duterte orders travel ban from China province amid coronavirus scare, *CNN Philippines*, January 31. https://www.cnnphilippines.com/news/2020/1/31/Philippines-novel-coronavirus-China-travel-ban.html. Accessed 4 September 2020.

CNN Philippines. 2020b. Duterte appeals for calm, vigilance amid coronavirus scare. *CNN Philippines*, February 13. https://cnnphilippines.com/news/2020/2/13/Novel-coronavirus-disease-Philippines-Duterte.html. Accessed 6 September 2020.

CNN Philippines. 2020c. Metro Manila be placed on 'lockdown' due to Covid-19, March 12. https://cnnphilippines.com/news/2020/3/12/COVID-19-Metro-Manila-restrictions-Philippines.html. Accessed 6 September 2020.

CNN Philippines. 2020d. DOLE to extend cash aid to employees who can't go to work amid Covid-19 travel restrictions, March 16. https://cnnphilippines.com/news/2020/3/16/DOLE-cash-aid-coronavirus.html. Accessed 7 September 2020.

CNN Philippines. 2020e. Testing for coronavirus disease is free—Duque, March 11. https://www.cnnphilippines.com/news/2020/3/11/coronavirus-testing-free-.html. Accessed 8 September 2020.

CNN Philippines. 2020f. DepEd official: Close to 4 million learners did not enroll for next year due to Covid-19 crisis, August 12. https://www.cnnphilippines.com/news/2020/8/12/4-million-out-of-school-youth-covid-crisis.html. Accessed 10 September 2020.

Britto, De, and Tatiana Feitosa. 2008. The emergence and popularity of conditional cash transfer in Latin America. In *Social protection for the poor and poorest: Concepts, policies and politics*, ed. Armando Barrientos and David Hulme, 181–193. Basingstoke: Palgrave Macmillan.

Devereux, Stephen, and Rachel Sabates-Wheeler. 2007. Editorial introduction: Debating social protection. *IDS Bulletin* 38 (3): 1–7. https://doi.org/10.1111/j.1759-5436.2007.tb00363.x.

Esmael, Lisbet. 2020. DoTr: Thousands of PUV drivers to receive cash aid. *The Manila Times*, April 9. https://www.manilatimes.net/2020/04/09/business/business-top/dotr-thousands-of-puv-drivers-to-receive-cash-aid/711579/. Accessed 10 September 2020.

Holzmann, Robert, and Richard Hinz. 2005. *Old age income support in the 21st century: An international perspective on pension system and reform*. Washington, DC: World Bank.

International Labour Organization. 2020. Social protection responses to the Covid-19 pandemic in developing countries: Strengthening resilience by building universal social protection. *ILO Brief*, May 2020. https://www.ilo.org/wcmsp5/groups/public/—ed_protect/—soc_sec/documents/publication/wcms_744612.pdf. Accessed 6 September 2020.

GMA News. 2020a. Manila Mayor Isko Moreno implements Covid-19 action plan, March 13. https://www.gmanetwork.com/news/news/metro/729490/manila-mayor-isko-moreno-implements-covid-19-action-plan/story/. Accessed 11 September 2020.

GMA News. 2020b. 100% of cash aid distributed in Marikina; LGU gives more aid, March 11. https://www.gmanetwork.com/news/news/metro/737774/100-of-cash-aid-distributed-in-marikina-lgu-distributes-more-aid/story/. Accessed 12 September 2020.

GMA News. 2020c. Covid-19 cases in Cebu province reach 5,008, September 12. https://www.gmanetwork.com/news/news/regions/755333/covid-19-cases-in-cebu-province-reach-5-008/story/. Accessed 12 September 2020.

GMA News. 2020d. Nearly 400 locally stranded individuals provided transportation assistance – Palace, June 15. https://www.gmanetwork.com/news/news/nation/742686/nearly-400-locally-stranded-individuals-provided-transportation-assistance-palace/story/. Accessed 13 September 2020.

Gregorio, Xave. 2020a. Movement of people in Luzon restricted as island placed under 'enhanced' community quarantine. *CNN Philippines*, March 16. https://www.cnnphilippines.com/news/2020/3/16/luzon-enhanced-community-quarantine-covid-19.html. Accessed 11 September 2020.

Gregorio, Xave. 2020b. Philippines confirms first case of novel coronavirus. *CNN Philippines*, January 30. https://cnnphilippines.com/news/2020/1/30/Philippines-coronavirus-case.html. Accessed 8 September 2020.

Gubalani, Richelyn. 2020. Gensan declares Covid-19 local transmission. *Philippine News Agency*, August 31. https://www.pna.gov.ph/articles/1113931. Accessed 12 September 2020.

LGUvsCOVIDPH. 2020. Drug surrenderees tapped by LGU for essential services. https://www.lguvscovid.ph/content/drug-surrenderees-tapped-by-lgu-for-essential-services. Accessed 12 September 2020.

Jubelag, Joseph. 2020. Gensan seeks GCQ status to address growing number of Covid-19 cases. *Manila Bulletin*, September 11. https://mb.com.ph/2020/09/11/gensan-seeks-gcq-status-to-address-growing-number-of-covid-19-cases/. Accessed 12 September 2020.

Kabagani, Lade Jean. 2020. Gov't sends off 400 more LSIs as 'Hatid Tuong' resumes. *Philippine News Agency*, August 20. https://www.pna.gov.ph/articles/1112878. Accessed 12 September 2020.

Kabeer, Naila. 2004. Imagining 'the social': Social policy analysis for the poor in poor countries. IDS Working Paper 191.

Lopez, Melissa Luz. 2020. Roque on 27 M Filipinos reported jobless: 'It could've been worse'. *CNN Philippines*, August 17. https://www.cnnphilippines.com/news/2020/8/17/Harry-Roque-SWS-survey-45.5-percent-Pinoys-jobless.html. Accessed 13 September 2020.

Manuel, Pilar. 2020. Balik Probinsya program temporarily suspended to prioritize locally stranded individuals. *CNN Philippines*, June 11. https://cnnphilippines.com/news/2020/6/11/Balik-Probinsya-program-temporarily-suspended.html. Accessed 13 September 2020.

Marquez, Consuelo. 2020. Pasay LGU gives aid to family of stranded mon who died waiting for bus ride. *Philippine Daily Inquirer*, June 10. https://newsinfo.inquirer.net/1289524/pasay-lgu-gives-aid-to-family-of-stranded-mom-who-died-after-waiting-for-bus-ride. Accessed 13 September 2020.

Merrien, Francois-Xavier. 2013. Social protection as development policy: A new international agenda for action. *International Development Policy*: 89–106. https://doi.org/10.4000/poldev.1525.

Medenilla, Vina. 2020. Maguindanao LGU buys vegetables produced by local women farmers for relief goods. *Monthly Agriculture*, April 7. https://www.agriculture.com.ph/2020/04/07/maguindanao-lgu-buys-vegetables-produced-by-local-women-farmers-for-relief-goods/. Accessed 12 September 2020.

Mindanews. 2020. Gensan LGU imports 7,200 metric tons of rice. *Mindanews*, April 9. https://www.mindanews.com/top-stories/2020/04/gensan-lgu-imports-7200-metric-tons-of-rice/. Accessed 12 September 2020.

Munro, Lauchlan. 2008. Risks, needs and rights: Compatible or contradictory bases for social protection. In *Social protection for the poor and poorest: Concepts, policies and politics*, ed. Armando Barrientos and David Hulme, 27–46. Basingstoke: Palgrave Macmillan.

Nakpil, Danielle. 2020. Duterte rejects Metro Manila lockdown despite rising coronavirus cases in PH. *CNN Philippines*, March 9. https://cnnphilippines.com/news/2020/3/9/Duterte-rejects-Metro-Manila-lockdown-despite-rise-PH-coronavirus-cases.html. Accessed 6 September 2020.

Ofreneo, Rosalinda. 2012. Addressing social dimension of climate change through adaptive social protection. In *Strengthening social protection components and strategies in the Philippines: A compilation of social protection think papers*, 1–17. Manila: Department of Social Welfare and Development, United Nations Development Programme and National Economic and Development Authority.

Orbeta, Aniceto Jr. 2012. Social protection in the Philippines: Current state and challenges. Discussion Paper Series No. 2011-02. Philippine Institute for Development Studies. https://dirp4.pids.gov.ph/ris/dps/pidsdps1102.pdf. Accessed 13 September 2020.

Ornedo, Julia Mari. 2020. QC dangles cash reward for barangays with effective anti-Covid-19 programs. *GMA News Online*, September 7. https://www.gmanetwork.com/news/news/metro/754615/qc-dangles-cash-reward-for-barangays-with-effective-anti-covid-19-programs/story/. Accessed 11 September 2020.

Peralta, Janine, Catherine Modesto, and Eimor Santos. 2020. Duterte declares public health emergency due to coronavirus–spokesperson. *CNN Philippines*, March 8. https://cnnphilippines.com/news/2020/3/8/Philippines-public-health-emergency.html. Accessed 10 September 2020.

Philippine Navy. 2020. Navy ferries locally stranded individuals bound for Iloilo, Cebu. *Philippines News Agency*, June 21. https://pia.gov.ph/news/articles/1045425. Accessed 13 September 2020.

Philippines. 1991. Official Gazette of the Philippines, Republic Act No. 7160 or the Local Government Code. https://www.officialgazette.gov.ph/1991/10/10/republic-act-no-7160/. Accessed 13 September 2020.

Philippines. 2001. Official Gazette of the Philippines. Republic Act No. 9155 or the Governance of Basic Education. https://www.officialgazette.gov.ph/2001/08/11/republic-act-no-9155/. Accessed 13 September 2020.

Philippines. 2010. Official Gazette of the Philippines, Republic Act No. 10121 or the Philippine Disaster Risk Reduction and Management Act. https://www.officialgazette.gov.ph/2010/05/27/republic-act-no-10121/. Accessed 13 September 2020.
Philippines. 2016. Official Gazette of the Philippines. Republic Act No. 10931 or the Universal Access to Quality Tertiary Education Act. https://www.officialgazette.gov.ph/downloads/2017/08aug/20170803-RA-10931-RRD.pdf. Accessed 13 September 2020.
Philippines. 2020a. Department of Health, COVID-19 Case Tracker. https://www.doh.gov.ph/2019-ncov/. Accessed 14 September 2020.
Philippines. 2020b. Official Gazette of the Philippines. Republic Act No. 11469 or the Bayanihan to Heal as One Act. https://officialgazette.gov.ph/downloads/2020/03mar/20200324-RA-11469-RRD.pdf. Accessed 6 September 2020.
Philippines. 2020c. Department of Social Welfare and Development, Memorandum Circular No. 9, series of 2020, Omnibus Guidelines in the Implementation of the Emergency Subsidy Program of the Department of Social Welfare and Development. https://www.ncda.gov.ph/wp-content/uploads//2020/04/MC-09-s2020-OMNIBUS-GUIDELINES-EMERG-SUBSIDY-PROG-DSWD.pdf. Accessed 6 September 2020.
Philippines. 2020d. Department of Labour and Employment, About TUPAD. https://www.dole.gov.ph/tupad-contents/. Accessed 6 September 2020.
Philippines. 2020e. Balik Probinsya, Bagong Pag-asa Program. https://balikprobinsya.ph/. Accessed 6 September 2020.
Philippines. 2020f. Department of Labour and Employment, 86 K OFWs get DOLE cash aid. https://www.dole.gov.ph/news/86k-ofws-get-dole-cash-aid/. Accessed 6 September 2020.
Philippines. 2020g. Philippine Health Insurance Corporation, Advisory No. 2020-022. https://www.philhealth.gov.ph/advisories/2020/adv2020-0022.pdf. Accessed 6 September 2020.
Philippines. 2020h. Research Institute for Tropical Medicine, Department of Health, RITM strengthens subnational labs, Covid-19 response. http://ritm.gov.ph/itm-strengthens-subnational-labs-covid-19-response/. Accessed 8 September 2020.
Philippines. 2020i. National Economic and Development Authority, Philippine Development Plan 2017-2022. http://www.neda.gov.ph/wp-content/uploads/2017/12/Abridged-PDP-2017-2022_Final.pdf. Accessed 13 September 2020.
Philippines. 2020j. Department of Social Welfare and Development, Monthly Report on Pantawid Pamilya Coverage as of March 31, 2020. https://pantawid.dswd.gov.ph/wp-content/uploads/2020/07/1st-Quarterly-Report-2020.pdf. Accessed 13 September 2020.

Philippines News Gazette. 2020. SAP 2 Payouts 72.4% Complete: DSWD. August 6. https://www.philippinesnewsgazette.com/sap-2-payouts-72-4-complete-dswd/. Accessed 8 September 2020.

Pineda, Leonard. 2020. 250 LGBT members get cash aid from city gov't. *Philippine Information Agency*, May 18. https://pia.gov.ph/news/articles/1042137. Accessed 12 September 2020.

Punzalan, Jamaine. 2020. Pasig to give P 1 billion cash aid to residents: Vico Sotto. *ABS CBN News*, April 15. https://news.abs-cbn.com/news/04/15/20/pasig-vico-sotto-give-p1-billion-cash-all-residents. Accessed 11 September 2020.

Santos, Eimor. 2020a. DepEd moves opening of classes to October 5. *CNN Philippines*, August 14. https://cnnphilippines.com/news/2020/8/14/deped-class-opening-october-5.html. Accessed 10 September 2020.

Santos, Jel. 2020b. Nat'l Security adviser lauds Makati's Covid-19 programs. *Manila Bulletin*, August 19. https://mb.com.ph/2020/08/19/natl-security-adviser-lauds-makatis-covid-19-programs/. Accessed 10 September 2020.

Schelzig, Karin. 2015. Social protection brief: The social protection support project in the Philippines. Asian Development Bank. https://www.adb.org/publications/social-protection-support-project-philippines. Accessed 13 September 2020.

Schubert, Bernd. 2008. Protecting the poorest with cash transfers in low income countries. In *Social protection for the poor and poorest: Concepts, policies and politics*, ed. Armando Barrientos and David Hulme, 211–223. Basingstoke: Palgrave Macmillan.

Schubert, Bernd, and Rachel Slater. 2006. Social cash transfer in low-income African countries: Conditional or unconditional? *Development Policy Review* 2006 (24): 571–578. https://doi.org/10.1111/j.1467-7679.2006.00348.x.

Social Watch Philippines. 2017. Philippines: The transformative potential of a universal social protection floor. https://www.socialwatch.org/node/17624. Accessed 13 September 2020.

Ulriksen, Marianne Sandvad. 2012. Questioning the pro-poor agenda: Examining the links between social protection and poverty. *Development Policy Review* 30 (3): 261–281. https://doi.org/10.1111/j.1467-7679.2012.00576.x.

Voipio, Timo. 2007. Social protection for poverty reduction: The OECD/DAC/POVNET View. *IDS Bulletin* 38 (3): 45–50. https://doi.org/10.1111/j.1759-5436.2007.tb00374.x.

World Bank. 2001. Social protection sector strategy: From safety net to springboard. http://documents1.worldbank.org/curated/en/299921468765558913/pdf/multi-page.pdf. Accessed 14 September 2020.

World Bank. 2018. Philippines: Social protection review and assessment. http://documents1.worldbank.org/curated/en/420821539338371335/pdf/Philippines-Social-Protection-Review-and-Assessment-October-8-2018.pdf. Accessed 13 September 2020.

Yumol, David Tristan. 2020. DOLE estimates 10 million workers will lose jobs this year due to Covid-19 pandemic. *CNN Philippines*, March 21. https://www.cnnphilippines.com/news/2020/5/21/dole-estimates-ten-million-workers-will-lose-jobs-covid-pandemic.html. Accessed 14 September 2020.

CHAPTER 10

The Original Instructions of Accountability: Pandemic Response as Old Ways and New Means

Matthew Scobie

In Aotearoa New Zealand, Te Tiriti/The Treaty of Waitangi, signed in 1840 between representatives of the British Crown and representatives of autonomous Māori kinship groupings, sets up two spheres of authority. These are kāwanatanga (government) and tino rangatiratanga (unqualified exercise of chieftainship). This creates possibilities for *at least* dual legal systems and therefore *at least* dual economic systems (Godfery 2016). Responses to COVID-19 have revealed the enabling potential of this understanding based on a more authentic partnership between the Crown and Māori. Māori economies based on mana (authority/prestige) and tikanga (normative ethics) operate within, against and beyond a general understanding of 'economy' based on duties to protect. While the conventional economic effects from COVID-19 within the global capitalist economy have and will be devastating, Māori economies based on

M. Scobie (✉)
University of Canterbury, Christchurch, New Zealand
e-mail: matthew.scobie@canterbury.ac.nz

S. Ratuva et al. (eds.), *COVID-19 and Social Protection*,
https://doi.org/10.1007/978-981-16-2948-8_10

Māori values have huge potential for imagining and implementing alternative Indigenous economies. This chapter explores the potential for scaling out economies based on present practices and future possibilities with a focus on the concept and practice of accountability. That is, how is accountability understood and exercised within Māori thought, and how can this be harnessed in a post-COVID present and future?

A key feature of Māori thought around developing future economies is inspired by the common proverb *ka mua, ka muri*, walking backwards into the future. This means that many of the instructions for how to imagine and implement other economies will be in the enduring Indigenous traditions of that place. To focus my argument, I will concentrate on a word that has come to mean everything and nothing—accountability. I will delve into the concept and practice of accountability in Māori society, taking Ngāi Tahu, my iwi, as the focus, and continue to develop a theory of grounded accountability (see Scobie et al. 2020) inspired by old ways and new means that is being enacted in practice as a response to the COVID-19 crisis. The focus is on accountability because this word has been appropriated by accounting and accountants in mainstream economic thought with a focus on rights and accounts. In Māori thought and practice, rights are determined largely by obligations, which suggests a system of mutual aid. The term 'mutual aid' has emerged in popular discourse as a response to COVID, and here we explore the parallels between Māori grounded accountability and contemporary mutual-aid practices.

This chapter is structured as follows. First, we explore pre-colonial accountability structures, which I term grounded accountability, by following Māori and Indigenous thought and practice. This is to outline the original instructions of accountability (Reid and Rout 2016). We then briefly explore historical and contemporary perspectives on mutual aid to acknowledge the parallels, and then use this framework to examine the contemporary moment and future possibilities. I finish the chapter with concluding thoughts and guiding questions for future research and practice.

Pre-colonial Grounded Accountability

In order to understand the significance of an institution, such as accountability, it must be studied along with the 'social fabric into which it is woven' (Firth 1959, p. 402). The forms of accountability and organisation about to be explored are thought to have emerged in Aotearoa New Zealand in the three centuries between 1500 and 1800. They are largely based on a combination of information provided to European observers in the late eighteenth and early nineteenth centuries (Firth 1959; Anderson et al. 2016) and the oral histories and enduring practices that have been passed down through generations of Māori.

Obligations between people are best understood through the concepts of whakapapa and mana. Whakapapa is broadly defined as genealogy, but more broadly, it recognises kinship relations between contemporary Māori and one another, ancestors, descendants and land. It is a structured genealogical line to all things. Whakapapa is the fabric that holds the world together and provides an ontological understanding of relationships between people and the world (Tau 2001). Tau (2001) maintains that today the primary purpose of whakapapa is to reinforce communal solidarity, kinship and identity. The concept is therefore a mediator of relationships between people and place. The whakapapa obligations established from creation through today's kinship and environmental obligations make up an important part of accountability for Ngāi Tahu. These concepts establish links between the cosmological world, reinforce tribal identity and create obligations across generations between the land and people. They are the beginning of accountability relations, and this has been given statutory acknowledgement in the Ngāi Tahu Claims Settlement Act 1998. Whakapapa has a close relationship with mana (authority/prestige) because mana can be inherited through whakapapa.

Mana is widely referred to as prestige, authority, control, power, influence, status, spiritual power and charisma. It is a supernatural force in a person, place or object, but people and objects are agents of mana rather than sources. There are several sources of mana including mana atua (authority from Gods); mana tīpuna (authority from ancestors); and mana tangata (authority derived from personal attributes) (Gallagher 2003, as cited in Rout et al. 2017). This multi-source nature of mana 'explains the dynamics of Māori status and leadership and the lines of accountability between leaders and their people' (Gallagher 2003). Rout et al. (2017) continue and argue that a loss or gain in mana tangata would result in an equivalent loss or gain of authority, so that mana 'functioned as the meritocratic stabiliser against inherited status' (p. 863). Anderson (1998) explains that 'Ngāi Tahu liked to avoid dynastic aspirations by balancing the mana conferred by whakapapa with that acquired by service' (Anderson 1998, p. 100, as cited in Rout et al. 2017).

Obligations were organised around the two most important aspects of life: land and people. These were governed by a web of interrelations guided by mauri (life force), whakapapa and mana. All aspects of life were anchored to the environment where the hapū, which now make up what we know as Ngāi Tahu, lived and moved around and across (Firth 1959; Beattie and Anderson 2009). Economic and social relations were inextricably intertwined with the natural environment that acted both as inspiration and limitation for these relationships (Firth 1959). Food, clothing, tools and arts were drawn from the land to the extent that significant parts of the land, like the mountain and the river, share kinship through whakapapa with those who share its produce (Firth 1959). This creates a complex web of obligations and interrelations. Every craft and food production process contains a number of regulation practices in order to acknowledge the importance of these natural ancestors in providing sustenance—the more important the practice to economic and cultural life, the more regulatory forces there are (Firth 1959; Mead 2003). Mauri is the essence that exists in all living things. In relation to natural resources, damaging the mauri of the river damages both the mana of the hapū who draw from that river, and also their ability to subsist with the river. These values are inextricably linked to wellbeing and authority through mana because the wellbeing of the land was intertwined with the wellbeing of the people. Therefore, 'culture steps in to keep pace with environment as a co-determinant of the economic process' (Firth 1959, p. 89).

'There was in Māori society a definite tendency for the kinship principle to pervade the economic grouping–or, to look at the question from the other angle, for the kinship group to exert comprehensive economic functions' (Firth 1959, p. 224). Whakapapa connects all living things, past and present, together and encourages individuals within a kinship grouping to make 'uneconomic' (for their individual, short-term position) decisions in favour of the collective progress of the whānau or hapū (Firth 1959). Whanaungatanga is the practice of benevolent, and even familial, relationships bound by whakapapa. This is a virtual acknowledgement of mutual aid as a factor of evolution (Kropotkin 1902), or at the very least, a recognition of the importance of social approval or sanction in kinship-based settings to regulate economic activities (Mead 2003). Pre-colonial Māori economic affairs were regulated by reinforcing economic interests with powerful social and cultural forces. An individual within a hapū is obliged to meet economic responsibilities because of social relationships that are difficult to undermine in the given circumstances. According to Firth (1959), economic cooperation was achieved more easily when members of a working group shared kinship ties, as this strengthened their obligations to one another in achieving a common economic aim. The binding forces of the social world were deployed to enhance production in the economic world. Thus, obligations were enforced by careful attention to both tradition and public opinion (Firth 1959).

Paramount leaders accrued wealth and mana predominantly through gifts, the quality and value of which were correlated with their mana and number of 'followers' (Firth 1959). Although the chief was able to accrue a store of assets above what others were able to accumulate, these assets came with serious obligations to maintain the mana of position (Firth 1959; Rout et al. 2017). Rather than accumulating excesses of wealth, the chief's mana was recognised through the level of wealth that passed through their hands. It is in use rather than in hollow possession that the value was held (Firth 1959). The chief's personal wealth creation did advance their own status, influence and mana, but at the same time, it materially benefitted the mana of the people. The chief's economic position is buttressed by their social status (Firth 1959, p. 298), and their authority was regulated by mana (Rout et al. 2017).

The manifestation of kinship bonds in practice is most easily observed in the social and economic organisation of the village. Firth (1959) boldly asserts that the claims of the group upon an individual were rarely denied, but the exact contribution of each individual towards common pursuits was rarely considered. This is not to be mistaken for a kind of 'primitive communism', but rather it should be seen that the obligations of each individual to the group were strengthened by necessity of survival as well as strong kinship bonds (Firth 1959). The power of public opinion within whānau and hapū regulated against idleness as a 'simple and direct' practice of accountability (Day and Klein 1987). Because the chief's mana was intimately tied to their whakapapa and generosity to followers, the weight of public opinion was inextricably intertwined with the weight of the chief's mana. Chiefs therefore had to exercise manaakitanga, enhancing the mana of their people and even opponents in decision-making, in order to enhance their own mana (Firth 1959; Reid and Rout 2016).

This section has sought to illustrate how characteristics of accountability were organised in pre-colonial Māori, and where possible, Ngāi Tahu society. Obligations and rights emerge from whakapapa and mana, which are anchored in land. Therefore, accountability is grounded. This is grounded accountability. By exploring these characteristics and their interrelationships with the socio-cultural context, I sought to emphasise that we cannot extract accountability relationships from traditional values or the community/context in which these accountability relationships occur. In the next section I briefly turn towards mutual aid as a factor of evolution, as a global, but decentralised movement that swept the world as a response to COVID-19.

Mutual Aid—'Solidarity not Charity'

In *A Paradise Built in Hell* (2010), Rebecca Solnit illustrates that although the cliché of brutal human nature during times of disaster is pervasive, often people come together during these times in mutual support through bottom-up organising and altruism. Solnit (2020) continues along these lines in the contemporary moment. She writes that a dozen years ago, the term 'mutual aid' was generally only used by anarchists and researchers, but during the COVID-19 crisis, it is everywhere. Contemporary forms of mutual aid are dispersed and decentralised, numerous beyond counting, and are based on solidarity within communities, self-determination and usually with an eye towards wider social change.

Anarchist geographer Petyr Kropotkin's central question in *Mutual aid: A factor of evolution* is 'Who are the fittest: those who are continually at war with each other, or those who support one another?' (Kropotkin 1902, pp. 5–6). To address this question, he collected extensive bodies of evidence from the animal kingdom and the social world, using primary, secondary and historical empirical materials to come to the conclusion that rather than mutual struggle, sociability and mutual aid are of the greatest importance for maintaining life, preserving species and further evolution. He also specifically departs from suggestions that feelings of sympathy or love drive mutual aid and argues that these only contribute to a narrow comprehension of the moral feeling. Instead, he asserts that it is something infinitely wider than those feelings, an instinct of basic solidarity and sociability among humans and animals, which has developed over an extremely long evolution to drive humans and animals together towards a common good—maintenance, preservation and evolution. It is this factor of evolution—mutual aid—arising from reciprocal obligations that propels non-humans and humans alike forward.

In many cases, mutual support or a safety net and the maintenance of justice were carried out by guilds prior to state formalisation according to a 'brotherly element'. These functions were 'appropriated' by the state for its bureaucracy and police and formalised into codified relations. This absorption of social functions by the state favoured and fostered a narrow-minded individualism, and as obligations to the state grew, citizens were relieved from their obligations to one another (Kropotkin 1902, p. 227). Therefore, the state or state-like institutions create and protect monetary systems to formalise relationships and obligations between themselves and their individual citizens at the expense of the relationships that those individuals share with one another. Ngāi Tahu's experience of colonisation and being legislated out of economic activity by the state speaks to this. Despite 'the most ferocious theocracy or autocracy in the State' (Kropotkin 1902, p. 114), however, social organisation according to local conceptions of equity and mutual aid has been maintained in pockets of society over time. In these pockets, people tend to feel an enormous sense of responsibility towards each other. Despite the large-scale roll-out of state-sanctioned neoliberalism, these pockets of mutual aid based on customs and habits dating from the community period persevere. Throughout history, societies have consistently returned to that constant factor of evolution—mutual aid——and Kropotkin argues for a recognition of this to guide the development of contemporary and future institutions and relations:

> constructive genius always drew the elements and the inspiration for the new departure from that same ever-living tendency. New economical and social institutions, in so far as they were a creation of the masses, new ethical systems, and new religions, all have originated from the same source, and the ethical progress of our race, viewed in its broad lines, appears as a gradual extension of the mutual-aid principles from the tribe to always larger and larger agglomerations, so as to finally embrace one day the whole of mankind, without respect to its diverse creeds, languages, and races. (Kropotkin 1902, p. 223)

Therefore, if we agree that some fundamental reform of our current economic system, ravaged by COVID-19 and its response, and the organizations within is necessary, then in order to *evolve* these institutions, we must acknowledge and embrace a fundamental factor of evolution—mutual aid, not mutual struggle—to guide the reformation of these institutions. As far as accountability is concerned then, the multiple and shared obligations to one another that feature in accountability relationships is the first step towards this: obligations as enabling, giving meaning and a factor of evolution, rather than a constraint, a burden or a necessary hurdle on the road to progress.

In our contemporary moment, Solnit (2020) quotes a Fijian climate organiser, Thelma Young-Lutunatabua, saying 'the way we get through this is together'. Solnit also draws from Common Ground Relief (n.d.), who paraphrase Eduardo Galeano with their assertion of 'Solidarity not charity'. She asks what if rather than the clean-up crews picking up where business and government have failed, these forces were the ones setting the agenda, and she argues that the solidarity in the action of the present moment foreshadows a possible and necessary future. What I find most intriguing about the global proliferation of mutual aid movements is that, although I saw mutual aid all around me in Aotearoa New Zealand, it was very rarely called this. In the next section, I argue the reason for this is that mutual aid is already embedded in the enduring practices of Māori knowing and being, which stand on their own terms, in their own right. It is these that I argue have the capacity to enact alternative forms of solidarity and social protection as a response to the COVID-19 crisis based on existing grounded accountability within Māori thought, values and practices.

Grounded Accountability and Mutual Aid in Aotearoa New Zealand

Now that we have established the parallels between Māori grounded accountabilities and mutual aid, we can better understand our contemporary moment. Harris (2020), for example, refers to a proud history of Māori mobilisation during crisis, and Ngata (2020) refers to iwi community checkpoints established to protect communities as an enduring duty to protect. McMeeking et al. (2020) illustrate Te Pūtahitanga's model of social transformation as a catalyst for self-determination in response to COVID-19. There are two layers of mutual aid in the pandemic response of Aotearoa New Zealand. The first is not doing anything (staying at home to save lives). The other is doing something (banding together within the appropriate healthcare conditions to support one another). In this section, I will explore some aspects of the second layer enacted within my iwi, Ngāi Tahu, a large Indigenous kinship grouping that calls the majority of the South Island of Aotearoa New Zealand home. These are drawn from publicly available updates and newsletters (for example Te Pānui Rūnaka 2020; Te Rūnanga o Ngāi Tahu, n.d.).

It is worth pointing out at the beginning of this exploration that much of the national response to the pandemic in Aotearoa New Zealand drew from Māori thought and language. Proverbs including *noho atu ki te kāinga kia ora ai te iwi* (stay at home to save lives) and *he waka eke noa* (we are all in this together) were frequently used by Māori communities and organisations, but also used or misused by the government, businesses and other organisations. The lockdown was also referred to as a rāhui, which is a customary prohibition used in Te Ao Māori to make an area tapu (sacred) and/or preserve, protect and regenerate natural resources. While the lockdown was often referred to as a national rāhui, some remain unconvinced of the use of this term and prefer noho taratahi (quarantine) (Stephens 2020). Nonetheless, all of this would suggest that Māori grounded accountabilities are already geared towards the sort of response, or mutual aid, required to weather crises.

For the purposes of this chapter, there are two key layers of contemporary Ngāi Tahu organising to understand. Te Rūnanga o Ngāi Tahu (Te Rūnanga) was established following a settlement of grievance, as a central organisation to protect and enhance the collective interests of the Ngāi Tahu iwi (extended kinship grouping) (Te Rūnanga o Ngāi Tahu, n.d.). Within this organisational structure, 18 regional papatipu rūnanga (localised councils) exist to uphold the mana of their people over the land, the sea and the natural resources. In terms of crisis response, Te Rūnanga plays a centralised coordination role and provides support and services to papatipu rūnanga to look after their people in their regions:

> Our Papatipu Rūnanga continue to lead the way with the on-the-ground response, supporting whānau with deliveries of food, prescription medication, firewood and hygiene packs, while the Emergency Operations Centre at Te Rūnanga o Ngāi Tahu coordinates this mahi [work] and supports it with sourcing and providing supplies, data-gathering and research, alignment with Government, and forward planning for the medium- to long-term response and recovery.

The central organisation therefore uses economies of scale to support the localised papatipu rūnanga who have on-the-ground authority, but also uses its centralised authority to engage with the Crown around long-term crisis response and recovery. Lisa Tumahai, kaiwhakahaere (Chair) of Te Rūnanga reflects on the 'groundswell of collective kindness and goodwill, accompanied by a widespread willingness to support the government's strategy to protect our people and eliminate the virus' and states that:

> The purpose of Te Rūnanga o Ngāi Tahu remains unchanged in the wake of COVID-19, and has reminded us to hold true to the things that really matter–the wellbeing of our people, the revitalisation of our culture, the protection of our environment and mahinga kai. These things ground us, and will always be at the heart of who we are–mō tātou, ā, mō kā uri ā muri ake nei [for us and our children after us]. (Tumahai 2020)

This response model is somewhat akin to what Solnit (2020) describes as a 'distributed factory' where support, response and care is organised together from below, with support when needed from above. This, according to Solnit, is exemplary of mutual aid.

While the central organisation did conduct large-scale 'kaumatua calls' (3500 calls between March 23 and April 9) and centrally directed clear communications to facilitate connections, the majority of the care was directed by papatipu rūnanga. For example, Southern rūnanga are closely associated, and partnered with, Ngā Kete Mātauranga Pounamu, which supports people throughout Murihiku (Southland). This included an acknowledgement that self-isolation is not possible when food shortage is an issue, so the organisation worked carefully with food banks to provide food parcels of dry goods, fruit and vegetables, toilet paper and washing powder. Additional care packages included more food, medication, firewood, top-up cards for phones to stay connected and warm clothes. They also set up free COVID-19 mobile or drive-through testing whether or not an individual was a patient with the service. Ngā Kete Mātauranga, for example, made at least 918 food deliveries, 457 wellness checks, 383 medication deliveries, 33 food vouchers, 1250 hygiene and winter clothing parcels, which often made use of rūnanga facilities as preparation and distribution hubs. Otago-based rūnanga followed similar practices. They offered small cash grants to whānau affected by the crisis and extended welfare visits to the wider community by partnering with related organisations. Arowhenua Marae and Arowhenua Whānau Services set up a drive-through that distributed flu vaccinations, food and firewood. Some rūnanga also partnered with Crown agencies and other organisations to deliver fresh seafood and meat to families.

A key part of Te Rūnanga and papatipu rūnanga responses revolves around kaumātua (elder) care, recognising that the elders are both more vulnerable to COVID-19 and isolation/loneliness, but also that kaumātua hold a precious status within Ngāi Tahu. This included the aforementioned calls, as well as in one example three lots of care packages for kaumātua and families in need, one before lockdown, fruit and vegetables for Easter and a hygiene pack. Some rūnanga aimed to call elders once a week, sometimes more, and delivered food and medication daily. This was a lifeline of connectedness for some of these isolated elders. This connectedness was a key theme for the central organisation and papatipu rūnanga who increased communications, increased social-media use to facilitate two-way communication with whānau for updates and connections and moved meetings and social events to 'zui' (zoom hui (meetings)) to keep connected. These were often cherished by members, some of whom were able to attend from overseas for the first time.

The majority of these programmes are funded by Te Rūnanga and papatipu rūnanga distributions, which are in their own way supported by intergenerational commitments to grounded accountability through the settlement claim and negotiations. They are also supported by significant amounts of time given freely by members. Because of this, the majority of the programmes are aimed at Ngāi Tahu families and elders, but this does not preclude the organisation and rūnanga from extending their solidarity beyond kinship. Te Hapū o Ngāti Wheke, for example, write that in the spirit of *aroha ki te tangata, tētahi ki tētahi* (love to the people, love to one another), they will not just assist their own members, but anyone from any rūnanga because no one should be alone or vulnerable. In addition, a number of rūnanga report extending their care packages to neighbours and local community, including *all* residents living in the area over 60, one suggesting that the non-Māori elders of these communities were overwhelmed by the gestures, which led to more sharing and caring. The kaiwhakahaere remains unsurprised by these sorts of initiatives: 'The word "unprecedented" has been regularly used to describe this pandemic, but I can safely say that the prompt and capable response of our Papatipu Rūnanga is neither new nor surprising' (Te Pānui Rūnaka 2020).

While these support structures took quite a conventional approach, which involved kinship-based communities coming together to support one another in solidarity, drawing funding from communal pools and in-kind donations and time, the central organisation also managed to leverage its collective power to provide additional support. For example, small businesses run by Ngāi Tahu people were given support from Te Rūnanga staff to guide them through Personal Protective Equipment requirements and systems to meet government requirements for COVID response alert levels. This drew from Māori, Ngāi Tahu and Business Mentors New Zealand to support Ngāi Tahu business owners through the challenging circumstances. In addition, Te Rūnanga set up a Ngāi Tahu business directory *Te Aka Haumi o Tahu* to guide Ngāi Tahu people and others towards these businesses to provide extra custom. They also drew from their expertise to provide mentorship/support for workers facing redundancy, reduced hours or fewer employment opportunities as a result of the crisis. Finally, Te Rūnanga provided individual hardship grants and small business recovery grants in addition to this mentorship and planning advice (Te Rūnanga o Ngāi Tahu 2020a, b). These programmes are usually seen as ***additions*** to the Crown's packages because the Treaty guarantees that Ngāi Tahu and Māori be treated as citizens, and a lot of Te Rūnanga's work involves filling the gaps in Crown policy in addition to working alongside the Crown as Treaty partners to advocate for Ngāi Tahu.

These things that I am describing may not be new to you or may not seem wildly worthy of note, but this is the crux of my argument. There are values and practices within Māori and many other traditions that prioritise solidarity, social protection and connectedness. In this case, whakapapa, as a structured genealogical relationship between all things binds the layers of Ngāi Tahu that make up the iwi (individuals, whānau, hapū and rūnanga), and the contemporary institutions have design elements that reflect this. When required, these original instructions of accountability manifest as old ways and new means to provide mutual support according to mutual obligations. Along these lines, and to conclude, we return to Kropotkin (1902) and Solnit's (2020) insights, respectively. Kropotkin argues that despite state and other repression, mutual aid continues to rear its head as a key factor of evolution, and our contemporary and future institutions should be constructed on this foundation. Solnit asks what if rather than being a reactive response to fill the gaps left in the institutional structures of our contemporary society, mutual-aid principles and movements were setting the agenda? I have responded to these points by drawing from Māori thought to illustrate that Ngāi Tahu and many other pandemic responses are neither radical nor revolutionary, but are expectations within enduring traditions of mobilisation and duties to protect. Whenever a crisis occurs—tragically all too often in my hometown of Ōtautahi Christchurch–the country and the world watch in awe as Ngāi Tahu and Māori perspectives provide a framework for response, care and grieving (Kenney and Phibbs 2015; Daly 2019). Each time this happens, the norms of solidarity and social protection adjust at a national scale to learn a little from these enduring perspectives.

References

Anderson, Atholl. 1998. *The welcome of strangers: An ethnohistory of southern Māori AD 1650-1850*. Dunedin, New Zealand: University of Otago Press.

Anderson, Atholl, Judith Binney, and Aroha Harris. 2016. *Tangata Whenua*. Wellington, New Zealand: Bridget Williams Books.

Beattie, James Herries, and Atholl Anderson. 2009. *Traditional lifeways of the Southern Māori*. Dunedin, New Zealand: Otago University Press.

Common Ground Relief. n.d. Common ground relief. https://www.commongroundrelief.org. Accessed 21 September 2020.

Daly, Michael. 2019. Ngāi Tahu open marae to families of Christchurch mosque shooting victims. *Stuff.co.nz*. March 20. https://www.stuff.co.nz/national/christchurch-shooting/111415971/ngi-tahu-open-marae-to-families-of-christchurch-mosque-shooting-victims. Accessed 21 September 2020.

Day, Patricia, and Rudolph Klein. 1987. *Accountabilities: Five public services*. London, UK: Tavistock.

Firth, Raymond. 1959. *Economics of the New Zealand Māori*, 2nd ed. Wellington, New Zealand: Government Printer.

Gallagher, Timoti. 2003. *Tikanga Māori pre-1840*. http://nzetc.victoria.ac.nz/tm/scholarly/tei-Bid001Kahu-t1-g1-t1.html. Accessed 21 September 2020.

Godfery, M. 2016. The political constitution: From Westminster to Waitangi. *Political Science* 68 (2): 192–209. https://doi.org/10.1177/0032318716676291.

Harris, Aroha. 2020. Māori mobilisation in a crisis: A proud history. *The Spinoff*. May 7. https://thespinoff.co.nz/atea/07-05-2020/maori-mobilisation-in-a-crisis-a-proud-history/. Accessed 21 September 2020.

Kenney, C., and S. Phibbs. 2015. A Māori love story: Community-led disaster management in response to the Ōtautahi (Christchurch) earthquakes as a framework for action. *International Journal of Disaster Risk Reduction* 14 (1): 46–55. https://doi.org/10.1016/j.ijdrr.2014.12.010.

Kropotkin, Petyr. 1902. *Mutual aid: A factor of evolution*. London, UK: Heinemann.

McMeeking, S., H. Leahy, and C. Savage. 2020. *An Indigenous self-determination social movement response to COVID-19*. AlterNative: Situation report. https://doi.org/10.1177/1177180120967730.

Mead, Hirini Moko. 2003. *Tikanga Māori: Living by Māori values*. Wellington, New Zealand: Huia.

Ngāi Tahu Claims Settlement Act 1998. http://www.legislation.govt.nz/act/public/1998/0097/latest/DLM429090.html. Accessed 21 September 2020.

Ngata, Tina. 2020. COVID-19 and the Māori duty to protect. *Overland Journal*. May 7. https://overland.org.au/2020/05/covid-19-and-the-maori-duty-to-protect/. Accessed 21 September 2020.

Reid, John, and Matt Rout. 2016. Māori tribal economy: Rethinking the original economic institutions. https://ir.canterbury.ac.nz/handle/10092/12391. Accessed 21 September 2020.

Rout, M., J. Reid, B. Te Aika, R. Davis, and T. Tau. 2017. Muttonbirding: Loss of executive authority and its impact on entrepreneurship. *Journal of Management & Organization* 23 (6): 857–872. https://doi.org/10.1017/jmo.2017.78.

Scobie, Matthew, Bill Lee, and Stewart Smyth. 2020. Grounded accountability and Indigenous self-determination. *Critical Perspectives on Accounting*. https://doi.org/10.1016/j.cpa.2020.102198.

Solnit, Rebecca. 2010. *A paradise built in hell: The extraordinary communities that arise in disaster*. New York, NY: Viking.

Solnit, Rebecca. 2020. 'The way we get through this is together': The rise of mutual aid under coronavirus. *The Guardian*. May 14. https://www.theguardian.com/world/2020/may/14/mutual-aid-coronavirus-pandemic-rebecca-solnit. Accessed 21 September 2020.

Stephens, Māmari. 2020. Rāhui, mana, and Peter Ellis. *E-Tangata*. July 26. https://e-tangata.co.nz/comment-and-analysis/rahui-mana-and-peter-ellis/. Accessed 21 September 2020.

Tau, Te Maire. 2001. The death of knowledge: Ghosts on the plains. *New Zealand Journal of History* 35 (2): 131–152.

Te Pānui Rūnaka. 2020. Te Pānui Rūnaka: A monthly newsletter of Kāi Tahu news, views and events. https://tepanui.co.nz/. Accessed 21 September 2020.

Te Runanga o Ngai Tahu. n.d. Te Rūnanga o Ngāi Tahu. https://ngaitahu.iwi.nz/te-runanga-o-ngai-tahu/. Accessed 21 September 2020.

Te Rūnanga o Ngāi Tahu. 2020a. COVID-19 business support. https://ngaitahu.iwi.nz/runanga/tribal-economies/puna-pakihi/business-support/. Accessed 21 September 2020.

Te Rūnanga o Ngāi Tahu. 2020b. COVID-19: Unite for the recovery. https://ngaitahu.iwi.nz/whanau/covid-19/. Accessed 21 September 2020.

Tumahai, Lisa. 2020. He whakaaro: Rising to the challenge. *Te Karaka*. July 7. https://ngaitahu.iwi.nz/our_stories/rising-to-the-challenge-tk86/. Accessed 21 September 2020.

CHAPTER 11

Bartering as a Form of Resilience During COVID-19: Case Study of Barter for Better Fiji Facebook Page

Glenn Finau and Romitesh Kant

Introduction

The COVID-19 crisis has impacted all countries of the world, but some countries have fared much worse than others. Particularly vulnerable were small developing economies, burdened with high levels of public debt and highly dependent on tourism. Fiji meets all these criteria and has been particularly impacted from COVID-19 with almost a third of Fiji's total labour force either losing their jobs or having experienced a loss of income due to reduced hours or rates (Government of Fiji 2020). While developed countries have announced and implemented unprecedented economic stimulus packages, the Fiji government lacks the financial resources to provide such generous boosts to the economy. With

G. Finau (✉)
University of Tasmania, Hobart, TAS, Australia
e-mail: glenn.finau@utas.edu.au

R. Kant
University of the South Pacific, Suva, Fiji

S. Ratuva et al. (eds.), *COVID-19 and Social Protection*,
https://doi.org/10.1007/978-981-16-2948-8_11

the global closure of borders, Fiji's economic situation will only worsen as the crisis continues.

The crisis has led to a scarcity of cash, and people have become desperate to find alternative means to sustain and support themselves and their families. From the crisis, a Facebook page called "Barter for Better Fiji" (BFBF) has emerged that has revived what some have claimed to be an ancient Indigenous Fijian practice of bartering. Barter is the exchange of commodities without the use of money. For neo-classical economists, barter was an integral part of their narrative on the evolution of money. They argue that barter preceded modern forms of money, but was highly inefficient as it required there to be a "double co-incidence of wants" (Starr 1989). That is, both the traders must want what the other has and be willing to exchange the commodities at that rate. Economists argue that the inefficiencies of barter would naturally lead to the creation of money as a medium of exchange. However, anthropologists argue that the economist's tale is mere fantasy and constructed to create the ideology of money (Graeber 2012). The late Graeber made this claim in his highly celebrated book "*Debt: The First 5,000 Years*". In it, he argues that there has been no anthropological evidence to verify that barter indeed preceded money. Rather, barter economies emerge from a financial crisis where money becomes scarce or its value becomes worthless. Anthropologists have viewed barter as part of a complicated social process rather than as a purely economic transaction (Humphrey and Hugh-Jones 1992).

The emergence of the barter economy in Fiji is more consistent with the anthropological claims of barter economies (Finau and Scobie 2021). While studies have examined emerging barter economies from economic crisis (Cellarius 2000), Fiji's new barter economy is unique in that it has emerged from Facebook. The affordances of this social media platform such as virality, sharing and connectedness facilitated the spread and growth of the barter economy not only within Fiji, but also in other countries around the world (Boodoosingh 2020). This chapter explores the emergence of Fiji's barter economy as an alternative form of community-based and internet-mediated social protection during the COVID-19 crisis.

The Barter for Better Fiji (BFBF) Page

The Barter for Better Fiji (BFBF) page was created by Marlene Dutta who came up with the concept in February 2020, when she quite accurately predicted that the COVID-19 crisis would have a devastating impact on Fiji leading to mass unemployment and scarcity of cash (Kuinikoro 2020). She believed that a barter platform would be useful for those who have lost jobs and possessed little cash, but were able to trade goods or services (Tora 2020). She also believed that barter would be successful in Fiji as this was an ancient practice in the Pacific (UNAIDS 2020). The page was officially launched on April 21, and within a day, the page had over 2,000 members. In a few weeks, that number increased to 100,000 (Fogarty 2020). Currently, the page has 180,000 members and there have also been outgrowths with different pages in Fiji, pages in other Pacific Island countries and also in developed countries with large Pacific Island diasporic populations (Boodoosingh 2020). Because of the widespread success of the page, Marlene enlisted the assistance of her friends—who were involved in the early conceptualisations of the idea—to assist as admins of the page.

Marlene and her associates have described the motivations of creating the page as fostering an economy of kindness (UNAIDS 2020). This economy of kindness is focused on helping those who have been particularly affected by the economic impact of COVID-19. In the early weeks of the page's creation, many of the most popular posts or posts that garnered the greatest attention in terms of Facebook reactions and comments were those by unemployed mothers who asked for items for their newborn infants in exchange for baked goods. Many people offered to provide these goods for free.

Other popular posts included a group of young men from the Western part of Viti Levu who had lost their jobs following COVID-19. They formed a group called K9E Brothers and posted on the page offering their services, which include cleaning of compounds, cleaning of exteriors of houses and other maintenance work in exchange for goods and services (Rakautoga 2020). The group have become so popular that they have created their own Facebook page called K9E Brothers. Some professionals have also offered their services in exchange for barter. Dr Ashank Naidu, a general practitioner based in Nadi, began accepting barter for medical services (RadioNZ 2020).

The most common items that are traded are baked goods, plant seedlings, clothes, books, household items and fresh produce (Boyle 2020). More exotic trades include a live pig for a kayak and one trader wishing to trade land for a pick-up truck (Tora 2020). However, the latter trade is not possible as there are tax implications when trading real estate property such as land. Furthermore, a lawyer is also required to complete the process of a transfer of property.

The BFBF page has become so popular and has spread so quickly because it used Facebook as a platform. While most of the Western world has become increasingly wary of Facebook due to the controversies of data privacy emanating from the Cambridge Analytica Scandal during the 2016 US Presidential elections (Isaak and Hanna 2018), Pacific Islanders are still avid users of social media (Titifanue et al. 2017). While the Pacific was the last frontier of the digital revolution, Pacific Islanders have been quick to join the new social media landscape and leverage the capabilities of this new suite of technologies in innovative ways. Finau et al. (2014) explore the emerging use of Facebook pages as a means of extracting greater accountability from governments in the Pacific Island countries of Fiji, Vanuatu and Solomon Islands. Facebook is the most popular social media platform in the Pacific by a wide margin, and its impact has been far-reaching. While others have examined Facebook's increasing use within the political sphere in the Pacific (Brimacombe et al. 2018; Kant et al. 2018; Tarai et al. 2015), few studies have explored the impact of Facebook on social and economic fields in the Pacific.

While Facebook groups and pages have proliferated in Fiji, the Facebook page that has the highest membership of Fijian members is the Chat (fiji) page that has over 250,000 members in and outside of Fiji. This page has very little, if any, regulation of what is actually posted, and the page is used by members to advertise, to share other posts or just to elicit conversation or discussion from members. The popularity of Chat (fiji) is due largely in part to its lack of censorship, regulation and any clear leadership structure. While this is an appealing feature of the page, it also produces posts that are vulgar, discriminatory, defamatory and contains graphic images of violence or explicit sexual content. Unlike BFBF, Chat (fiji) has been anything but a well-spring of positivity.

BFBF is still far behind Chat (fiji) as the most popular Facebook page in Fiji. However, Chat (fiji) has existed for a longer period of time, and BFBF's growth is much higher than Chat (fiji). From the period of April 2020 to May 2020, the page experienced a 4,900% growth rate, and this reduced to 50% in the following month in July and has steadied to an average of 6% till October 2020. This exponential surge followed by a gradual increase is common in social media platforms where early entrants are able to capitalise on the exponential user growth of network effects, and then this growth slows as fewer people join the platform (Katona et al. 2011). At its current growth rate, it is anticipated to exceed Chat (fiji) by February 2020.

The spread and popularity of the barter economy in Fiji could not have been so rapid and pervasive had it not been for the Facebook platform. The success of Facebook as a platform can be analysed in terms of its affordances that have attracted a large proportion of Fiji's population to the social media platform. These affordances, including content sharing, connectedness and virality, have led to the mass adoption of the platform and the unprecedented membership growth of the BFBF page in a short period of time. Traders on the BFBF page who have utilised the features of the platform such as sharing images, writing descriptive posts and tagging other people have been able to accumulate more reactions, comments and shares from users. Facebook's algorithm uses these metrics to increase the ranking of these posts so they will be shown more on the page's newsfeed (Bucher 2017).

While Facebook has played an integral part in reviving Fiji's barter economy, it is by no means the main reason for the BFBF page's success. If that was the case, then we would see Facebook barter pages emerging in other parts of the world. While there are similar pages in other countries, these pages were inspired by the BFBF page, but have not been as successful as the Fiji page. The following Table 11.1 presents a summary

Table 11.1 Pacific Island Barter pages

Country	*Page name*	*Type*	*Membership*	*% of population*
Fiji	Barter for Better Fiji	Private Group	190,000	21
Tonga	Barter for Change Tonga	Private Group	10,500	10
Samoa	Le Barter	Public Group	4,900	2
Vanuatu	Barter for Nambawan life Vanuatu	Public Group	1,500	.5
Solomon Islands	Barter for Better Solomon Islands	Public Page	N/A[1]	N/A
Papua New Guinea	Barter for Better PNG	Public Group	3,300	.04

[1] Published as a public page, which does not require membership.

of Facebook barter pages in the Pacific and their current membership.

The key reasons for the success of the BFBF page can be attributed to the fact that most Fijians believe that bartering was indeed part of traditional Fijian practice. This was mentioned by Marlene, and there was a related post on Facebook by Alisi W Daurewa:

> Synonymous with the English word barter, veisa is a transaction, an act of exchange. The forebears of the iTaukei practiced veisa in various situations; be it economical, political or social. Veisa is what modernity calls trade. The practice of veisa is birthed out of the value for reciprocity. Like other customary practices, veisa is premised on strengthening relationships for social cohesion and security. Above all, it is symbolic of our ancestors' religious believe (sic) in connectedness be it to their unseen God, or neighbor, or the environment. It was their way of life. (Daurewa 2020)

While many Fijians on the page do believe that barter represents a traditional way of living that predated the arrival of Europeans, their conception of historical barter practices are more akin to a gift economy. A gift economy represents an economy where the exchange of goods or services is embedded within a social relationship where there is an implied obligation to reciprocate the gifts (Mauss 1954). From our observations, barter and gift-giving seem to be conflated with most of the trades on the BFBF page. While an analysis of the nature and interpretations of barter by users on the BFBF page is important, it is beyond the scope of this chapter. Rather, we refer to it as what the previous quote highlights is the communal spirit and resilience exhibited by Fijians on the BFBF page in the wake of the COVID-19 pandemic. The next section will discuss the revival of the barter economy as a form of resilience and possibly resistance to modern-day capitalism.

Bartering as a Form of Resilience?

Unlike an earthquake or a flood, coronavirus (COVID-19) is a slowly unfolding disaster. The concept of *community resilience*—that is, the communities' capacity to withstand crises or disruptions—can help us understand what we need to do now to recover. Post-disaster studies, following the 2011 Japan earthquake and subsequent tsunami, the Christchurch earthquake in 2011 and Hurricane Katrina in 2005, revealed the most significant predictor of survival and recovery is the extent to which people know each other and feel a sense of duty and responsibility to each other (Aldrich and Meyer 2015).

People's social ties and bonds are critical to reducing losses and accelerating recovery. In some situations, this human connection is more important in saving lives than infrastructure and emergency supplies. Research tells us connected, trusting and cohesive communities where people know and care about each other survive and recover better than those less well-connected within households, neighbourhoods and other community networks. Social connections enable people to help each other and are literal lifelines for the disadvantaged and the elderly (Aldrich and Meyer 2015).

The global impacts of COVID-19 are unprecedented and extend beyond the realm of health into the social, economic and psychological aspects of people's lives. Although the number of infections in Pacific Island Countries (PICs) may be low because of their relative isolation, they still cannot escape the consequences of the economic free-fall emanating from the lockdowns. The sudden demise of tourism, a major money earner for many island states; loss of jobs and income; decline in remittance and the dramatic shrinking of investment and economic opportunities have left families devastated and governments' resources stretched to the limit (UNDP 2020).

In many ways, the pandemic merely exacerbates the existing economic challenges and further deepens the poverty and vulnerability that many Fijians have been experiencing. It exposes, in more blatant ways, some pre-existing social, economic and gender inequities. Those in vulnerable employment (such as the hospitality industry, infrastructure, construction and manufacturing), and those in the informal sector are among the first victims of the economic squeeze. The aid-, debt- and remittance-based Pacific economies are struggling to respond effectively as many do not have the means to provide wage subsidy and stimulus packages similar to those implemented by industrialised neighbours like Australia and New Zealand. This should signal the need for new innovative strategies and models of development that have the capacity to respond effectively to disasters and crises; a strategy that requires identifying and building on local strengths and innovations.

One of the unique characteristics of Pacific communities is the dynamic interrelationship between the traditional subsistence production and the market system. The subsistence sector in the Pacific provides a significant subsidy for cash income, as well as a socio-economic cushion in times of crisis. When crises occur, there is almost a collective intuition to revert to community embedded survival values and strategies. The resurrection of the age-old reciprocity system, which is now being enthusiastically embraced by *Barter for Better Fiji* to counter the cash shortfall; the rush to promote backyard subsistence farming; and re-engineering of indigenous social protection systems of support shows that the basis of resilience is locked within local cultural and innovation systems. The challenge for Fiji and the Pacific is how to incorporate these values of resilience into the formal policy process.

Perhaps, it is time for a dialogue between the Indigenous systems of production and the formal sector in framing an innovative, equitable, resilient and sustainable system, which is capable of withstanding the potentially devastating impact of economic and social risks. Among some possible strategies for resilience, equity and sustainability would be utilising local resources and knowledge. Hence, rethinking new development strategies should also consider local innovations, community resources and indigenous knowledge and marry these with macro forms of institutional governance and development, which can be resilient yet empowering. As the remittance tap slows to a trickle, tourism and the travel industry collapses, and hundreds lose their jobs (as we witnessed with Fiji Airways and the hotel industry) and as poverty and inequality increases, it is time to rethink innovatively about our future development strategies.

The pandemic has also put the spotlight on the need for PICs to strengthen their social protection strategies, seriously address the issues of inequity and cut down on their national debts and expenditure to respond more effectively to major disasters such as the one we are facing now. What we need is not incremental or token adjustments that only serve the interest of a few, but major conceptual and structural transformations for the betterment of entire communities.

BFBF as a Community-Based "Digital Sharing Economy"

The term community-based sharing economy refers to initiatives coordinating through non-contractual, non-hierarchical or non-monetised forms of interaction (to perform work, participate in a project or form exchange relationships). Rather than the creation and maximisation of economic value, the primary purpose of initiatives belonging to the community-based economy is to contribute to a community project, to create social bonding, to promote values or to achieve a social mission through a collective project (Acquier et al. 2017).

The digital culture has birthed new forms of communal sharing (both for production and distribution). ICT-enabled sharing platforms have changed individual practices in connecting, exchanging and cooperating. Online platforms have established and scaled up peer-to-peer relationships to an unprecedented level and altering societal structures, which in turn has changed economic structures as an important special case. As technological providers, digital platforms endorse sharing practices by coordinating the social, including economic, dynamics of sharing. They provide connectivity through which they enable structural changes by creating networked societies (Martin 2016; Hamari et al. 2015).

The digital sharing economy has formalised sharing practices that before were informally done among friends and within communal ties of smaller scopes. By enabling this formalisation, digitalisation has made sharing scalable to an unprecedented extent. In the digital sharing economy, actors, connections, transactions and other components of a sharing process are recorded and tracked and are thus, to some extent, transparent. Digital sharing is an enabler of bringing the economy to the level of social practices whereby people become economic actors in their social bonds (Acquier et al. 2017).

Local neighbourhood interactions have become the backbone of social connection in times of lockdown as neighbours check in on each other from a distance and turn to each other for support when in need. Online neighbourhood networks had mixed success in the first wave of the sharing economy due to the absence of a burning imperative to drive them towards mainstream adoption. Communication tools and infrastructure that facilitate both online and offline interaction at a hyper-local level will be key to building resilient communities in a COVID era.

Conclusion

The BFBF page has been one of the few positive stories to have emerged from the COVID-19 pandemic. It is a page created to spread an economy of kindness, to create opportunities for those who lack the cash but are able to trade their goods and services. This barter economy has highlighted the resilience of the Fijian community, especially as Fiji is an economy that is particularly exposed to the economic impact of

COVID-19 due to the Fijian economy being heavily dependent on the tourism industry, which is the industry that has been affected the most by the pandemic. The barter economy has also flourished because it was initiated on the popular social media platform of Facebook. Social media's affordances of content sharing, ease of content creation, perceived democratised structure and virality helped in the page's rapid growth.

This chapter has examined the emergence of this Facebook-mediated barter economy in Fiji and explored its potential contribution to our understanding of resilience during crisis situations. The barter economy has been extremely successful and has even led to outgrowths in other Pacific Island countries and developed countries, although not as popular as the original Fiji page. The chapter has highlighted how the barter economy contributes to our existing knowledge on collective action and resilience during a crisis. However, more literature is required to further examine the impact, potential and evolution of a barter economy in a post-COVID world.

References

Acquier, Aurélien, Thibault Daudigeos, and Jonatan Pinkse. 2017. Promises and paradoxes of the sharing economy: An organizing framework. *Technological Forecasting and Social Change* 125: 1–10. https://doi.org/10.1016/j.techfore.2017.07.006.

Aldrich, Daniel P., and Michelle A. Meyer. 2015. Social capital and community resilience. *American behavioral scientist* 59 (2): 254–269. https://doi.org/10.1177%2F0002764214550299.

Boodoosingh, Ramona. 2020. Bartering in Samoa during COVID-19. *DevPolicy Blog*: 4.

Boyle, Maggie. 2020. Revising the barter trade in Fiji on Facebook. *FBC news*, 4 October 2020. https://www.fbcnews.com.fj/news/covid-19/revising-the-barter-trade-in-fiji-on-facebook/. Accessed 4 October 2020.

Brimacombe, Tait, Romitesh Kant, Glenn Finau, Jope Tarai, and Jason Titifanue. 2018. A new frontier in digital activism: An exploration of digital feminism in Fiji. *Asia & the Pacific Policy Studies* 5 (3): 508–521.

Bucher, Taina. 2017. The algorithmic imaginary: Exploring the ordinary affects of Facebook algorithms. *Information, Communication & Society* 20 (1): 30–44. https://doi.org/10.1080/1369118X.2016.1154086.

Cellarius, Barbara A. 2000. You can buy almost anything with potatoes: An examination of barter during economic crisis in Bulgaria. *Ethnology*: 73–92. https://doi.org/10.2307/3773796.

Daurewa, Alisi W. 2020. Just saying.....VEISA and KEREKERE. *Facebook*, https://www.facebook.com/groups/2964591663604507/permalink/2968744183189255. Accessed 23 April 2020.

Finau, Glen, Romitesh Kant, Sarah Logan, Acklesh Prasad, Jope Tarai, and John Cox. 2014. Social media and e-democracy in Fiji, Solomon Islands and Vanuatu. Presented at the 20th Americas Conference on Information Systems.

Finau, Glenn, and Matthew Scobie. 2021. Old ways and new means: Indigenous accountings during and beyond the pandemic. *Accounting, Auditing & Accountability Journal*. In Press.

Fogarty, Nick. 2020. Ancient bartering system finds new life on Facebook. *Australia Broadcasting Commission*, 5 May. Accessed June 6. https://www.abc.net.au/radio-australia/programs/pacificbeat/barter-for-better-fiji/12214544.

Government of Fiji. 2020. Economic and fiscal update supplement to the 2020–2021 budget address, ed. Ministry of Economy.

Graeber, David. 2012. *Debt: The first 5000 years*. New York: Palgrave.

Hamari, Juho, Kai Huotari, and Juha Tolvanen. 2015. Gamification and economics. In S. P. Walz & S. Deterding (Eds.), *The gameful world: Approaches, issues, applications* (pp. 139–161). Cambridge, MA: MIT Press.

Humphrey, Caroline, and Stephen Hugh-Jones. 1992. *Barter, exchange and value: an anthropological approach*. Cambridge: Cambridge University Press.

Isaak, Jim, and Mina J. Hanna. 2018. User data privacy: Facebook, Cambridge analytica, and privacy protection. *Computer* 51 (8): 56–59.

Kant, Romitesh, Jason Titifanue, Jope Tarai, and Glenn Finau. 2018. Internet under threat?: The politics of online censorship in the Pacific Islands. *Pacific Journalism Review: Te Koakoa* 24 (2): 64–83.

Katona, Zsolt, Peter Pal Zubcsek, and Miklos Sarvary. 2011. Network effects and personal influences: The diffusion of an online social network. *Journal of Marketing Research* 48 (3): 425–443. https://doi.org/10.1509%2Fjmkr.48.3.425.

Kuinikoro, Lucy. 2020. 8 pm Inspire on Prime. *Facebook*. https://www.facebook.com/lucy.kuinikoro/videos/10163724696840710. Accessed on 4 June 2020.

Martin, Chris J. 2016. The sharing economy: A pathway to sustainability or a nightmarish form of neoliberal capitalism? *Ecological Economics, 121*, 149–159.

Mauss, Marcel. 1954. *The Gift: Forms and Functions of Exchange in Archaic Societies*. Translated by I. Cunnison. London: Routledge

RadioNZ. 2020. Fiji-based doctor drops cash fees, switches to barter. *Radio New Zealand*. Accessed 4 October 2020.

Rakautoga, Venina. 2020. K9E Brothers hope to venture into business. *FBC News*. Accessed October 4, 2020. https://www.fbcnews.com.fj/news/k9e-brothers hope-to-venture-into-business/.

Starr, Ross M. 1989. The structure of exchange in barter and monetary economies. *Quarterly Journal of Economics* 86 (2): 12. https://doi.org/10.2307/1880564.

Tarai, Jope, Romitesh Kant, Glen Finau, and Jason Titifanue. 2015. Political social media campaigning in Fiji's 2014 elections. *Journal of Pacific Studies* 35 (3): 89–114.

Titifanue, Jason, Romitesh Kant, Glen Finau, and Jope Tarai. 2017. Climate change advocacy in the Pacific: The role of information and communication technologies. *Titifanue, J., Kant, R., Finau, G., & Tarai, J. (2017). Climate change advocacy in the Pacific: The role of information and communication technologies. Pacific Journalism Review* 23 (1): 133–149.

Tora, Talei. 2020. Two piglets for a kayak: Fiji returns to barter system as Covid-19 hits economy. *The Guardian*. Accessed June 6. https://www.theguardian.com/world/2020/may/08/two-piglets-for-a-kayak-fiji-returns-to-barter-system-as-covid-19-hits-economy.

UNAIDS. 2020. Fostering an economy of kindness through traditional bartering in Fiji. Accessed October 3. https://www.unaids.org/en/resources/presscentre/featurestories/2020/july/20200717_bartering_fiji.

UNDP. 2020. *Socio-economic impact assessment of COVID-19 in Fiji*. Fiji: Suva.

CHAPTER 12

West Papuan Students' Responses to Educational and Economic Challenges During the COVID-19 Pandemic

Jhon Urasti Blesia, Efraim Lokden, and Renny Sulelino

Introduction

The novel coronavirus disease, COVID-19, and its impacts have caused significant challenges for education around the world. Since the World Health Organisation (WHO) declared the COVID-19 outbreak a pandemic in March 2020, many educational institutions have made drastic changes in their teaching and learning activities. School closures have been implemented to reduce social contacts between students and to slow further transmission of the disease in the community (Van Lancker

J. U. Blesia (✉)
University of Canterbury, Christchurch, CT, New Zealand
e-mail: jhoe_bless@yahoo.com

J. U. Blesia · R. Sulelino
Universitas Cenderawasih, Jayapura, Papua, Indonesia

E. Lokden
Sekolah Tinggi Bio Sains Swadiri, Jayapura, Papua, Indonesia

S. Ratuva et al. (eds.), *COVID-19 and Social Protection*,
https://doi.org/10.1007/978-981-16-2948-8_12

and Parolin 2020; Viner et al. 2020). As a result, face-to-face educational activities were avoided (Chick et al. 2020), and online classrooms have served as a model for uninterrupted teaching and learning during these times (Chick et al. 2020; Kapasia et al. 2020; Singh et al. 2020). However, challenges are inevitable, particularly in countries where the lack of a learning infrastructure remains the main problem (Kapasia et al. 2020).

In the Province of Papua, the most eastern province of Indonesia, COVID-19 and its effects have reached all regions. There are huge concerns about the inadequate healthcare facilities and the inefficient testing processes in this province. The Government of Indonesia's health policy of increased social restrictions has been translated by educational institutions into the termination of physical learning interactions between students and staff. Traditional learning methods that have been used for many decades also needed to be shifted to the online learning method. These immediate transitions have triggered various challenges, particularly involving students' difficulties in adapting to the new learning methods with the lack of learning facilities and unprepared lecturers when designing learning activities. These challenges have also occurred within the wider context of students' existing challenges in their livelihoods. Nine indigenous students in a public university in West Papua share their testimonies of learning challenges while also facing strains on their livelihoods. Besides the various efforts made and the support students received from the government, the university, and the church, communal gardening has provided one alternative to traditional family agriculture to meet their daily economic needs and support their studies.

The study was undertaken in West Papua, the western half of New Guinea island, bordered by Papua New Guinea. In 2013, West Papua was administratively divided into two provinces: the western part is the Province of West Papua, and the eastern part is the Province of Papua. Most people refer to both of these provinces as West Papua to distinguish themselves from those from the eastern part of the New Guinea island (Widjojo et al. 2010). To reduce the confusion with the term "West Papua", we report West Papua in this research as referring to the Province of Papua (Brundige et al. 2004). The study took place in Universitas Cenderawasih (hereafter Cenderawasih University), Papua's oldest public university, located in Jayapura, the capital province of Papua. Currently, Cenderawasih University is the leading university in eastern Indonesia. With nine faculties, this university has graduated many Papuans across 28 regencies and one city of the province. This chapter begins with a discussion of COVID-19 in both the national and regional contexts. It continues with the government's higher education policies in response to the pandemic. The findings discuss learning challenges, including economic and other external challenges, and the efforts taken to minimise these challenges.

COVID-19 Impacts and Policies: National and Regional Contexts

COVID-19 in Indonesia

The Government of Indonesia first declared that the spread of COVID-19 had reached the archipelago in March 2020 (Conversation 2020b). While many countries had been alarmed by its rapid transmission when it started as a viral outbreak in Wuhan, China in December 2019 (Viner et al. 2020), Indonesia denied the presence of the infection within the country and rejected the Harvard University report confirming that Indonesia must have had unreported cases (Conversation 2020b). Indonesia was more concerned with the global threats the virus posed to its trade, investment, and tourism. While other countries had imposed tough restrictions on travel since February 2020 (Gonzalez et al. 2020), Indonesia allocated US$8 million to pay for social media and offered discounts of up to 30% to promote tourism (Conversation 2020b).

In early April, Indonesia reported more than 2,400 infections and 209 deaths based on 11,500 tests, a tiny sample from a nation with a population of nearly 270 million (COVID-19 Indonesia 2020; Health Ministry 2020; Conversation 2020a). This was an increase from 136 deaths (around 8.9%) from a total of 1,528 confirmed cases at the end of March (COVID-19 Indonesia 2020). Conversation (2020a) reported Indonesia as having one of the highest COVID-19 death rates in the world, just below Italy's (10% of the confirmed cases), and a death rate of almost double the global mortality rate of 4.8%. Scientists at the University of Indonesia predicted an increase of 240,000 deaths by the end of April if stricter measures were not started immediately (Conversation 2020a). One of the reasons triggering the increasing number of COVID-19 deaths is that very few people have been tested (Conversation 2020a). With more than eight million people living in its capital city of Jakarta—the epicentre of the outbreak, Indonesia reported the total test numbers of only 6,683 people as of 1 April 2020 (see also COVID-19 Indonesia

2020). The government focussed on testing people who had been in contact with confirmed patients, travelled to infected areas in the last 14 days, and showed symptoms of a fever (more than 38°C), cough, sore throat, and shortness of breath.

In order to respond to potential consequences, the government formulated several policies: including imposing so-called "large-scale social restrictions" (in Indonesian translation: Pembatasan Sosial Berskala Besar—PSBB) and barring foreigners from entering the country (Paat et al. 2020). Mass gatherings were then prohibited, triggering the release of 30,000 prisoners from the country's notoriously overcrowded and unhealthy prisons (Conversation 2020b; Yasmin 2020). Stricter lockdowns would further depress the country's economic activity. Under the 2018 Health Quarantine Law, the government would incur huge costs from being responsible for all the basic needs of the citizens in those areas (Conversation 2020b; Paat et al. 2020; Tambun et al. 2020). To protect from the social consequences, the government spent US$40 billion on medical needs, social support, and relief for small and medium business and imposed a nationwide ban on the traditional visits home for Muslims in the lead-up to the Idul Fitri (Eid) celebration in May 2020 (Conversation 2020b; Tambun et al. 2020).

Unfortunately, the government's efforts to prepare its health systems were considered to be an impossible task. Indonesia only had four doctors and 12 hospital beds per 10,000 people and fewer than three intensive care beds per 100,000 (Health Ministry 2020). As a result, the extreme shortage of ventilators resulted in many avoidable deaths, especially in regional areas. A serious lack of protective equipment for medical workers also caused the deaths of at least 24 medical doctors (Conversation 2020b). Social isolation was also extremely difficult to implement in such a densely populated country as around 70% of the workforce in Indonesia is employed in the informal sectors, and many people live hand-to-mouth. Conversation (2020c) reported that in 2019, people working in the informal sector accounted for 57.2% of the workforce (74 million people), and 25.14 million people live under the poverty line, that is, about 9% of Indonesia's population. Those working in the informal sectors and as casuals do not have the luxury of working from home and cannot perform their jobs remotely (Conversation 2020c). Indonesia's current health and social support system (called Badan Penyelenggara Jaminan Sosial—BPJS) is also considered inadequate to be called universal health coverage since it requires people to pay a monthly premium, and informal workers are unable to pay these monthly charges (Conversation 2020c).

COVID-19 in West Papua

Papua has had a continuing increase in the number of COVID-19 cases with the first case reported on 23 March 2020 in the regency of Merauke, a region bordering with Papua New Guinea (Mawel 2020). The total of confirmed cases in the province was 2,365 people with 22 deaths as of 14 July 2020 and an increasing trend among medical workers at 222 confirmed cases (Liputan6 2020; Tobing 2020). This sharp jump has seen the province move into the top eight regions with the largest number of COVID-19 cases in Indonesia (Devi 2020; Tobing 2020). From a total of 3.4 million people in 2020 (only 1% of the total national population) (Statistics of Papua Province 2020), the increase in COVID-19 cases in Papua is very different from many other Indonesian regions. The ratio of testing in Papua is only 5,440 tests per one million people, compared to Jakarta with 26,527 tests per one million; West Sumatra had 9,124 tests, and Bali had 8,870 tests per one million (Tobing 2020). The President of Indonesia in his official press release on 13 August 2020 highlighted the increase in COVID-19 cases in the province of Papua, instructing that the province should be given priority for testing, tracing, and treatment.

In order to combat the rapid transmission of the pandemic, the provincial government contributed 77 billion rupiahs to all the regencies and cities in the province (Papua Bangkit 2020). However, its policies are considered chaotic. Mawel (2020) reports that the provincial policy to blockade all means of transportation is not followed by some regencies. When the province gave orders to close air transport, the Regencies of Mimika, Jayapura, and Keerom still allowed access to theirs. The military also continued to transport passengers to the Regencies of Mimika, Wamena, and Jayapura where several passengers were confirmed positive for COVID-19. There was also no transparency in the data, causing great difficulty in tracing cases, and the community often ignored the suggested health protocols (see also Amindoni 2020). There have also been self-denials from COVID-19 patients who rejected the requirement to self-isolate. As confirmed by one Papuan epidemiologist, some Papuans refused to self-quarantine and requested fines for the medical workers who asked them to do so (Amindoni 2020). The Head of the Health Department in Nduga claimed that COVID-19 is still considered a cursed disease in the community. Some felt that the community has a strong immune system (Amindoni 2020). This false feeling of safety comes from the assumption that Papuans have more resistance towards the virus (Tobing 2020).

Inadequate Healthcare Facilities and Testing Processes

The difficulties in handling COVID-19 in Papua are mainly caused by the lack of health facilities. While the transmission of the disease has spread to almost 17 regencies in Papua, and while 16 hospitals have been approved as referral hospitals, the whole province has only two isolation rooms that meet the WHO standards (Tobing 2020). People in the highland regencies experience more difficulty in reaching the central hospitals (Amindoni 2020; Tobing 2020). Mountainous regencies, such as Lanny Jaya, Tolikara, Maberamo Tengah, and Yalimo, have to rely on only one central hospital in the Regency of Jayawijaya. This regency has an extremely difficult geographical location, and it has been confirmed as the region with the highest number of cases (Amindoni 2020). Nduga, another mountainous regency, has the same issues. Eleven municipalities in this regency can only be accessed using air transport. With only four general practitioners, those with the disease must be immediately referred to the Jayawijaya hospital, which gives rise to high transportation costs (Tobing 2020).

There are also problems with the inefficient testing process for COVID-19. Suwandi (2020) claims that the rapid test is confirmed as effective in identifying COVID-19 cases. However, based on expert reports, Devi (2020) questions the accuracy of the rapid test to detect COVID-19 cases. The test has often failed to detect positive COVID-19 patients and should not be used to diagnose the virus, and the results of that test need to continue undertaking a PCR (polymerase chain reaction) test. However, people with non-reactive results are not necessarily safe. Another problem is related to testing costs. The rapid test in Papua's public hospitals should be free as it is subsidised by the provincial government (Ratumakin 2020). While the test is mandatory for those who plan to travel, it is paid for by the passengers, and the highest tariff of 150,000 rupiahs was determined by the Health Ministry (Devi 2020). However, in Papua, some private hospitals can charge up to 650,000 rupiahs per person. Due to the rapid test policy, Devi (2020) claims that fake reports of the negative rapid test are being traded in Jayapura.

Furthermore, according to the WHO recommendations, the PCR testing standard should be one test per 100 persons, and the ideal for PCR testing in Indonesia should be 50,000 tests per day. However, Indonesia can only provide 11,000 PCR tests per day (Devi 2020). The province of Papua can only provide a small number of tests (see Sect. 2.2) (Devi 2020). The issue becomes more complicated in mountainous regions. Amindoni (2020) reports that to confirm COVID-19 reactive patients, the testing samples need to be sent to the Health Research and Development Board in Jayapura. The Regencies of Jayawijaya, Mimika, and Biak only began to do PCR tests from the end of May.

Higher Education Policy

As alluded to in Sect. 2.1, the central government imposed large-scale social restrictions to prevent a significant increase in the transmission of COVID-19. The 2018 Law on Health Quarantine Number 6 defines the restriction as a limitation of certain activities for residents in an area suspected of being infected with a disease and/or contaminated in such a way as to prevent the possibility of spreading the disease or contamination. This is considered as the most effective way to stop the transmission of COVID-19 (see Viner et al. 2020). Some activities are still allowed to take place, except for schools and offices, public transport, religious activities, and other mass gatherings (Paat et al. 2020). The regions under this restriction must prohibit all teaching and learning activities in schools and universities, and the police will take care of the duty of keeping law and order (Paat et al. 2020).

The Ministry of Education and Culture released Circular Letter 3 in 2020 about the prevention of COVID-19 in education units, mandating both public and private higher education move from traditional learning to online learning (Media Indonesia 2020). In only one week, around eight million students were suddenly needing to use online learning (Media Indonesia 2020). Massive Open Online Courses (MOOCs) were then established for both students and lecturers to gain high-quality learning and teaching materials from both national and international institutions (Gonzalez et al. 2020; Herlina 2020). Online learning has served as an alternative modern learning method, and it is purported to have a similar learning quality as traditional methods (see Chick et al. 2020; Gonzalez et al. 2020). Thus, the indicators to ensure the learning quality will rely on institutional support, learning activities, learning development processes, lecturer and student support, assessment, and evaluation (Herlina 2020). According to the Ministry of Education and Culture's online learning evaluation in May 2020, 33.51% of students were able to understand, 30.90% had "good" understanding, and 5.64% had a "better" understanding of the learning materials. The results also showed 25.34% of students had satisfactory experiences with lecturers' teaching, 45.56% having "good" and 15.84% "better" experiences with the teaching (Media Indonesia 2020). While this evaluation does not mention the location of the samples (Media Indonesia 2020), online learning in other Papuan universities will probably have different stories.

To support the students and educational institutions, the Ministry of Education and Culture released several policies, such as higher institutions reducing tuition fees, enacting new tuition fees, paying no tuition fees for those who take study leave, and paying 50% of tuition fees for final year students. Students can also pay tuition fees in installments, delay payments, receive a reduction in tuition fees, and receive scholarships and infrastructure support for internet data and credit (Alkalis 2020). The Ministry also provides funding support to 410,000 students in private educational institutions, not including 467,000 students with low economic levels and with high grades who receive financial support. Those who receive financial support have to fulfil criteria, such as students with financial difficulties and students with no scholarships (Alkalis 2020).

Research Method

The following responses to COVID-19 in West Papua have come from the testimonies of nine indigenous Papuan students who are currently studying at Cenderawasih University. Due to the large-scale social restriction policy, data were collected through online communication using phone recordings. The participants who agreed to be audio-recorded shared their experiences through open-ended questions, categorised as semi-structured interviews (Patton and Cochran 2002). From the nine participants, five are male, four are female, and all are indigenous Papuans aged from 20 to 26. Five are highlanders, and the other lowlanders; all come from regions outside Jayapura and are enrolled in undergraduate studies at the university. Participants are studying from Year 1 to Year 4 across the medicine, social sciences and politics, economics, education, engineering, and law faculties. Most of their parents are farmers, and

Table 12.1 Characteristics of the participants

Gender	*Age*	*Year*	*Faculty*	*Region*	*Parent work*	*Average spending*	*Dates*
Male	26	4	Medicine	Serui	Entrepreneur	500,000	10 August
Male	20	1	Law	Ngalum	Farmer	1,000,000	4 July
Male	23	4	Engineering	Sorong	Farmer	500,000	6 July
Male	23	4	Accounting	Sorong	Farmer	500,000	6 July
Male	22	2	Public Administration	Yali	Farmer	1,000,000	4 July
Female	20	3	Public Administration	Dani	Public servant	1,000,000	9 August
Female	22	4	Civics	Sorong	Farmer	500,000	9 August
Female	21	3	Public Administration	Yali	Farmer	500,000	9 August
Female	24	4	Medicine	Mee	Teacher	300,000	10 August

their average monthly spending is around 300,000 to 1,000,000 rupiahs. Table 12.1 depicts participants' characteristics as explained below.

Of the three researchers, two are Papuan and one non-Papuan, two are working as lecturers at Cenderawasih University, and one is on the administrative staff at Swadiri Bioscience Institute in Papua. All researchers contributed to the data collection, but the second researcher performed the majority of the interviews. The first researcher performed the data analysis and interpreted the data in relation to recent literature on COVID-19 from around the world. The three researchers then evaluated findings and wrote the discussion.

The researchers considered potential issues related to the use of new technology as a means of cultural imperialism against the indigenous participants in this study. Cultural imperialism refers to any values, practices, and meanings from a powerful foreign culture that are imposed upon one or more indigenous cultures (Roach 1997; Tomlinson 2012). However, the researchers' strong attachment to each participant freed any potential issues related to the use of phone recordings (Kovach 2010). All in-depth interviews went smoothly, and there were no participants who were forced to be interviewed. Although the first researcher found some words difficult to understand in the transcription process, the contents of the interviews were generally understood quite well.

The data collected were analysed using coding. Initial and selective coding was continuously performed to find meaningful interpretations of the data. Charmaz (2014) claims that coding is a pivotal link between the process of collecting data and developing an emergent theory to explain the data. All the data gathered from the interviews were coded while writing notes, taking categories apart, and breaking the categories into their components. The coding process increased the researchers' familiarity with the collected data. The findings were then presented using a thematic interpretation of the data and placing explicit values on these interpretations (Scotland 2012).

Learning Challenges

In this section, we present the learning challenges faced by the participants. The challenges are categorised into student difficulties in adapting to new learning methods, the lack of learning facilities, and unclear communication about online learning activities.

First, adapting to new learning methods was challenging for almost all participants. Most participants acknowledged that the teaching and learning process took place using Zoom, Microsoft Teams, WhatsApp, and Google Classroom. Students learnt to adopt new learning systems and use social media to interact with lecturers and classmates. A few participants saw the changes as a new way of learning for personal growth and engaged in their learning quite well. They did not feel comfortable in the beginning and had difficulties with online learning, but then learned to adapt to this new learning style. However, online learning has caused most participants to feel left behind in keeping up to date with learning activities and their objectives. Some did not entirely understand how to access online materials. Some students expressed feeling sad, stressed, disappointed, and confused about using media for online learning. One public administration student (Year 3) could not finish all her papers this semester; from eight papers in which she was enrolled, she only completed four. A civics student (Year 4) felt angry but had no choice and must accept the situation, saying:

> I feel very left behind. This semester is not as effective as out of eight papers, I could only complete four papers while I did not know how to use the application for the other four papers. So, lecturers only give us assignments, [and] replaced examinations with small research-assignments. These research assignments are hard to do as we do not meet directly to

> discuss them; (Public administration student, Year 3, female, 20 YO, Dani, 9 August 2020)

> I am disappointed. We cannot be angry but must accept to learn the situation. My classmates are still confused with how to use social media to access online learning. (Civics student, Year 4, female, 22 YO, Sorong, 6 July 2020)

This finding aligns with Singh et al. (2020) who found encouraging feedback from students who engaged in online learning, although almost 50% of the students believed that physical classrooms were better than e-classrooms. Most students in this study chose face-to-face learning, but they realised that online learning could keep them from the disease and, thus, they must learn to adapt to this new way of learning. Using the case of higher education in Spain, which we can apply to our case, Gonzalez et al. (2020) also found that the positive sides of online learning during the COVID-19 pandemic can change students' learning habits and improve their grades. However, as Singh et al. (2020) claimed, students learnt more from face-to-face learning methods than online learning. The findings from this study showed that most students have faced serious problems related to stress, depression, and anxiety in their learning process during the lockdown. This coincided with Kapasia et al. (2020) and Manzoor (2020) who stated that online learning can be emotionally harmful to students.

Similar to Kapasia et al. (2020), this study found that the adaptation challenges were massively experienced by students from the remote highlands. Students from remote areas and marginalised sections faced more challenges during the pandemic. Kapasia et al. (2020) argue that online learning is often discriminatory as many could not undertake online learning. In this study, a public administration student (Year 2) admitted the learning challenges faced by the highland students compared to lowland ones. A law student (Year 1) from Ngalum, a highland region, could not finish two papers he enrolled in that semester. An administration student (Year 3) from Yali, another highlander, expressed her confusion with online learning and struggled with financial difficulties. Those who were unhappy with the online learning affirmed that the education they had encountered so far also did not run as expected. Learning activities did not run well, and students did not study for long periods. Instead of receiving lectures, students were required to constantly do more assignments without receiving further guidance from the lecturers:

> Online learning is not good compared to traditional learning. I see many students being left far behind with their online learning. New students from [the] highlands are left behind more than those from coastal areas as they have not been exposed to the online system. To be fair, education must use traditional learning methods … Some students were angry as many new students from highlands cannot enrol at the university as they do not know how the enrolment is processed online … I feel left behind. I can go home but because of COVID-19. I must stay here; (Public administration student, Year 2, male, 22 YO, Yali, 4 July 2020)

> I am confused. I do not know how to answer whether I am ready or not. For us from highland regions, many of our parents do not have good financial ability, so this type of learning has caused more burdens for us. Lecturers are probably ready but not [the] students. (Public administration student, Year 3, female, 21 YO, Yali, 9 August 2020)

Second, most participants experienced problems with their learning facilities. The university did not have any clear solutions to support students having issues with access to facilities. Students with no internet access at their homes cannot be facilitated to complete their assignments at the university. The university did not provide spaces for students to do their assignments, and the internet available required a password to access. A public administration student (Year 2) and a civics student (Year 4) shared that their faculties did not provide spaces for students to work on their assignments:

> It all depends on each faculty, but my faculty does not provide places for students to do their assignments. They do not provide internet access for us to do online learning. (Civics student, Year 4, female, 22 YO, Sorong, 9 August 2020)

> In our faculty, we have internet access, but students cannot access it as it requires passwords, and the faculty does not give us the passwords to access. This has affected our ability to do the assignments. We also do not have any computer for students in our department. (Public administration student, Year 2, male, 22 YO, Yali, 4 July 2020)

Most students further claimed they had poor internet connectivity in the regions. For example, an accounting student (Year 4) had issues with internet connectivity. A public administration student (Year 2) claimed that the internet connectivity in his hometown was not as good as that in Jayapura (the city where the university is located). For those who were afraid of the outbreak, having to go home and live in remote areas had more difficulties in accessing online learning. Some students disclosed issues of internet access in their towns that meant they were unable to access learning materials, attend online teaching, and complete their assignments. This finding coincides with Chick et al.'s (2020) findings that limitations in using technology to maintain education during the pandemic include the participants having difficulties with poor bandwidth connections. Kapasia et al. (2020) also confirmed that poor internet connections and unfavourable study environments have challenged students in their access to online learning. Like the findings from that study, the study found that students from remote and marginalised areas had difficulties in accessing online materials due to the lack of electricity. Students were more likely to share their materials than to attend online lectures due to poor internet connectivity.

The lack of a technology infrastructure is another issue in learning facilities. Online learning requires a laptop or a smartphone and internet data credit, which many students do not have. The law student (Year 1) expressed that students cannot participate in online learning as they do not have a phone to access learning materials. A public administration student (Year 2) and a civics student (Year 4) also expressed that they were not ready to do online learning as they did not have laptops. A medical student (Year 4) told her story, saying that many of her friends were unable to study due to not having smartphones and their parents were unable to support them. This finding aligns with Kapasia et al.'s (2020) finding that more than 50% of the students surveyed attended fewer classes due to issues in technology; so, some must borrow phones or money for phones from their family members or neighbours. Manzoor (2020) also found similar cases about how students were challenged by the need for laptops to access online learning, and there were no resources to arrange for online equipment:

> To respond to this type of education, I am probably not ready as I do not have a laptop and any money to purchase internet data credit, not to

> mention other things I am lacking. (Law student, Year 1, male, 20 YO, Ngalum, 4 July 2020)

> No change at all. Many of my friends do not have smartphones and internet data credit to do online learning. Our parents do not have much money to support us while the faculty forced us to attend online learning. (Medical student, Year 4, female, 24 YO, Mee, 10 August 2020)

> I have a laptop and mobile phone now, but I can only attend the online teaching when I have internet data credit, otherwise, I cannot. It all depends on family income, and I need to wait for them to transfer my monthly living costs. I do not have significant issues with food, but am challenged most by the internet access. (Public administration student, year 3, female, 21 YO, Yali, 9 August 2020)

Internet data credit is another challenge for most students. An engineering student (Year 4) expressed that although he has a laptop to use to complete his final project, he was challenged by getting internet data credit, and it all depended on his parents' financial support. A public administration student (Year 3) also said that he can only do online study if he has internet data credit, otherwise, he cannot. Another public administration student (Year 3) claimed that she needs double her usual data credit to do online learning. She previously only spent 200,000 rupiahs to purchase internet data credit, but now spends around 400,000 rupiahs. An accounting student (Year 4) added that students choose offline methods so everyone can have access to a fair education. It was also confirmed by Kapasia et al. (2020) and Manzoor (2020) that online learning created challenges for students in their learning process.

Third, unclear communication between lecturers and students constituted another learning challenge. Some lecturers did not clearly communicate learning activities with the students. A public administration student (Year 3) expressed his confusion with the online learning process. Students did not receive clear information about how to use the online learning applications. While McLoughlin and Oliver (2000) emphasised the importance of clear course instructions and learning outcomes for indigenous students (see also Sahu 2020), many students in this study were left confused with no clear solutions to their problems. For those who did not have smartphones, lecturers only gave them paper assignments and assigned one student leader to collect the assignments. An engineering student (Year 4) expressed being uncomfortable with online learning. Lecturers asked them to learn independently, but students still needed some time to adjust to the new learning methods and environment. Gonzalez et al. (2020) argue that problems with online learning also include teachers and teaching strategies. Teachers should be able to modify their teaching and assessment methods. In this study, lecturers were overwhelmed with the new online methods and that affected their teaching quality. The lack of well-structured training for the lecturers has also affected their teaching process (Singh et al. 2020). As a result, students were asked to learn the materials themselves, and they had difficulties in understanding the learning materials.

Issues with undisciplined lecturers have been another learning challenge for students. The quotes below exemplify the issues of undisciplined lecturers:

> What I see is that lecturers do not work based on the time arranged by the faculty. I am not happy with way lecturers treat us. (Public administration student, Year 2, male, 22 YO, Yali, 4 July 2020)

> Online study is not effective, I cannot enjoy and understand the learning materials. Lecturers have discipline problems. For example, we have a lecture at 8 am but then [it] changed to 3 or 5 pm. We do not feel comfortable to be treated that way. (Medical student, year 4, female, 24 YO, Mee, 10 August 2020)

A public administration student (Year 2) confirmed that lecturers were undisciplined with the agreed teaching schedules. He was unhappy with lecturers changing class times without taking into consideration students' situations. Gonzalez et al. (2020) found that rewards and extra motivation were important for students to change their learning behaviour and study continuously. When lecturers were occupied with their schedules and were undisciplined in following their schedules, students were likely to be reluctant to study. McLoughlin and Oliver (2000) argue that lecturers should engage with indigenous students using various online dialogues, and students should be able to access multiple channels of communication with the lecturers. Failure to do this may cause students to have a lower desire to meet learning objectives.

Economic and Other Challenges

Besides learning challenges, participants in this study also encountered economic and other external challenges, such as concerns about the effect of COVID-19 on their families, communities, and regional development.

Most participants encountered economic challenges that gave rise to their inability to eat every day or do any necessary actions to solve this. A medical student (Year 4) said that during the pandemic, his monthly transfer from his parents was reduced causing him to be unable to eat every day. To support his economic needs, he needed to earn extra income from casual work. However, instead of using this money to buy food, he purchased internet data credit to enable him to study. A public administration student (Year 3) also had a reduction in her parents' monthly transfer. Her parents reduced 50% of their transfers in the last three months and even did not send her money for a few months. A public administration student (Year 2) had difficulties paying his tuition fees. Although the government has reduced the tuition fees by 50%, he still found it difficult to pay. Strielkowski (2020) confirms how economic shutdowns during the months-long quarantine have affected most students participating in higher education. Kapasia et al. (2020) found a similar issue in India: that out of 232 students surveyed, 181 reported that COVID-19 has affected their economic situation, and 178 reported that low-income families were affected badly by this pandemic. In developed countries, such as the United States, Dorn et al. (2020) also found that lower-income students have minimal access to online learning as well as conducive learning environments (see also Van Lancker and Parolin 2020). Similar to this study, these students have various distractions to their learning activities and issues with learning facilities and high-speed internet:

> COVID-19 has affected my monthly transfer being reduced as my parents' salaries are also reduced. I need to think about how to support my life. I am looking for extra work to support myself here. (Medical student, Year 4, male, 26 YO, Serui, 10 August 2020)

> My parents still send me money although in the past they sent me around 800,000 to 1,000,000 rupiahs, now they only send me 500,000. In the past three months, they only sent me [it] once. Nevertheless, they keep supporting me financially and physiologically. (Public administration student, Year 3, female, 20 YO, Dani, 9 August 2020)

Participants were also concerned about the transmission of COVID-19 to their families. As Dorn et al. (2020) added, other harder aspects that could exacerbate the situation were social and emotional disruptions, such as parents losing their jobs or falling ill. Living far from their families, most students in this study shared how the pandemic has increased their stress and concern about their family. One public administration student (Year 3) is worried about her parents living in their old age. The airports and harbours were closed for a long period, and she was concerned about whether or not there was food distribution to the town where her family lived. Another public administration student (Year 3) also revealed that her parents had economic difficulties and have now started to sell cakes and crackers to support themselves. Sahu (2020) finds similar issues facing international students living far from home, in that, besides worrying about their health, safety, and education, students have high concerns for the wellbeing of their parents. In contrast, a few students, particularly those from the highlands, were not concerned about their parents. For example, a law student (Year 1) shared that his family was not economically affected as they lived in a very remote area so they did not need money, instead they can use their agricultural production to meet their daily needs.

Most participants were concerned with the impact of the pandemic on the community in the region where they currently studied (in Jayapura) and in those where their parents lived (for the regions where students are originally from, see Table 12.1). As Dorn et al. (2020) argue, the pandemic may cause further long-term harm for both the individual and society. A medical student (Year 4) expressed his concern with the lack of education about COVID-19 and its impact on the community giving rise to people disobeying the government's health guidance. A public administration student (Year 2) shared his worries about the increasing number of deaths because of COVID-19 in the community. Most students were also concerned with the impact of COVID-19 on the community's economy. An engineering student (Year 4) and a public administration student (Year 3) also expressed their concern about the economic crisis in the whole country. They saw that many micro-businesses have been significantly affected. This aligns with Van Lancker and Parolin's (2020) finding that the ongoing pandemic can lead to a severe economic recession. Some participants were also concerned about the impact of the pandemic on regional development and government activities. A civics student (Year 4) was worried about the government being unable to run normally and its ability to provide public services to society. A public administration student (Year 2) was also concerned with the lack of development as the impact of the virus has caused his region to be unable to function. In his village, people are afraid to go out.

Various Efforts to Minimise the Challenges

We now present the efforts made to minimise the learning and economic challenges. We have divided the section into the students' efforts to minimise their challenges and the various support they received from the government, the university, and churches. We then propose participants' suggestions for communal gardening as an alternative solution to solve their economic challenges while supporting their online learning.

Students should actively participate and take responsibility for their own learning. Despite the challenges, students need to understand their responsibilities and can find their own ways to solve their problems (Gonzalez et al. 2020). For example, the medical student (Year 4) needed to make extra efforts to learn, such as actively asking questions of lecturers or their classmates. In regard to the issue of the lack of learning facilities, students made efforts by asking for help from friends for internet access. The law student (Year 1) and public administration student (Year 3) used their classmates' houses with internet access and completed their assignments together. An engineering student (Year 4) shared his experience of finding ways to solve his problems of having no data credit. He went to some stores or cafes with internet connections for several hours to consult about his final projects with his supervisors. These findings reflect those of Kapasia et al. (2020) who stated that students borrow smartphones and use internet access from their relatives and neighbours to do online learning.

Students have also made a number of efforts to minimise their economic challenges, such as doing casual work. A medical student (Year 4) and an accounting student (Year 4) needed to engage in some casual work to support their economic needs. An accounting student (Year 4) and an engineering student (Year 4) worked for their relatives. Although they received little money from the work, it was enough to meet their daily needs. A public administration student (Year 2) said that to support his economic needs, he needed to sell all that he grew in his gardens, such as corn, taro, and chilli, in the traditional markets, which he also used to pay for his tuition fees. Unlike these students, a public administration student (Year 4) said that to support her life, she has been doing online business with her classmates:

> We need to make extra efforts to work. I have worked casually and am now looking for casual work, such as helping other people in order to get some money. (Medical student, Year 4, male, 26 YO, Serui, 10 August 2020)

> I am working for my relatives to support my daily needs. They give me some money after finishing my work there, so I use it to buy rice and vegetables. (Accounting student, Year 4, male, 23 YO, Sorong, 6 July 2020)

Besides all their efforts, participants in this study acknowledged receiving various support from the government, the church, and the university. Most participants received local government support in the form of face masks, and food, such as rice and noodles. For example, a medical student (Year 4) received face masks and a law student (Year 1) received food support. A public administration student (Year 3) received financial and food support directly from the church. Some students also received financial support from the regencies they came from. For example, a public administration student (Year 3) and a civics student (Year 4) received financial support from the government's regencies.

Some participants also received support from the university. An engineering student (Year 4) and a medical student (Year 4) said that the university listed students who did not have smartphones and internet data credit so the university can provide support. Some students confirmed receiving financial support to buy internet data credit. However, others, such as a public administration student (Year 2), did not receive any support. Instead of giving data credits to all students, the central government reduced tuition fees to all students (Alkalis 2020) (see Sect. 3). A medical student (Year 4) and a law student (Year 1) acknowledged that the Minister released an official letter to reduce the student's tuition fees by 50%. One public administration student (Year 3) then acknowledged that the university has released a policy to reduce tuition fees so that the money saved from the 50% reduction can be used to buy data credit.

Furthermore, one solution suggested by almost all participants to solve their economic challenges while supporting their learning activities was to establish a communal garden. It was an effort made by the students themselves to address the scarcity of food while supporting their learning activities. Gersky (2015) argues that gardening among the community can address food insecurity and develop community cohesion, which then creates positive implications for the community. It serves to meet well-being and increase the resilience of the community on multiple levels that involve individuals, social groups, and the natural environment (Okvat and Zautra 2011). In this study, one engineering student (Year 4) claimed that gardening had a positive impact on him as he can also share the produce with other people who need food. He has used his backyard for communal gardening with his dormitory friends, and he planted vegetables, cassava, and sweet taro. His parents also opened a big farm in his village to support their lives during the pandemic in the community. He supported his parents to continue the farming habits they had built up over a long time. Due to not having areas to make gardens, a public administration (Year 2) and a civics student (Year 4) have joined gardens of their friends:

> In my opinion, gardening is useful for us and our families to support our daily economic needs. We can do gardening to also support other people. People are helped if we can share the results of what we planted in our gardens. (Engineering student, Year 4, male, 23 YO, Sorong, 6 July 2020)

> I think gardening is a good thing to do because we can get some sources of food from vegetables, taro, corns, etc. It is one of the ways to support our daily life. (Public administration student, Year 3, female, 21 YO, Yali, 9 August 2020)

A public administration student (Year 3) and an accounting student (Year 4) said that gardening is good to support their lives while doing their studies during the pandemic. An accounting student decided to make a garden so he can solve his economic problems. To open the garden, he needs to prepare the land (a small area), use some fertiliser, and then plant water spinach and other vegetables. A public administration student (Year 3) agreed with the benefits of gardening, adding that gardening is one of the government's recommendations to help the community. The central government, through its food security policy, has instructed all society to return to agriculture so gardening can help the community's economy during the lockdown. This student started her garden in her backyard by planting green onions, chilli, vegetables, and pandanis in small polythene bags.

Conclusions

In conclusion, West Papuan students faced difficulties in adapting to a new way of learning, the lack of learning facilities, such as unavailability of study spaces, technology infrastructure, and internet data credit, as well as poor internet connectivity, unclear instructions for courses and evaluations, and an issue with undisciplined lecturers. Economic issues were also challenging when continuing their online learning while also being concerned about the impact of the pandemic on their families, communities, and regions. Efforts to deal with the COVID-19 pandemic should be considered as a fine balance between protecting public health and preventing economic and social challenges while respecting human rights (Viner et al. 2020). In this study, indigenous students experienced fear and frustration in keeping up with their online learning while working hard to meet their daily economic needs. These students were not supported by a conducive study environment, and their lecturers did not provide clear guidance and instructions or adequate supervision.

We recommend that the university should develop strategies for a resilient educational system to ensure indigenous students can continue to develop their knowledge and skills during a future university closure. The university needed to ensure that lecturers provided clear online guidance and instructions for the online learning process. Lecturers should also be flexible in modifying their teaching strategies and assessment processes (Gonzalez et al. 2020). McLoughlin and Oliver (2000) argued that online learning for indigenous students should be created with flexible tasks and tools for knowledge sharing. Thus, there should also be a greater flexibility for students who faced difficulties with online courses due to the reasons explained above. The university should also provide students with suitable mental health support to deal with their stress during online study (Manzoor 2020; Sahu 2020). The university and other authorities, such as the local government, should consider strategies to solve the students' problems with their learning facilities. Authorities should also ensure food and accommodation for students and continuously promote communal gardening in the community. Cooperation between institutions will also help the university achieve these objectives.

References

Alkalis, Galuh. 2020. Kebijakan Pemerintah untuk Pendidikan Indonesia di Tengah Pandemi. Portonews. Accessed August 21, 2020. https://www.portonews.com/2020/covid-19/kebijakan-pemerintah-untuk-pendidikan-indonesia-di-tengah-pandemi/.

Amindoni, Ayomi. 2020. Covid-19 di Papua: Waspada Gelombang Kedua, 'Ini Bukan Kutukan Tuhan tapi Virus yang Mudah Sekali Menyebar'. BBC News. Accessed August 24, 2020. https://www.bbc.com/indonesia/indonesia-53220200.

Brundige, Elizabeth, Winter King, Priyneha Vahali, Stephen Vladeck, and Xiang Yuan. 2004. Indonesian human rights abuses in West Papua: Application of the law of genocide to the history of Indonesian control. Accessed August 24, 2020. http://www.g-a-l.info/Yale%20Report%20on%20West%20Papuah%20rights.pdf.

Charmaz, Kathy. 2014. *Constructing grounded theory*, 2nd ed. London, England: Sage.

Chick, R.Connor, Guy T. Clifton, Kaitlin M. Peace, Brandon W. Propper, Diane F. Hale, Adnan A. Alseidi, and Timothy J. Vreeland. 2020. Using technology to maintain the education of residents during the COVID-19 pandemic. *Journal of Surgical Education* 77 (4): 729–732. https://doi.org/10.1016/j.jsurg.2020.03.018.

Conversation. 2020a. "3 Overlooked facts behind Indonesia's high COVID-19 death rate". Accessed August 21, 2020. https://theconversation.com/3-overlooked-facts-behind-indonesias-high-covid-19-death-rate-135223.

Conversation. 2020b. Indonesia was in Denial over Coronavirus. Now it may be facing a looming disaster. Accessed August 21, 2020. https://theconversation.com/indonesia-was-in-denial-over-coronavirus-now-it-may-be-facing-a-looming-disaster-135436.

Conversation. 2020c. No work, no money: How self-isolation due to COVID-19 pandemic punishes the poor in Indonesia. Accessed August 21, 2020. https://theconversation.com/no-work-no-money-how-self-isolation-due-to-covid-19-pandemic-punishes-the-poor-in-indonesia-134141.

COVID-19 Indonesia. 2020. Data Sebaran. Accessed August 21, 2020. https://covid19.go.id/.

Devi. 2020. Rapid Test Kontroversial, di Papua Selain Mahal juga Bisa Dipalsukan. Suara Papua. Accessed August 25, 2020. https://suarapapua.com/2020/07/17/rapid-test-kontroversial-di-papua-selain-mahal-juga-bisa-dipalsukan/.

Dorn, Emma, Bryan Hancock, Jimmy Sarakatsannis, and Ellen Viruleg. 2020. COVID-19 and student learning in the United States: The Hurt Could last a lifetime. *McKinsey and Company*, September 7, 2020. https://fresnostate.edu/kremen/about/centers-projects/weltycenter/documents/COVID-19-and-student-learning-in-the-United-States-FINAL.pdf.

Gersky, Kathleen Marie. 2015. Exploring community gardening: Motivations and impacts. Master's thesis, Wayne State University.

Gonzalez, Teresa, M. A. de la Rubia, Kajetan P. Hincz, M. Comas-Lopez, L. Subirats, S. Fort, and G. M. Sacha. 2020. *Influence of COVID-19 confinement in students performance in higher education*. Cornell University. Accessed August 24, 2020. https://arxiv.org/abs/2004.09545.

Health Ministry. 2020. Publikasi Data dan Informasi. Accessed August 21, 2020. https://www.kemkes.go.id/folder/view/01/structure-web-content-publikasi-data.html.

Herlina, Neni. 2020. Strategi dan Kebijakan Ditjen Dikti Terhadap Keberlanjutan Pendidikan Tinggi di Indonesia dalam Hadapi Pandemi Covid-19. Direktorat Jenderal Pendidikan Tinggi Kementerian Pendidikan dan Kebudayaan Republik Indonesia. Accessed September 5, 2020. http://dikti.kemdikbud.go.id/kabar/strategi-dan-kebijakan-ditjen-dikti-terhadap-keberlanjutan-pendidikan-tinggi-di-indonesia-dalam-hadapi-pandemi-covid-19/.

Kapasia, Nanigopal, Pintu Paul, Avijit Roy, Jay Saha, Ankita Zaveri, Rahul Mallick, Bikash Barman, Prabir Das, and Pradip Chouhan. 2020. Impact of lockdown on learning status of undergraduate and postgraduate students during COVID-19 pandemic in West Bengal, India. *Children and Youth Services Review* 116: 105–194. https://doi.org/10.1016/j.childyouth.2020.105194.

Kovach, Margaret. 2010. Conversation method in Indigenous research. *First Peoples Child and Family Review: an Interdisciplinary Journal Honouring the Voices, Perspectives, and Knowledges of First Peoples Through Research, Critical Analyses, Stories, Standpoints and Media Reviews* 5 (1): 40–48. https://doi.org/10.7202/1069060ar.

Liputan6. 2020. 52 Tenaga Medis di Papua Terpapar Virus Corona Covid-19. Accessed August 21, 2020. https://www.liputan6.com/regional/read/4273290/52-tenaga-medis-di-papua-terpapar-virus-corona-covid-19.

Manzoor, Afaf. 2020. Online teaching and challenges of COVID-19 for inclusion of PWDs in higher education. *Daily Times*. Accessed September 12, 2020. https://dailytimes.com.pk/595888/online-teaching-and-challenges-of-covid-19-for-inclusion-of-pwds-in-higher-education/.

Mawel, Benny. 2020. Penanganan COVID-19 di Papua Kacau Balau. Jubi. Accessed August 30, 2020. https://jubi.co.id/penanganan-covid-19-di-papua-kacau-balau/.

McLoughlin, Catherine, and Ron Oliver. 2000. Designing learning environments for cultural inclusivity: A case study of indigenous online learning at tertiary level. *Australasian Journal of Educational Technology* 16 (1). https://doi.org/10.14742/ajet.1822.

Media Indonesia. 2020. Revolusi Pendidikan Tinggi di Tengah Pandemi Covid-19. Accessed August 24, 2020. https://mediaindonesia.com/read/detail/313911-revolusi-pendidikan-tinggi-di-tengah-pandemi-covid-19.

Okvat, Heather A., and Alex J. Zautra. 2011. Community gardening: A parsimonious path to individual, community, and environmental resilience. *American Journal of Community Psychology* 47 (3–4): 374–387. https://doi.org/10.1007/s10464-010-9404-z.

Paat, Yustinus, Lenny Tristia Tambun, and Diana Manafe. 2020. Jakarta to Limit Private Vehicles on the road as city imposes large-scale social restriction. Jakarta Globe. Accessed August 25, 2020, https://jakartaglobe.id/news/jakarta-to-limit-private-vehicles-on-the-road-as-city-imposes-largescale-social-restriction.

Papua Bangkit. 2020. Pemprov Papua Berikan Bantuan Uang Cash Rp 77 M Untuk Kabupaten Kota. Accessed November 24, 2020. https://www.papuabangkit.com/2020/04/30/pemprov-papua-berikan-bantuan-uang-cash-rp-77-m-untuk-kabupaten-kota/.

Patton, Michael Quinn, and Michael Cochran. 2002. *A guide to using qualitative research methodology*. Paris, France: Médecins Sans Frontières.

Ratumakin, Roylinus. 2020. Pemprov Papua Tegaskan Tes Covid-19 Gratis. Medcom. Accessed August 29, 2020. https://www.medcom.id/nasional/daerah/3NOGde2N-pemprov-papua-tegaskan-tes-covid-19-gratis.

Roach, Colleen. 1997. Cultural imperialism and resistance in media theory and literary theory. *Media, Culture and Society* 19 (1): 47–66. https://doi.org/10.1177/016344397019001004.

Sahu, Pradeep. 2020. Closure of universities due to coronavirus disease 2019 (COVID-19): Impact on education and mental health of students and academic staff. *Cureus* 12 (4): e7541. https://doi:10.7759/cureus.7541.

Scotland, James. 2012. Exploring the philosophical underpinnings of research: Relating ontology and epistemology to the methodology and methods of the scientific, interpretive, and critical research paradigms. *English Language Teaching* 5 (9): 9–16. https://doi:10.5539/elt.v5n9p9.

Singh, Kuldeep, Shival Srivastav, Abhishek Bhardwaj, Abhinav Dixit, and Sanjeev Misra. 2020. Medical education during the COVID-19 pandemic: A single institution experience. *Indian Paediatrics* 57 (7): 678–679. https://doi.org/10.1007/s13312-020-1899-2.

Statistics of Papua Province. 2020. Papua Dalam Angka. Accessed September 5, 2020. https://papua.bps.go.id/publication/2020/05/20/ebf212dd68f6d6905aadc626/provinsi-papua-dalam-angka-2020.html.

Strielkowski, Wadim. 2020. COVID-19 pandemic and the digital revolution in academia and higher education. Preprints 2020040290. https://doi:10.20944/preprints202004.0290.v1.

Suwandi, Dhias. 2020. Temukan Kasus Positif Covid-19, Pemprov Papua Pesan 5.000 Alat Rapid Test. Kompas. Accessed August 28, 2020. https://regional.kompas.com/read/2020/03/23/08343871/temukan-kasus-positif-covid-19-pemprov-papua-pesan-5000-alat-rapid-test.

Tambun, Lumanauw, and Putuhena. 2020. Jokowi Bans Mudik as police prepare to close off roads in and out of Jakarta. Jakarta Globe. Accessed August 25, 2020. https://jakartaglobe.id/news/jokowi-bans-mudik-as-police-prepare-to-close-off-roads-in-and-out-of-jakarta/.

Tobing, Sorta. 2020. Mengurai Permasalahan Penanganan Covid-19 di Papua. Kata Data. Accessed September 5, 2020. https://katadata.co.id/sortatobing/berita/5f0d4bd6ba390/mengurai-permasalahan-penanganan-covid-19-di-papua.

Tomlinson, John. 2012. *Cultural imperialism*. Oxford, UK: Blackwell. https://doi.org/10.1002/9780470670590.wbeog129.

Van Lancker, Wim, and Zachary Parolin. 2020. COVID-19, school closures, and child poverty: A social crisis in the making. *The Lancet Public Health* 5 (5): e243–e244. https://doi.org/10.1016/S2468-2667(20)30084-0.

Viner, Russell M., Simon J. Russell, Helen Croker, Jessica Packer, Joseph Ward, Claire Stansfield, Oliver Mytton, Chris Bonell, and Robert Booy. 2020. School closure and management practices during coronavirus outbreaks including COVID-19: A rapid systematic review. *The Lancet Child and Adolescent Health* 4 (5): 397–404. https://doi.org/10.1016/S2352-4642(20)30095-X.

Widjojo, Muridan S., Adriana Elizabeth, Amirudin Al Rahab, Cahyo Pamungkas, and Rosita Dewi. 2010. *Papua road map: Negotiating the past, improving the present, and securing the future*. Jakarta, Indonesia: Yayasan Pustaka Obor Indonesia.

Yasmin, Nur. 2020. "Indonesian Netizens critical of Gov't handling of pandemic: Study". Jakarta Globe. Accessed August 29, 2020. https://jakartaglobe.id/news/indonesian-netizens-critical-of-govt-handling-of-pandemic-study/.

CHAPTER 13

The Public Health Response of the US Federal Government to the Coronavirus Crisis and the Narrative of Donald J. Trump

Jeffrey Willis

Introduction

On September 9, 2020, the *Washington Post* released tapes of interviews conducted with American President Donald J. Trump in the early days of the novel coronavirus pandemic. In one interview conducted on February 7, 2020, Trump admitted that he was aware that the virus is transmitted primarily through the air rather than through physical contact, and that, "It's also more deadly than even your strenuous flus" (Trump, qtd. in Costa and Rucker 2020). This private statement stands in stark contrast to the public statements made by Trump about the coronavirus throughout February and March 2020—statements that frequently downplayed the severity of the virus or even suggested that it was *less* deadly than the common flu. Relaying what he knew to be misinformation to the public was apparently a deliberate strategy on Trump's part, as in another of the taped interviews conducted on March 19, Trump stated that he "wanted

J. Willis (✉)
University of Canterbury, Christchurch, CT, New Zealand

S. Ratuva et al. (eds.), *COVID-19 and Social Protection*,
https://doi.org/10.1007/978-981-16-2948-8_13

to always play it [the severity of the coronavirus] down" so as to avoid creating a panic (Trump, qtd. in Costa and Rucker 2020).

The same day that the tapes were released, Trump Administration Press Secretary Kayleigh McEnany directly stated to the White House press corps that Trump had "never downplayed the virus" and "never lied to the American public on COVID", despite Trump's on-the-record statements to the contrary (McEnany 2020). In isolation, this was perhaps not unusual—the Press Secretaries of the Trump Administration have a documented history of misleading the American public. McEnany's immediate predecessor, Sarah Huckabee Sanders, admitted under oath to fabricating information "in the heat of the moment" that had no factual basis (Sanders, qtd. in Mueller 2019, p. 334), and McEnany has disseminated falsehoods on a variety of topics throughout her tenure as Press Secretary (Rupar 2020). However, this particular statement was not about foreign election interference or President Trump's exploits on Twitter—important but not acutely life-threatening topics. It was about an ongoing pandemic from which nearly 200,000 Americans have lost their lives.[1]

The events surrounding the release of the *Washington Post* tapes—Trump's admission that he deliberately downplayed the threat of the coronavirus and McEnany's subsequent falsehood in defence of the President—are largely demonstrative of how Trump and those in the Trump White House have communicated about the coronavirus and the pandemic that it has caused. Since the coronavirus first came to the public's attention in January 2020, Trump has constructed a public narrative about the virus that has often been divorced from the facts on the ground, from the conclusions of public health experts, and, at times, from the public health recommendations of his own government. By one analysis, as of mid-September 2020, Trump has downplayed the severity of the virus 109 times since January (Blake and Rieger 2020). By another, the US ranks last in "fact-based communications" about the coronavirus when compared to other nations with advanced economies (FP Analytics 2020).

Regardless of the occupant of the White House, the coronavirus pandemic is a sprawling, complex, and deadly challenge that touches upon almost every area of American life. As one political scientist has noted, the coronavirus crisis "is perfectly set up for perception to matter a lot and

[1] 186,162 Americans have died from Coronavirus Disease 19 (COVID-19) as of September 13, 2020 (US Daily Cumulative Totals 2020).

be manipulatable" (Azari, qtd. in Klein 2020). It is for these reasons that understanding the way that Trump and his Administration have communicated about the coronavirus, and the narrative that has emerged from those communications, is critical. Narratives are a key means for political actors to define the challenges that they face and to attempt to manipulate perceptions about those challenges. They are not simply stories—they are political tools through which politicians and other actors attempt to construct a shared understanding of unfolding events and give meaning to past and future actions (Miskimmon et al. 2013; Hertner and Miskimmon 2015). Thus, they are a means of communication that can ultimately impact behaviour—and in a crisis situation where individual actions such as social distancing or wearing a face-covering can have a major impact on how events unfold, they can have a tremendous impact on public health.

With these facts in mind, this chapter provides a chronological overview of how the coronavirus pandemic has unfolded in the United States through September 2020, with a particular focus on the various comments made by President Donald J. Trump. While it is outside the scope of this work to comprehensively document and analyse every statement made by Trump regarding the coronavirus, the goal of this chapter is to draw out and piece together Trump's broader narrative about the virus and how this has impacted the federal response to the crisis. The chapter particularly focuses on the early months of the pandemic—as most of the actions taken by the US federal government in response to the coronavirus have thus far been confined to January through approximately early May. In concluding, it finds that Trump's narrative has been erratic, divisive, and misleading and that this, combined with a chaotic federal response to the crisis, has undermined public health in the United States.

January–February

On December 31, 2019, the World Health Organization (WHO) reported an outbreak of a "pneumonia of unknown cause" in Wuhan, a city of 11 million located in the Hubei province of interior China (World Health Organization 2020). Shortly after, on January 3, the Director of the US Center for Disease Control (CDC) was notified by authorities in the People's Republic of China (PRC) that a mysterious respiratory illness was spreading through the city. This information was relayed to the White House, and American officials within the CDC, State Department, and other federal agencies and departments began preliminary discussions regarding how to respond to the emerging viral threat (Abutaleb et al. 2020). On January 17, the CDC held its first public briefing on the virus, stating that while the risk to the American public was low, "the situation could change quickly" (Center for Disease Control 2020). The following day, President Trump met with Health and Human Services (HHS) Secretary Alex Azar. Although Azar had been trying to arrange a meeting with Trump since earlier in January, this was Trump's first significant briefing on the virus (Harris et al. 2020). On January 21, the first coronavirus case in the United States was confirmed near Seattle, Washington (Taylor 2020).

While attending the World Economic Forum in Davos, Switzerland, on January 22, President Trump made his first public comments about the coronavirus, stating that his government was not worried about a pandemic, and that "It's one person coming in from China. We have it under control. It's going to be just fine" (Trump, qtd. in Belvedere 2020). He also noted that he had a "great relationship with President Xi" of China, and that he trusted China to be open and transparent regarding the viral outbreak. Around the same time, China instituted a major lockdown of Wuhan city and the surrounding province, and, in formal briefings prepared by the US intelligence community, Trump was informed that the PRC was not providing accurate data regarding coronavirus infections and deaths (Harris et al. 2020; Rascoe and Dwyer 2020). Despite the warnings he received in late January, Trump continued to praise the PRC's handling of coronavirus issues throughout January and February, including in his State of the Union Address on February 4.[2] (see Trump 2020b, c, e, g).

On January 30, just over a week after Trump's initial public comments on the virus, the WHO declared a global health emergency, and the following day, HHS Secretary Azar declared the coronavirus a public health emergency in the United States (Department of Health and Human Services 2020; Taylor 2020). The same day as Azar's declaration, Trump took one of his first concrete actions to limit the spread of the virus by barring some travellers from the PRC from entering the United States. This event would go on to become a key element of Trump's coronavirus narrative. In later months, he would incorrectly describe the

[2] An annual event, the State of the Union is one of the most high-profile domestic speeches delivered by the American president.

travel restrictions as a "China Ban" (Trump 2020c) and frame them as a signature element of his coronavirus response, eventually claiming that had he not instituted the restrictions, the United States "would have lost hundreds of thousands more lives" (Trump 2020z). There is little to no evidence to support this claim,[3] and despite Trump's later assertion that he "closed [traffic] down to all of China" (Trump 2020z), the restrictions had many exemptions. Between January 30 and April 1, approximately 40,000 travellers entered the United States after flying direct from China (Kessler 2020; Robertson 2020).

Despite the new travel restrictions, entering February, it was becoming increasingly obvious to some in the federal government that coronavirus spread inside the United States was possible—although many still felt that a widespread outbreak in the US was unlikely (Abutaleb et al. 2020; Shear et al. 2020). During this time, the CDC began to develop the capacity to deploy widespread coronavirus testing[4] across the US. However, this effort was quickly beset by bureaucratic confusion and infighting, and ultimately the CDC failed in its first attempt to create a working test that could be distributed to states (Abutaleb et al. 2020). Additionally, as some in the CDC and other federal agencies advocated for more proactive action, the Trump White House signalled its concern that increasing federal efforts to respond to the virus could appear alarmist (Abutaleb et al. 2020). This attitude resulted in impeded federal efforts to stockpile medical supplies and equipment that officials were beginning to identify a need for (Abutaleb et al. 2020; Grady 2020; Shear et al. 2020; Sommer 2020). Public health officials both inside and outside of the federal government have since acknowledged February as a "lost month"

[3] Multiple studies have found that while travel restrictions were modestly useful at slowing the spread of the coronavirus in the early days of the pandemic, only other public health interventions, such as social distancing, rapid contact tracing, and widespread testing, can significantly curb its transmission (Chinazzi et al. 2020; Tian et al. 2020; Wells et al. 2020).

[4] Experts consider widespread testing to be one of the most critical tools for containing an infectious disease like the coronavirus (Tromberg et al. 2020).

and stated that the lack of early testing[5] significantly reduced the United States' ability to effectively respond to the virus[6] (Shear et al. 2020).

By the end of the month, spread of the coronavirus was accelerating around the globe, with major outbreaks taking hold in Iran and Italy (Blake 2020). Studies have since indicated that spread was accelerating inside the United States as well, though the lack of a systematic testing regime meant that it was going mostly undetected (Carey and Glanz 2020). Lacking reliable data, fear of a potential pandemic prompted a series of massive losses on the US stock exchange in late February, including the largest single-week loss of the Dow Jones Industrial Average in its history (Imbert and Huang 2020). Around the same time, the Trump White House requested $2.5 billion from the US Congress to "accelerate vaccine development, support preparedness and response activities and to procure much-needed equipment and supplies" (Falconer 2020). This amount was heavily criticized by both Democrats and Republicans as being far below what was required to significantly increase the US' ability to respond to the challenges posed by the virus[7] (Roubien and Olstein 2020).

For his part, throughout February, President Trump offered a consistent narrative that downplayed the threat posed by the virus. As the days passed, he often made comments such as "[the coronavirus] is very much under control in the USA" (Trump 2020d), and, "One day, it's like a miracle, [the coronavirus] will disappear" (Trump, qtd. in Blake 2020).

[5] Indicative of both the United States' sluggish testing rollout and how the Trump Administration has often amplified misinformation, on Wednesday, March 4, Vice-President Mike Pence—who by that time was leading a federal coronavirus task force—stated that 1.5 million tests would be available across the country by the end of that week. Two days later, Trump stated "Anybody that wants a test can get a test. That's what the bottom line is" (Trump 2020v). Available data indicates that approximately 3,128 tests had been completed in the United States at the time of Trump's March 6 statement, and 1.5 million tests would not be completed until one month later on April 4 (US Daily Cumulative Totals 2020).

[6] Both epidemiological projections and independent analysis comparing the United States to peer nations have indicated that a high percentage of the American coronavirus deaths to occur in the first several months of the pandemic could have been averted with more efficient testing, quicker lockdown orders, and national social distancing guidelines (Sebenius and Sebenius 2020).

[7] Congress ultimately rejected the Trump Administration's proposal and instead approved an $8 billion funding package with overwhelming bipartisan support, which Trump signed on March 6 (Axios 2020b).

In response to losses on the stock market, Trump accused "Low Ratings Fake News" of "doing everything possible to make the Caronavirus *[sic]* look as bad as possible, including panicking markets, if possible" (Trump 2020t). Similarly, two days after the bipartisan criticism of his Administration's funding request, he described the coronavirus crisis as a "new hoax" perpetrated by Democrats in an attempt to discredit him (Trump 2020u).

Again, by his own admission, Trump was aware that the coronavirus was extremely deadly and highly transmissible at the time that he was making these statements. He had been warned by both public health and national security officials that the coronavirus could result in a pandemic, and as early as January 30 his Deputy National Security Advisor had warned him that the world was facing a public health emergency equal to the flu of 1918, which killed an estimated 50 million people worldwide (Costa and Rucker 2020). While Trump could not have known how the coming months would unfold, he had more than enough data to know that his narrative that all was under control was divorced from the reality of the threat facing the United States. While not causing panic is a reasonable goal, Trump was actively attempting to seed a false sense of security and leaving the American people highly vulnerable to what was to come.

March–April

On March 11, the WHO formally declared the coronavirus crisis a pandemic, and the National Basketball Association (NBA) shut down its season indefinitely, a move that signalled one of the first major disruptions of American life (Cacciola and Deb 2020; Ghebreyesus 2020). Shortly after, on March 19, the State of California became the first state to issue a general stay-at-home order (Office of the Governor of the State of California 2020). By the end of the month, more than 30 states had followed suit, and most were moving forward with their own coronavirus response plans. However, these plans were hampered by a lack of coronavirus testing across the United States. As of mid-March, the United States was conducting less than 10,000 tests per day—a number which it would expand to around 100,000 per day by the beginning of April. This was far below what most experts said was required to contain the spread of the virus (Lopez 2020a, b). New daily coronavirus cases increased throughout March before plateauing around approximately 30,000 per day through most of the following month (Johns Hopkins Coronavirus Resource Center 2020a).

With the pandemic accelerating, on March 11, Trump delivered an Oval Office address in which he blamed the European Union for failing to take adequate precautions in addressing the virus, thus allowing it to spread to the United States (Trump 2020e). In addition to several other measures, Trump announced during the address that the United States would be suspending all travel from Europe.[8] As with the move to bar some travellers from China from entering the United States, Trump would later go on to claim the European restrictions as evidence of his Administration's decisiveness. However, high-ranking officials within the Administration had been advocating for European travel restrictions for more than a month and been rebuffed on the basis that such restrictions would prove too disruptive to the American economy (Abutaleb et al. 2020).

Oval Office addresses are considered particularly important rhetorical tools for American presidents (Elving 2020), and Trump's decision to speak to the American people in such a manner was, after weeks of downplaying the threat, an attempt to signal that his Administration was taking the pandemic seriously. However, it was also evidence of a shift in Trump's public narrative away from praising international actors and towards blaming them for challenges faced by the United States. In particular, following his March 11 address, Trump pivoted particularly strongly towards blaming the PRC for the global spread of the coronavirus. In a tweet on March 16, Trump used the phrase "Chinese Virus" to describe the coronavirus for the first time (Trump 2020f). A few days later, photographs revealed that Trump had crossed off the word coronavirus and replaced it with "Chinese Virus" in notes for his daily press briefing[9] (Peters 2020).

[8] Confusion over Trump's wording and a failure to consult with the EU beforehand meant that Trump's speech created a minor panic, as Americans living abroad—many in COVID hotspots—rushed to try and return to the United States. Markets also faced uncertainty about whether trade goods were subject to the new restrictions (Miller et al. 2020). Over the next few days, the Administration was forced to clarify that European restrictions would be significantly less stringent than Trump had implied (Lopez 2020c).

[9] Academics and social justice experts have argued that this type of racialized terminology promotes anti-Asian bias and exclusion. Additionally, at least one study identified that media reports of hate incidents committed against Asian-Americans increased as public officials began to adopt such terminology in Trump's wake. In March, Trump stated that

Terms like "China Virus" have since become a staple of Trump's public coronavirus narrative, and since mid-March, the pivot towards assigning blame to international actors has become entrenched in US policy. Notably, in late April, Trump instructed the US to place a funding hold on the WHO—a move that received widespread condemnation from public health experts and international officials (Smith 2020). Although Trump spent months praising China and publicly accepting its claims at face value, in his announcement of the move to defund the WHO, Trump's primary contention was that the global health organization was overly "China-centric", and that it amplified misinformation from the Chinese Communist Party (Trump 2020g).

There is ample evidence that this pivot was a deliberate strategy on the part of the Trump Administration, and the Republican Party more generally, to shore up domestic political support, rather than to advance any particular public health goal. For instance, a leaked memo sent by the National Republican Senatorial Committee to Republican congressional candidates advised candidates to address the coronavirus crisis by aggressively attacking China rather than defending the domestic pandemic response (Isenstadt 2020). Additionally, Republican pollsters have identified amplifying tough-on-China rhetoric as an effective strategy for Trump's re-election campaign to pursue (Kumar 2020).

Outside of efforts to shift blame for the coronavirus onto international actors, during March and April, the federal government in some ways did move to respond to the pandemic more proactively. In large part, this "reset" of the federal response began with Trump's aforementioned Oval Office address on March 11. Shortly after that address, on March 13, Trump declared the coronavirus pandemic a national emergency, freeing up federal disaster relief funding. Three days later he announced "15 Days to Slow the Spread" public health guidelines developed by the CDC (The White House 2020). Perhaps most significantly, on March 27, Trump signed the $2.2 trillion-dollar Coronavirus Aid, Relief, and Economic Security (CARES) Act—economic relief legislation that had passed both

Asian-Americans should not be blamed for the coronavirus (Gover et al. 2020). However, as the pandemic has continued, he has continued to use racialized language, notably describing the coronavirus as the "kung-flu" at a campaign rally in June (Nakamura 2020).

the House of Representatives and Senate with overwhelming bipartisan support.[10]

Contemporaneously, Trump, essentially for the first time, began to frame the coronavirus as a serious challenge for the United States. Indicative of his new rhetorical approach, on March 31, Trump described the coronavirus as "vicious" and stated that it was "not the flu" while warning that Americans were about to go through a "very, very painful two weeks" in early April (Trump 2020y). This was a significant shift in a short period of time, as just over one week earlier Trump had compared the coronavirus to the flu in a series of interviews, though public health experts had publicly debunked that comparison and Trump knew it to be false (Karni and McNeil Jr.).

In public health terms, this shift in narrative on the part of Trump was undoubtedly positive. Following the reorientation of Trump's narrative, public concern about the coronavirus rose considerably in the United States—a helpful development in a situation where public health outcomes rely on individual actions such as wearing a face-covering. While this cannot be entirely attributed to Trump, public approval of his handling of coronavirus issues also shifted in his favour following his change of tone—indicating that many were aware of his narrative about ongoing events (Bycoffe et al. 2020). However, all of this came following months of amplifying misinformation and downplaying threats. While we cannot know exactly how the earliest months of the pandemic would have unfolded if Trump had communicated more honestly in the early days, it is possible that more Americans would, at the least, have behaved more cautiously in their daily lives, perhaps slowing the virus' spread.

Despite these generally positive developments, as March continued into April, proactive federal actions gave way to a more reactive and chaotic approach to dealing with the virus, and the Trump Administration increasingly shifted the burden of America's public health response

[10] In April—after many states instituted stay at home orders—the US unemployment rate spiked to 14.7%. This was a record single-month increase since record keeping began in 1948 (U.S. Bureau of Labor Statistics 2020). The CARES act provided for direct cash payments to American citizens, funding for hospitals, loans for small and large businesses, and funding for state and local governments in an attempt to respond to the economic disruption (Grisales et al. 2020). While, as the largest emergency spending measure in US history, the CARES Act was undoubtedly significant, its overall effectiveness is disputed, and it has faced significant criticism due to its inclusion of sizeable tax breaks for wealthy individuals and large corporations (Brown and Ozoguz 2020; Sloan 2020).

onto the backs of individual states. This began on March 16, when, as fears that coronavirus infections could overwhelm healthcare facilities were increasing, Trump instructed states to attempt to procure their own medical supplies independent of the federal government (Martin 2020). Three days later, he stated that the federal government was "not a shipping clerk" and that "The governors are supposed to be—as with testing, the governors are supposed—are supposed to be doing it" (Trump 2020w). As a result of this guidance, which effectively shifted the bulk of the burden of conducting a public health response away from the federal government, state and local officials turned to the private market to acquire needed supplies and increasingly developed their own coronavirus testing regimes.

In late March, with so many actors flooding the medical supply market, reports of supply shortages, price gouging, and the hoarding of medical products quickly emerged (Devaiah et al. 2020). Further complicating matters, federal authorities did attempt to complement state efforts by empowering the Federal Emergency Management Agency (FEMA) to manage a federal pipeline of Personal Protective Equipment (PPE) to states (Falzone 2020). However, in late March and throughout April, FEMA was beset by transparency issues, and both Republican and Democratic governors claimed that federal authorities were at times seizing shipments of PPE that their states had purchased and distributing them elsewhere in the country. As Democratic Governor Gretchen Whitmer and Republican Governor Larry Hogan put it in a joint op-ed on March 30: "The lack of any centralized coordination is creating a counterproductive competition between states and the federal government to secure limited supplies, driving up prices and exacerbating existing shortages" (Hogan and Whitmer 2020).

In an attempt to alleviate some of these issues, on March 18, Trump invoked the Defense Production Act (DPA)—a 1950 law allowing the federal government to compel private companies to produce specific supplies.[11] As of September, use of the DPA has allowed the United States to replenish supplies of some types of critical medical equipment (Kobokovich 2020). Also, during this time, federal authorities at FEMA

[11] However, he did not actually make use of it until the end of the month, only taking action following urgent requests from the American Hospital Association, American Medical Association, and American Nurses Association for the federal government to force the production of medical supplies (Edelman 2020).

authorized the Army Corps of Engineers to construct field hospitals in New York and other locations, and two US Naval Hospital ships were deployed in New York and Los Angeles (Barrett 2020; Ewing 2020). However, these actions, while positive, were essentially on the margins of the major public health challenges being faced across the United States. They were reactive, rather than proactive, and during this time, federal authorities did not institute the large-scale public health interventions—such as a national testing protocol—that public health experts called for. Often, when pressed by governors on challenges that they were facing, Trump's response was to double down on his previous guidance that states take the lead and to criticize states that he felt were not "appreciative" enough of federal efforts. On March 26, Trump publicly identified several states (all with Democratic governors) who he felt fit this description and stated that he had instructed Vice-President Mike Pence not to return calls from authorities in those states (Trump 2020x).

Beyond supply issues, friction between Trump and state governors manifested in other ways throughout March and April. Notably, it came through in Trump's arguments *against* state lockdown orders. These arguments not only directly contradicted his statements shifting the responsibility for public health decisions to state governments, but also the federal "15 Days to Slow the Spread" guidelines that directly instructed Americans to "Listen to and follow the directions of your *state and local authorities*" (The White House 2020, original emphasis). This dynamic was particularly apparent in two instances. The first came when, on March 22, following another series of stock losses, Trump tweeted "WE CANNOT LET THE CURE BE WORSE THAN THE PROBLEM ITSELF" (Trump 2020h). This was only three days after California had become the first state to institute a stay-at-home order, and it was just after Trump had declared that states should be acting independently, as the federal government was "not a shipping clerk" (Trump 2020w). After his Twitter proclamation, Trump went on to state in a Fox News interview that he would like to "have the country opened up" by Easter—April 12 (Trump, qtd. in Karni and McNeil Jr.). These comments ran counter to the recommendations of public health experts, who, at that time, were expecting the virus to peak in mid-April (Karni and McNeil Jr.).

The second major event came a few weeks later, during an outbreak of anti-lockdown protests largely supported by right-wing political groups (Wilson 2020). Just after protests began to spring up around the United

States, on an April 16 conference call with state governors discussing new federal guidelines for reopening state economies, Trump told the governors that while the federal government would support them "You're going to call your own shots" with regards to reopening plans (Trump, qtd. in Baker and Shear 2020). On April 17, the day immediately after he made those comments, Trump directly contradicted that sentiment when he again expressed support for the idea of lifting lockdown orders by tweeting calls to "LIBERATE" Michigan, Minnesota, and Virginia—again, all states with Democratic governors (Trump 2020i, j, k). Calls to end lockdown orders have since remained a fairly consistent element of Trump's coronavirus narrative, and he has often accused Democratic governors of keeping them in place not for public health reasons, but to sabotage his re-election efforts.[12]

In many ways, mid-March through mid-April was Trump at his most erratic. He swung wildly from comparing the coronavirus to the flu, to arguing that it was "vicious" and "not the flu". He shifted the burden of responsibility for the American public health response to the coronavirus to individual states and told them they would "call their own shots", and then immediately made extremely public calls for states to rescind their stay-at-home orders. All of this sowed confusion and division, and the specific targeting of Democratic governors seemed calibrated to appeal to Trump's political base, rather than to address any particular public health imperative.[13] Perhaps more importantly, as Trump vacillated, the federal government largely failed to develop clear and consistent pandemic response plans. For every positive action taken by federal authorities in March and April, another generated chaos and confusion. As one prominent epidemiologist stated in early April: "We don't have a national plan. We are going from press conference to press conference and crisis to crisis ... trying to understand our response" (Osterholm, qtd. in Science News Staff 2020).

[12] For example, comments from Trump's daily press conference on September 4: "I think North Carolina, I think that Michigan and Pennsylvania and other states, they should open. The governors—the Democrat governors—should open their states. They'll open them [the day after the US general election] on November 4th. But they should open them now. It's very unfair to the people to have those shutdowns continuing at the level that they're continuing" (Trump 2020p).

[13] By July, polling conducted by Pew Research Center found that only 46% of Republicans considered the coronavirus to be a major threat to public health, compared to 85% of Democrats (Tyson 2020).

May–September

On April 30, the Trump Administration allowed the national "15 Days to Slow the Spread" guidelines, instituted in mid-March and extended through April, to expire (Kenen 2020). In congressional testimony shortly after, epidemiologist Caitlin Rivers of Johns Hopkins University became the latest in a long line of public health experts to argue that the federal government urgently needed to develop national plans for coronavirus testing, contact tracing, and other critical virus containment measures.[14] However, since that time, the US federal government has taken none of these actions, nor has it passed new legislation to address the economic impact of the pandemic.[15] In mid-May, the Trump Administration rejected more detailed reopening guidance prepared by the CDC as "overly prescriptive", and, further signalling its desire to move on from the pandemic, said that it would end daily coronavirus press conferences.[16]

As a result of the unwillingness of the federal government to take any new actions to address the coronavirus crisis, the United States' fragmentary state-led public health response has persisted. Throughout May, with coronavirus cases declining slowly around the country, many states

[14] While it was not widely known until later in the summer, in the early months of the pandemic, the President's son-in-law Jared Kushner led a secretive team working to develop these types of long called for national plans. However, the plans that were developed were ultimately scrapped in favour of continuing the state-led patchwork approach. A public health expert in frequent contact with the federal coronavirus task force stated that this was because "The political folks believed that because it was going to be relegated to Democratic states, that they could blame those governors, and that would be an effective political strategy" (Eban 2020).

[15] On May 15, the House of Representatives passed the Health and Economic Recovery Omnibus Emergency Solutions (HEROES) Act, a $3 trillion-dollar stimulus package designed to follow-on from the CARES Act. However, largely as the result of ideological divisions within the Republican party, the Senate has failed for months to advance any new legislation, and the prospect of any new economic relief legislation for American citizens appears dim as of September 2020 (Zhou and Nilsen 2020). On August 11, President Trump signed four Presidential memorandums and executive orders to provide enhanced unemployment, defer payroll taxes, prevent evictions and foreclosures during the pandemic, and defer payments on federal student loans. These faced immediate legal questions and bipartisan criticism, and have thus far been of marginal benefit (Keith 2020; Millhiser 2020).

[16] Public outcry caused the Administration to quickly reinstate them (Goodnough and Haberman 2020).

moved to begin reopening their economies (Lee et al. 2020). On May 26, the United States reported 16,830 new coronavirus cases—the lowest number since March 25. However, by June, cases began to increase again, and by mid-July, the United States saw more than 76,000 cases in a single day—more than double the "first wave" peak of 35,870 on April 25.[17] At the time of the writing of this chapter in early September, cases have plateaued around a 7-day average of 41,000 per day, with a 7-day average of approximately 1,000 coronavirus deaths per day. Throughout July, August, and September, high case numbers have forced some states that began the reopening process to pause or reverse their plans, and currently there is little to no centralized coordination of state actions (Lee et al. 2020; US Daily Cumulative Totals 2020).

For his part, since May, Trump has maintained a more consistent coronavirus narrative than he did throughout March and April. Using racialized language, he has continued to blame China and other external actors for allowing the virus to spread globally (Trump 2020l). Despite the guidance of his own Administration and his previous statements that states should "call their own shots", he has consistently attacked Democratic governors for instituting their own state-specific public health measures.[18] And, although as of early September 2020 the United States leads the world in coronavirus cases and deaths,[19] he has described

[17] On July 25, the United States saw 78,427 new confirmed coronavirus cases. For comparison, the United Kingdom saw 731, Germany 781, and France 1,130 (Coronavirus (COVID-19) Cases 2020).

[18] For example, on a visit to the state of Maine in June, Trump stated of Democratic Governor Janet Mills: "You have a governor that doesn't know what she's doing. She's like a dictator. Why isn't she reopening up the state?" (Trump, qtd. in Andrews 2020). Throughout the pandemic, Maine has been one of the most successful US states in terms of containing the coronavirus when measured by common metrics such as per capita infections and deaths.

[19] During a widely publicized interview on August 3, Trump stated to *Axios* Jonathan Swan that, in terms of the coronavirus, the United States was "lower than the world" in "numerous categories" (Axios 2020a). Seeking to clarify the President's statement, Swan identified that Trump was using statistics that measured coronavirus deaths as a proportion of total coronavirus cases. He then asked Trump about American deaths as a proportion of the population of the United States, a category in which the US fairs poorly relative to its peer nations. Trump responded: "You can't do that".

While Trump was partially correct that the US' case fatality rate of 3.0% is fairly good (though it does not come close to leading the world), Swan was equally correct that the United States' per capita death rate of 58.61 per 100,000 population is among the worst in the world. According to statistics compiled by Johns Hopkins University, in that

his Administration's pandemic response in glowing terms (see Trump 2020m). In recent days, Trump has claimed that the US has "rounded the final turn" with regards to the coronavirus crisis (Trump 2020n). Doctor Anthony S. Fauci, the top infectious disease expert in the federal government, has explicitly disagreed with this sentiment and called the consistently high number of coronavirus cases and deaths "disturbing" heading into the Autumn and Winter (Oprysko 2020).

Perhaps most notably in terms of new additions to his narrative, since May, Trump has often argued that the US leads the world in coronavirus cases because it conducts more tests than other countries[20] (Vazquez 2020). It is true that the United States has expanded coronavirus testing significantly, albeit unevenly, across the country since April. However, epidemiologists and infectious disease experts have refuted Trump's claim and stated that test positivity rates—the percentage of tests conducted that return positive—provide a better indicator of how the virus is spreading. For instance, as one epidemiologist put it in late June during a nationwide surge in new cases, analyses of testing positivity rates "suggests that community transmission [of the virus] is increasing, and that increasing case counts are not simply an artifact of testing" (Ellingson, qtd. in McDonald 2020).

This element of Trump's narrative is particularly significant, as it has been reported that as a result of Trump's desire to lower reported coronavirus cases in the United States, the White House has engaged in a pattern of political interference with the CDC (Stolberg 2020). The most widely reported instance of this came in late August, when, amidst accusations of interference from the White House, the CDC abruptly changed its non-binding coronavirus testing guidance to recommend that potential asymptomatic carriers of the virus *not* be tested—a move widely opposed by public health experts (Wu 2020). More recently, internal emails obtained by the news organization *Politico* have seemed to confirm that the Trump White House has engaged in a pattern of pushing the CDC to soften its coronavirus reports in order to support the President's

category, the United States ranks 158th of 169 countries for which data is readily available (Johns Hopkins Coronavirus Resource Center 2020b).

[20] For example, Trump stated in an interview with Chris Wallace in July: "Chris, [cases numbers are high] because we have great testing, because we have the best testing in the world. If we didn't test, you wouldn't be able to show that chart. If we tested half as much, those numbers would be down" (Trump 2020q).

narrative downplaying the virus (Diamond 2020). In June, Trump also stated that he had asked "his people" to slow testing throughout the country so as to keep case numbers down (Trump 2020l). Though he later denied that he made such a request (Vazquez 2020), taken in their totality, Trump's statements and actions indicate a personal preference that the United States engage in less coronavirus testing so as to artificially suppress case numbers.[21]

Conclusion

Donald J. Trump is not responsible for the coronavirus. He could not have prevented it from arriving in the United States, nor could he have prevented some Americans from contracting and perishing from the virus. However, Trump is responsible—not entirely, but to a large extent—for how the US federal government has responded to the virus' spread in the United States. Unfortunately, available evidence suggests that by presiding over an overwhelmingly ineffective federal response to the coronavirus pandemic, Trump has failed to safeguard the public health interests of American citizens.

Trump had warning from officials in his Administration as early as January that the coronavirus could present a serious threat to the United States, and, by his own admission, he knew in early February that the virus was extremely deadly and difficult to contain (Costa and Rucker 2020). Nonetheless, the US federal government failed in the early months of the coronavirus crisis to develop the appropriate public health capacities necessary to respond to the arrival of the virus in the country (Abutaleb et al. 2020). When the federal government did begin to respond in mid-March, it did so in ways that were erratic, confused, and inefficient (Falzone 2020). Individual states were left to forge their own paths on matters of public health—though for states with Democratic administrations, Trump often publicly undermined them when they did so (Andrews 2020). As one public health expert summed up the Trump Administration's approach: "The federal government wants to shift all the political responsibility on the states. If something is going wrong,

[21] For example: "Uhh, if it did slow down, frankly, I think we're way ahead of ourselves, if you want to know the truth. We've done too good a job, because every time we go up — with 25 million tests, you're going to find more people. So then they say, 'oh we have more cases in the United States'" (Trump, qtd. in Allassan 2020).

blame the governor. But they still want to take the credit for getting the win" (Konyndyk, qtd. in Lopez 2020a). The result of this has been that, as of September 2020, the United States has never had national coronavirus testing or contact tracing protocols outside of non-binding federal guidance, nor has it had a national mask mandate, nor any number of other critical public health interventions at the national level. Further, the lack of centralized coordinating activity has resulted in a fragmentary system of overlapping public health responses that vary from jurisdiction to jurisdiction and often conflict with one another.

Beyond these governance issues, Trump is also responsible for how he has communicated about the threat posed by the virus and the narrative that he has advanced in relation to it. This is key, since, despite the ineffectiveness of the federal response, a patchwork state-led approach could perhaps have stood a chance of greater success if paired with clear and consistent communication about the pandemic from the Trump White House. However, Trump has consistently downplayed the virus (Blake and Rieger 2020). Additionally, he has often undermined state public health orders and amplified falsehoods, all while framing the federal response as an overwhelming success. He has done this by taking credit for "travel bans" that were, in fact, fairly moderate travel restrictions (Trump 2020c); by pointing to his Administration's efforts to supply PPE and medical equipment, while ignoring the chaos and confusion those efforts caused (Trump 2020m); by highlighting misleading statistics that support his claims, while ignoring those that show the United States leading the world in coronavirus cases and deaths (Axios 2020a); and by mocking the public health guidance of his own Administration. All of this, and this chapter has not even touched upon his promotion of unproven drugs and miracle cures that have scant scientific backing, or his consistent amplification of misinformation about the masks and face coverings that experts say are crucial to halting the virus' spread (see Dale 2020 and Trump 2020o). In short, Donald Trump has offered a coronavirus narrative that is divorced from the reality of the coronavirus crisis. This has hindered the ability of the American public to obtain a clear picture of the pandemic and ultimately put public health in the United States at risk.

In August, when pushed by interviewer Jonathan Swan about how he has downplayed the virus and whether the virus was under control in the United States, Trump stated of Americans who continue to perish from the coronavirus: "They are dying. That's true. And you—it is what it is. But that doesn't mean we aren't doing everything we can" (Axios 2020a). In terms of public health governance, there is almost no standard by which the US federal government is doing everything that it can to address the coronavirus crisis. As the pandemic continues, likely into 2021 and perhaps beyond, if Donald Trump continues to helm the US federal government, there is little reason to expect that federal authorities will start to take the steps that public health experts say are necessary to contain the pandemic, that Trump's communications about the virus will become more honest or grounded in facts, or even that Trump himself will show more respect for the public health guidance of his own Administration. For Americans whose health will continue to be put at risk by this, in the words of the President of the United States: it is what it is.

References

Abutaleb, Yasmeen, Josh Dawsey, Ellen Nakashima, and Greg Miller. 2020. The U.S. was beset by denial and dysfunction as the coronavirus raged. *Washington Post*. https://www.washingtonpost.com/national-security/2020/04/04/coronavirus-government-dysfunction/. Accessed 14 September 2020.

Allassan, Fadel. 2020. Trump declines to say he was joking about slowing down coronavirus testing. *Axios*. https://www.axios.com/trump-slowing-down-coronavirus-testing-joking-19cccd3d-7895-4a55-900e-caee1fe215bd.html. Accessed 14 September 2020.

Andrews, Caitlin. 2020. Trump called Mills a 'dictator' over reopening. Her plan is relatively middle of the road. *Bagnor Daily News*. https://bangordailynews.com/2020/06/05/politics/trump-called-mills-a-dictator-over-reopening-her-plan-is-relatively-middle-of-the-road/. Accessed 13 September 2020.

Axios. 2020a. Donald Trump interview transcript with Jonathan Swan of Axios on HBO. *Rev*. https://www.rev.com/blog/transcripts/donald-trump-interview-transcript-with-axios-on-hbo. Accessed 13 September 2020.

Axios. 2020b. Trump signs $8 billion emergency coronavirus funding package, March 6. https://www.axios.com/coronavirus-emergency-funding-congress-deal-8c9e7b5a-30a5-48a8-97ec-9bfc13dbe6f6.html. Accessed 13 September 2020.

Baker, Peter, and Michael D. Shear. 2020. Trump says states can start reopening while acknowledging the decision is theirs. *New York Times*. https://www.nytimes.com/2020/04/16/us/politics/coronavirus-trump-guidelines.html. Accessed 5 September 2020.

Barrett, Brian. 2020. The race to turn hotels into Coronavirus hospitals. *Wired*. https://www.wired.com/story/us-army-corps-of-engineers-deploys-against-coronavirus/. Accessed 12 September 2020.

Belvedere, Matthew J. 2020. Trump says he trusts China's Xi on coronavirus and the US has it 'totally under control.' *CNBC*. https://www.cnbc.com/2020/01/22/trump-on-coronavirus-from-china-we-have-it-totally-under-control.html. Accessed 12 September 2020.

Blake, Aaron. 2020. 2 months in the dark: the increasingly damning timeline of Trump's coronavirus response. *Washington Post*. https://www.washingtonpost.com/politics/2020/04/07/timeline-trumps-coronavirus-response-is-increasingly-damning/. Accessed 12 September 2020.

Blake, Aaron, and JM Rieger. 2020. Timeline: The 109 times Trump has downplayed the coronavirus threat. *Washington Post*. https://www.washingtonpost.com/politics/2020/03/12/trump-coronavirus-timeline/. Accessed 12 September 2020.

Brown, Greg, and Arzu Ozoguz. 2020. Who CARES? Assessing the impact of the CARES Act. *Kenan Insights*. https://kenaninstitute.unc.edu/kenan-insight/who-cares-assessing-the-impact-of-the-cares-act/. Accessed 9 September 2020.

Bycoffe, Aaron, Christopher Groskopf, and Mehta Dhrumil. 2020. How Americans view the Coronavirus crisis and Trump's response. *FiveThirtyEight*. https://projects.fivethirtyeight.com/coronavirus-polls/. Accessed 9 September 2020.

Cacciola, Scott, and Sopan Deb. 2020. N.B.A. suspends season after player tests positive for coronavirus. *New York Times*. https://www.nytimes.com/2020/03/11/sports/basketball/nba-season-suspended-coronavirus.html. Accessed 9 September 2020.

Carey, Benedict, and James Glanz. 2020. Hidden outbreaks spread through U.S. cities far earlier than Americans knew, estimates say. *New York Times*. https://www.nytimes.com/2020/04/23/us/coronavirus-early-outbreaks-cities.html. Accessed 9 September 2020.

Center for Disease Control. 2020. Transcript of 2019 novel Coronavirus response telebriefing, January 17. https://www.cdc.gov/media/releases/2020/t0117-coronavirus-screening.html. Accessed 9 September 2020.

Chinazzi, Matteo, Jessica T. Davis, Marco Ajelli, Corrado Gioannini, Maria Litvinova, Stefano Merler, Ana Pastore y Piontti, Kunpeng Mu, et al. 2020. The effect of travel restrictions on the spread of the 2019 novel coronavirus (COVID-19) outbreak. *Science* 368: 395–400. http://10.1126/science.aba9757.

Coronavirus (COVID-19) Cases. 2020. *Our world in data*. https://ourworldindata.org/covid-cases. Accessed 13 September 2020.

Costa, Robert, and Philip Rucker. 2020. Woodward book: Trump says he knew coronavirus was 'deadly' and worse than the flu while intentionally misleading Americans. *Washington Post*. https://www.washingtonpost.com/politics/

bob-woodward-rage-book-trump/2020/09/09/0368fe3c-efd2-11ea-b4bc-3a2098fc73d4_story.html. Accessed 13 September 2020.

Dale, Daniel. 2020. Fact check: Digging into Trump's false claim that CDC found that 85% of people who wear masks get the coronavirus. *CNN*. https://www.cnn.com/2020/10/16/politics/fact-check-trump-cdc-masks-85-percent/index.html. Accessed 20 October 2020.

Department of Health and Human Services. 2020. Secretary Azar declares public health emergency for United States for 2019 novel coronavirus. https://www.hhs.gov/about/news/2020/01/31/secretary-azar-declares-public-health-emergency-us-2019-novel-coronavirus.html. Accessed 14 September 2020.

Devaiah, Anand, Michael Wijaranakula, Chinmay Kommuru, and Rena M. Conti. 2020. Medical product procurement in a time of federalism: The COVID-19 challenge. *Health Affairs*. https://www.healthaffairs.org/do/10.1377/hblog20200515.360276/full/. Accessed 12 September 2020.

Diamond, Dan. 2020. Trump officials interfered with CDC reports on Covid-19. *Politico*. https://www.politico.com/news/2020/09/11/exclusive-trump-officials-interfered-with-cdc-reports-on-covid-19-412809. Accessed 13 September 2020.

Eban, Katherine. 2020. How Jared Kushner's secret testing plan "went poof into thin air." *Vanity Fair*. https://www.vanityfair.com/news/2020/07/how-jared-kushners-secret-testing-plan-went-poof-into-thin-air. Accessed 13 September 2020.

Edelman, Adam. 2020. Fact check: Ivanka Trump mischaracterizes father's use of Defense Production Act. *NBC News*. Fact check: Ivanka Trump mischaracterizes father's use of Defense Production Act. Accessed 13 September 2020.

Elving, Ron. 2020. Trump opts for gravitas of the oval office as he's in need of a game-changing moment. *NPR*. https://www.npr.org/2019/01/08/683084143/trump-opts-for-gravitas-of-the-oval-office-as-hes-in-need-of-a-game-changing-mom. Accessed 9 September 2020.

Ewing, Philip. 2020. Hospital ship USNS comfort scheduled to sail from New York City. *NPR*. https://www.npr.org/sections/coronavirus-live-updates/2020/04/28/847457974/hospital-ship-usns-comfort-scheduled-to-sail-from-new-york-city. Accessed 12 September 2020.

Falconer, Rebecca. 2020. Trump administration asks Congress for $2.5 billion to fight coronavirus. *Axios*. https://www.axios.com/coronavirus-trump-congress-coronavirus-request-c7ed2f68-1dd9-468c-8f9a-b5bfe7510b3a.html. Accessed 14 September 2020.

Falzone, Debra. 2020. "Like a Bully at the lunchroom": How the Federal Government took control of the PPE pipeline. *Vanity Fair*. https://www.

vanityfair.com/news/2020/05/how-the-federal-government-took-control-of-the-ppe-pipeline. Accessed 12 September 2020.

FP Analytics. 2020. The COVID-19 global response index. *Foreign Policy*. https://globalresponseindex.foreignpolicy.com/. Accessed 14 September 2020.

Ghebreyesus, Tedros Adhanom. 2020. WHO director-general's opening remarks at the media briefing on COVID-19—11 March 2020. *World Health Organization*. https://www.who.int/dg/speeches/detail/who-director-general-s-opening-remarks-at-the-media-briefing-on-covid-19—11-march-2020. Accessed 14 September 2020.

Goodnough, Abby, and Maggie Haberman. 2020. White House rejects C.D.C.'s coronavirus reopening plan. *New York Times*. https://www.nytimes.com/2020/05/07/us/politics/trump-cdc.html. Accessed 14 September 2020.

Gover, Angela R., Shannon B. Harper, and Lynn Langton. 2020. Anti-Asian hate crime during the COVID-19 pandemic: Exploring the reproduction of inequality. *American Journal of Criminal Justice*: 1–21. http://10.1007/s12103-020-09545-1.

Grady, Denise. 2020. Coronavirus test kits sent to states are flawed, C.D.C. says. *New York Times*. https://www.nytimes.com/2020/05/07/us/politics/trump-cdc.html. Accessed 14 September 2020.

Grisales, Claudia, Kelsey Snell, Susan Davis, and Barbara Sprunt. 2020. President Trump Signs $2 trillion coronavirus rescue package into law. *NPR*. https://www.npr.org/2020/03/27/822062909/house-aims-to-send-2-trillion-rescue-package-to-president-to-stem-coronavirus-cr. Accessed 14 September 2020.

Harris, Shane, Greg Miller, Josh Dawsey, and Ellen Nakashima. 2020. U.S. intelligence reports from January and February warned about a likely pandemic. *Washington Post*. https://www.washingtonpost.com/national-security/us-intelligence-reports-from-january-and-february-warned-about-a-likely-pandemic/2020/03/20/299d8cda-6ad5-11ea-b5f1-a5a804158597_story.html. Accessed 14 September 2020.

Hertner, Isabelle, and Alister Miskimmon. 2015. Germany's strategic narrative of the Eurozone crisis. *German Politics and Society* 33: 42–57. https://doi.org/10.3167/gps.2015.330104.

Hogan, Larry, and Gretchen Whitmer. 2020. Larry Hogan and Gretchen Whitmer: What governors need from Washington during this health emergency. *Washington Post*. https://www.washingtonpost.com/opinions/2020/03/30/larry-hogan-gretchen-whitmer-what-governors-need-washington-during-this-health-emergency/. Accessed 14 September 2020.

Imbert, Fred, and Eustance Huang. 2020. Dow falls 350 points Friday to cap the worst week for Wall Street since the financial crisis. *CNBC*. https://

www.cnbc.com/2020/02/27/dow-futures-fall-100-points-after-another-massive-rout-amid-coronavirus-fears.html. Accessed 14 September 2020.

Isenstadt, Alex. 2020. GOP memo urges anti-China assault over coronavirus. *Politico.* https://www.politico.com/news/2020/04/24/gop-memo-anti-china-coronavirus-207244. Accessed 14 September 2020.

Johns Hopkins Coronavirus Resource Center. 2020a. New cases of COVID-19 in world countries. https://coronavirus.jhu.edu/data/new-cases. Accessed 14 September 2020.

Johns Hopkins Coronavirus Resource Center. 2020b. Mortality analysis. https://coronavirus.jhu.edu/data/mortality. Accessed 14 September 2020.

Karni, Annie, and Donald G. McNeil Jr. Trump wants U.S. 'opened up' by Easter, despite health officials' warnings. *New York Times.* https://www.nytimes.com/2020/03/24/us/politics/trump-coronavirus-easter.html. Accessed 14 September 2020.

Keith, Tamara. 2020. A closer look at Trump's coronavirus relief executive actions. *NPR.* https://www.npr.org/2020/08/09/900603827/a-closer-look-at-trumps-coronavirus-relief-executive-orders. Accessed 14 September 2020.

Kenen, Joanna. 2020. End of Trump's social distancing policy spurs fears of virus rebound. *Politico.* https://www.politico.com/news/2020/04/29/end-of-social-distancing-rules-coronavirus-223505. Accessed 14 September 2020.

Kessler, Glenn. 2020. Trump's claim that he imposed the first 'China ban.' *Washington Post*, April 7. https://www.washingtonpost.com/politics/2020/04/07/trumps-claim-that-he-imposed-first-china-ban/. Accessed 14 September 2020.

Klein, Ezra. 2020. Can anything change Americans' minds about Donald Trump? *Vox.* https://www.vox.com/2020/9/2/21409364/trump-approval-rating-2020-election-voters-coronavirus-convention-polls. Accessed 14 September 2020.

Kobokovich, Amanda. 2020. Ventilator stockpiling and availability in the US. *Johns Hopkins Center for Health Security.* https://www.centerforhealthsecurity.org/resources/COVID-19/COVID-19-fact-sheets/200214-VentilatorAvailability-factsheet.pdf. Accessed 14 September 2020.

Kumar, Anita. 2020. Trump says blame China. His supporters are listening. *Politico.* https://www.politico.com/news/2020/05/03/trump-supporters-china-226309. Accessed 14 September 2020.

Lee, Jasmine C., Sarah Mervosh, Yuriria Avila, Barbara Harvey, and Alex Leeds Matthews. 2020. See how all 50 states are reopening (and closing again). *New York Times.* https://www.nytimes.com/interactive/2020/us/states-reopen-map-coronavirus.html. Accessed 14 September 2020.

Lopez, German. 2020a. April was another lost month for Trump's coronavirus response. *Vox*. https://www.vox.com/2020/5/5/21246327/coronavirus-trump-april-lost-month-jeremy-konyndyk. Accessed 14 September 2020.
Lopez, German. 2020b. The 4 plans to end social distancing, explained. *Vox*. https://www.vox.com/2020/4/14/21218074/coronavirus-plans-social-distancing-end-reopen-economy. Accessed 14 September 2020.
Lopez, German. 2020c. What Trump actually proposed in his coronavirus speech. *Vox*. https://www.vox.com/policy-and-politics/2020/3/11/21175953/trump-coronavirus-speech-response-policies. Accessed 14 September 2020.
Martin, Jonathan. 2020. Trump to Governors on ventilators: 'Try getting it yourselves.' *New York Times*, March 16. https://www.nytimes.com/2020/03/16/us/politics/trump-coronavirus-respirators.html.
McDonald, Jessica. 2020. Trump Falsely says COVID-19 surge 'only' due to testing, Misleads on deaths. FactCheck.org, June 25. https://www.factcheck.org/2020/06/trump-falsely-says-covid-19-surge-only-due-to-testing-misleads-on-deaths/. Accessed 14 September 2020.
McEnany, Kayleigh. 2020. Press briefing by press secretary Kayleigh McEnany | 9/9/2020. *The White House*. https://www.whitehouse.gov/briefings-statements/press-briefing-press-secretary-kayleigh-mcenany-9-9-2020/. Accessed 14 September 2020.
Miller, Greg, Josh Dawsey, and Aaron C. Davis. 2020. One final viral infusion: Trump's move to block travel from Europe triggered chaos and a surge of passengers from the outbreak's center. *Washington Post*. https://www.washingtonpost.com/world/national-security/one-final-viral-infusion-trumps-move-to-block-travel-from-europe-triggered-chaos-and-a-surge-of-passengers-from-the-outbreaks-center/2020/05/23/64836a00-962b-11ea-82b4-c8db161ff6e5_story.html. Accessed 14 September 2020.
Millhiser, Ian. 2020. The legal questions surrounding Trump's new executive orders, answered. *Vox*. https://www.vox.com/2020/8/11/21361879/trump-executive-orders-unemployment-benefits-student-loans. Accessed 14 September 2020.
Miskimmon, Alister, Ben O'Loughlin, and Laura Roselle, ed. 2013. *Strategic narratives: Communication power and the new world order*. New York: Routledge. Accessed 14 September 2020.
Mueller III, Robert S. 2019. *The Mueller Report*. Washington Post Edition. Washington, DC: Simon & Schuster. Accessed 14 September 2020.
Nakamura, David. 2020. With 'kung flu,' Trump sparks backlash over racist language—And a rallying cry for supporters. *Washington Post*. https://www.washingtonpost.com/politics/with-kung-flu-trump-sparks-backlash-over-racist-language–and-a-rallying-cry-for-supporters/2020/06/24/485d151e-b620-11ea-aca5-ebb63d27e1ff_story.html. Accessed 14 September 2020.

Office of the Governor of the State of California. 2020. Executive Order N-33-20. https://www.gov.ca.gov/wp-content/uploads/2020/03/3.19.20-attested-EO-N-33-20-COVID-19-HEALTH-ORDER.pdf. Accessed 14 September 2020.

Oprysko, Caitlin. 2020. Fauci: "I have to disagree" with Trump saying U.S. is rounding the corner on coronavirus. *Politico*. https://www.politico.com/news/2020/09/11/fauci-disagree-trump-coronavirus-rounding-corner-412558. Accessed 14 September 2020.

Peters, Cameron. 2020. A detailed timeline of all the ways Trump failed to respond to the coronavirus. *Vox*, June 8. https://www.vox.com/2020/6/8/21242003/trump-failed-coronavirus-response. Accessed 14 September 2020.

Rascoe, Ayesha, and Colin Dwyer. 2020. Trump received intelligence briefings on coronavirus twice in January. *NPR*. https://www.npr.org/sections/coronavirus-live-updates/2020/05/02/849619486/trump-received-intelligence-briefings-on-coronavirus-twice-in-january. Accessed 14 September 2020.

Robertson, Lori. 2020. Trump's snowballing China travel claim. *FactCheck.org*. https://www.factcheck.org/2020/04/trumps-snowballing-china-travel-claim/. Accessed 14 September 2020.

Roubien, Rachel, and Alice Miranda Olstein. 2020. Coronavirus triggers swift bipartisan backlash against Trump. https://www.politico.com/news/2020/02/25/trump-officials-defend-coronavirus-request-117329. Accessed 14 September 2020.

Rupar, Aaron. 2020. Minutes after pledging to not lie, the new White House press secretary lied a whole bunch. *Vox*. https://www.vox.com/2020/5/1/21244463/kayleigh-mcenany-first-press-briefing-lies. Accessed 14 September 2020.

Science News Staff. 2020. The United States leads in coronavirus cases, but not pandemic response. *Science*. https://www.sciencemag.org/news/2020/04/united-states-leads-coronavirus-cases-not-pandemic-response. Accessed 14 September 2020.

Sebenius, Isaac, and James K. Sebenius. 2020. How many needless Covid-19 deaths were caused by delays in responding? Most of them. *STAT*. https://www.statnews.com/2020/06/19/faster-response-prevented-most-us-covid-19-deaths/. Accessed 14 September 2020.

Shear, Michael D., Abby Goodnough, Sheila Kaplan, Sheri Fink, Katie Thomas, and Noah Weiland. 2020. The lost month: How a failure to test blinded the U.S. to Covid-19. *New York Times*. https://www.nytimes.com/2020/03/28/us/testing-coronavirus-pandemic.html. Accessed 14 September 2020.

Sloan, Allan. 2020. The CARES Act Sent You a $1,200 check but Gave Millionaires and Billionaires far more. *ProPublica*. https://www.propublica.org/article/the-cares-act-sent-you-a-1-200-check-but-gave-millionaires-and-billionaires-far-more. Accessed 14 September 2020.

Smith, David. 2020. Trump halts World Health Organization funding over coronavirus "failure." *The Guardian*. https://www.theguardian.com/world/2020/apr/14/coronavirus-trump-halts-funding-to-world-health-organization. Accessed 14 September 2020.

Sommer, Lauren. 2020. Why the warning that coronavirus was on the move in U.S. cities came so late. *NPR*. https://www.npr.org/sections/health-shots/2020/04/24/842025982/why-the-warning-that-coronavirus-was-on-the-move-in-u-s-cities-came-so-late. Accessed 14 September 2020.

Stolberg, Sheryl Gay. 2020. Top U.S. officials told C.D.C. to Soften coronavirus testing guidelines. *New York Times*. https://www.nytimes.com/2020/08/26/us/politics/coronavirus-testing-trump-cdc.html. Accessed 14 September 2020.

Taylor, Derrick Bryson. 2020. A timeline of the coronavirus pandemic. *New York Times*. https://www.nytimes.com/article/coronavirus-timeline.html. Accessed 14 September 2020.

The White House. 2020. 15 days to slow the spread. https://www.whitehouse.gov/articles/15-days-slow-spread/. Accessed 20 October 2020.

Tian, Huaiyu, Yonghong Liu, Yidan Li, Wu Chieh-Hsi, Bin Chen, Moritz U.G. Kraemer, Bingying Li, et al. 2020. An investigation of transmission control measures during the first 50 days of the COVID-19 epidemic in China. *Science* 368: 638–642. https://doi.org/10.1126/science.abb6105.

Tromberg, Bruce J., Tara A. Schwetz, Eliseo J. Pérez-Stable, Richard J. Hodes, Richard P. Woychik, Rick A. Bright, Rachael L. Fleurence, and Francis S. Collins. 2020. Rapid scaling up of Covid-19 diagnostic testing in the United States—The NIH RADx initiative. *New England Journal of Medicine*. https://doi.org/10.1056/nejmsr2022263.

Trump, Donald J. 2020a. @realDonaldTrump (January 29, 2020). *Twitter*. https://twitter.com/realDonaldTrump/status/1222672488934584324. Accessed 14 September 2020.

Trump, Donald J. 2020b. @RealDonaldTrump (February 7, 2020). *Twitter*. https://twitter.com/realDonaldTrump/status/1225728756456808448. Accessed 14 September 2020.

Trump, Donald J. 2020c. @RealDonaldTrump (September 9, 2020). *Twitter*. https://twitter.com/realDonaldTrump/status/1303368656680747008. Accessed 14 September 2020.

Trump, Donald J. 2020d. @RealDonaldTrump (February 24, 2020). *Twitter*. https://twitter.com/realDonaldTrump/status/1232058127740174339. Accessed 14 September 2020.

Trump, Donald J. 2020e. Remarks by President Trump in address to the nation. *The White House*. https://www.whitehouse.gov/briefings-statements/remarks-president-trump-address-nation/. Accessed 14 September 2020.

Trump, Donald J. 2020f. @RealDonaldTrump (March 16, 2020). *Twitter*. https://twitter.com/realDonaldTrump/status/1239685852093169664. Accessed 14 September 2020.

Trump, Donald J. 2020g. Remarks by President Trump in press briefing | April 14. *The White House*. https://www.whitehouse.gov/briefings-statements/remarks-president-trump-press-briefing/. Accessed 14 September 2020.

Trump, Donald J. 2020h. @RealDonaldTrump (March 22, 2020). *Twitter*. https://twitter.com/realDonaldTrump/status/1241935285916782593. Accessed 14 September 2020.

Trump, Donald J. 2020i. @RealDonaldTrump (April 17, 2020—11:25 AM). *Twitter*. https://twitter.com/realDonaldTrump/status/1251169987110330372. Accessed 14 September 2020.

Trump, Donald J. 2020j. @RealDonaldTrump (April 17, 2020—11:21 AM). *Twitter*. https://twitter.com/realDonaldTrump/status/1251168994066944003. Accessed 14 September 2020.

Trump, Donald J. 2020k. @RealDonaldTrump (April 17, 2020—11:22 AM). *Twitter*. https://twitter.com/realDonaldTrump/status/1251169217531056130. Accessed 14 September 2020.

Trump, Donald J. 2020l. Remarks by President Trump at Oklahoma Rally. *Rev*. https://www.rev.com/blog/transcripts/donald-trump-tulsa-oklahoma-rally-speech-transcript. Accessed 14 September 2020.

Trump, Donald J. 2020m. Transcript: Donald Trump's RNC speech. *CNN*. https://www.cnn.com/2020/08/28/politics/donald-trump-speech-transcript/index.html. Accessed 14 September 2020.

Trump, Donald J. 2020n. Remarks by President Trump in Press Briefing | September 10. *The White House*. https://www.whitehouse.gov/briefings-statements/remarks-president-trump-press-briefing-091020/. Accessed 14 September 2020.

Trump, Donald J. 2020o. Remarks by President Trump in press briefing | September 4, 2020. *The White House*. https://www.whitehouse.gov/briefings-statements/remarks-president-trump-press-briefing-september-4-2020/. Accessed 14 September 2020.

Trump, Donald J. 2020p. Transcript: "Fox News Sunday" interview with President Trump. *Fox News*. https://www.foxnews.com/politics/transcript-fox-news-sunday-interview-with-president-trump. Accessed 14 September 2020.

Trump, Donald J. 2020q. @RealDonaldTrump (January 24, 2020). *Twitter*. https://twitter.com/realDonaldTrump/status/1220818115354923009. Accessed 14 September 2020.

Trump, Donald J. 2020r. Remarks by President Trump in State of the Union Address, February 4. https://www.whitehouse.gov/briefings-statements/remarks-president-trump-state-union-address-3/. Accessed 14 September 2020.

Trump, Donald J. 2020s. @RealDonaldTrump (February 26, 2020). *Twitter.* https://twitter.com/realDonaldTrump/status/1232652371832004608. Accessed 14 September 2020.

Trump, Donald J. 2020t. Remarks by President Trump at South Carolina Campaign Rally. *Rev.* https://www.rev.com/blog/transcripts/donald-trump-charleston-south-carolina-rally-transcript-february-28-2020. Accessed 14 September 2020.

Trump, Donald J. 2020u. Remarks by President Trump after tour of the centers for disease control and prevention | Atlanta, GA. *The White House.* https://www.whitehouse.gov/briefings-statements/remarks-president-trump-tour-centers-disease-control-prevention-atlanta-ga/. Accessed 14 September 2020.

Trump, Donald J. 2020v. Remarks by President Trump, Vice President Pence, and members of the coronavirus task force in press briefing | March 19. *The White House.* https://www.whitehouse.gov/briefings-statements/remarks-president-trump-vice-president-pence-members-coronavirus-task-force-press-briefing-6/. Accessed 14 September 2020.

Trump, Donald J. 2020w. Remarks by President Trump, Vice President Pence, and members of the coronavirus task force in press briefing | March 28. *The White House.* https://www.whitehouse.gov/briefings-statements/remarks-president-trump-vice-president-pence-members-coronavirus-task-force-press-briefing-13/. Accessed 14 September 2020.

Trump, Donald J. 2020x. Remarks by President Trump, Vice President Pence, and members of the coronavirus task force in press briefing | March 31. *The White House.* https://www.whitehouse.gov/briefings-statements/remarks-president-trump-vice-president-pence-members-coronavirus-task-force-press-briefing-15/. Accessed 14 September 2020.

Trump, Donald J. 2020y. Remarks by President Trump, Vice President Pence, and members of the coronavirus task force in press briefing | April 7, 2020. *The White House.* https://www.whitehouse.gov/briefings-statements/remarks-president-trump-vice-president-pence-members-coronavirus-task-force-press-briefing-april-7-2020/. Accessed 14 September 2020.

Trump, Donald J. 2020z. Remarks by President Trump, Vice President Pence, and members of the coronavirus task force in press briefing | April 7, 2020. *The White House.* https://it.usembassy.gov/members-of-the-coronavirus-task-force-hold-a-press-briefing-april-7-2020/. Accessed 12 September 2020.

Tyson, Alec. 2020. Republicans remain far less likely than Democrats to view COVID-19 as a major threat to public health. *Pew Research Center.* https://www.pewresearch.org/fact-tank/2020/07/22/republicans-remain-far-less-likely-than-democrats-to-view-covid-19-as-a-major-threat-to-public-health/. Accessed 14 September 2020.

U.S. Bureau of Labor Statistics. 2020. Civilian unemployment rate. *Civilian unemployment rate*. https://www.bls.gov/charts/employment-situation/civilian-unemployment-rate.htm. Accessed 14 September 2020.

US Daily Cumulative Totals. 2020. *The Covid tracking project*. https://covidtracking.com/data/us-daily. Accessed 14 September 2020.

Vazquez, Maegan. 2020. Trump now says he wasn't kidding when he told officials to slow down coronavirus testing, contradicting staff. *CNN*. https://www.cnn.com/2020/06/22/politics/donald-trump-testing-slow-down-response/index.html. Accessed 14 September 2020.

Wells, Chad R., Pratha Sah, Seyed M. Moghadas Abhishek Pandey, Affan Shoukat, Yaning Wang, Zheng Wang, Lauren A. Meyers, Burton H. Singer, and Alison P. Galvani. 2020. Impact of international travel and border control measures on the global spread of the novel 2019 coronavirus outbreak. *Proceedings of the National Academy of Science of the United States of America* 117. http://10.1073/pnas.2002616117.

Wilson, Jason. 2020. The rightwing groups behind wave of protests against Covid-19 restrictions. *The Guardian*. https://www.theguardian.com/world/2020/apr/17/far-right-coronavirus-protests-restrictions. Accessed 14 September 2020.

World Health Organization. 2020. Pneumonia of unknown cause—China. https://www.who.int/csr/don/05-january-2020-pneumonia-of-unkown-cause-china/en/. Accessed 14 September 2020.

Wu, Katherine J. 2020. C.D.C. now says people without covid-19 symptoms do not need testing. *New York Times*. https://www.nytimes.com/2020/08/25/health/covid-19-testing-cdc.html. Accessed 14 September 2020.

Zhou, Li, and Ella Nilsen. 2020. Why Republicans are dragging their feet on more stimulus. *Vox*. https://www.vox.com/2020/8/6/21352939/senate-coronavirus-stimulus-republicans-national-debt. Accessed 14 September 2020.

CHAPTER 14

The Importance of Social Capital in New Zealand's COVID-19 Response

David Fielding and Stephen Knowles

Introduction

New Zealand has the eighteenth lowest death rate (deaths per million population) from COVID-19 of all countries in the world. By October 2020, New Zealand's cumulative death rate was 5.12 per million, compared to 670.23 per million in the United States (US), 656.29 per million in the United Kingdom (UK), 581.15 per million in Sweden and 36.21 per million in Australia (Statista 2020).[1] A key part of New Zealand's fight against COVID-19 was to go into a very strict lockdown when there was only a small number of cases in the country

[1] As can be seen in Fig. 14.1, Australia had a very similar death rate to New Zealand, until Australia experienced a second wave of deaths.

D. Fielding · S. Knowles (✉)
Department of Economics, University of Otago, Dunedin, New Zealand
e-mail: stephen.knowles@otago.ac.nz

D. Fielding
Global Development Institute, University of Manchester, Manchester, United Kingdom

S. Ratuva et al. (eds.), *COVID-19 and Social Protection*,
https://doi.org/10.1007/978-981-16-2948-8_14

and before there were any deaths, a strategy that became known as 'going hard and going early' (Jefferies et al. 2020). Fig. 14.1 illustrates the magnitude of the difference in outcomes between New Zealand and three other English-speaking countries (Australia, the US and the UK), plus two Nordic countries with economies that are often compared to that of New Zealand (Finland and Sweden). The figure shows the weekly moving average of reported COVID-19 deaths per million in each country; the data are taken from the Oxford Coronavirus Government Response Tracker dataset (see www.bsg.ox.ac.uk/research/research-projects/coronavirus-government-response-tracker).

In this chapter, we argue that New Zealand's high levels of social capital contributed to the success of the lockdown, in the sense that the vast majority of the population was happy to adhere to the rules. In a democratic country, restrictions this severe could not have been applied without the broad consent of the public, which requires a high degree of social capital. Our focus is on the link between social capital and adherence to the lockdown, not whether the lockdown was successful in

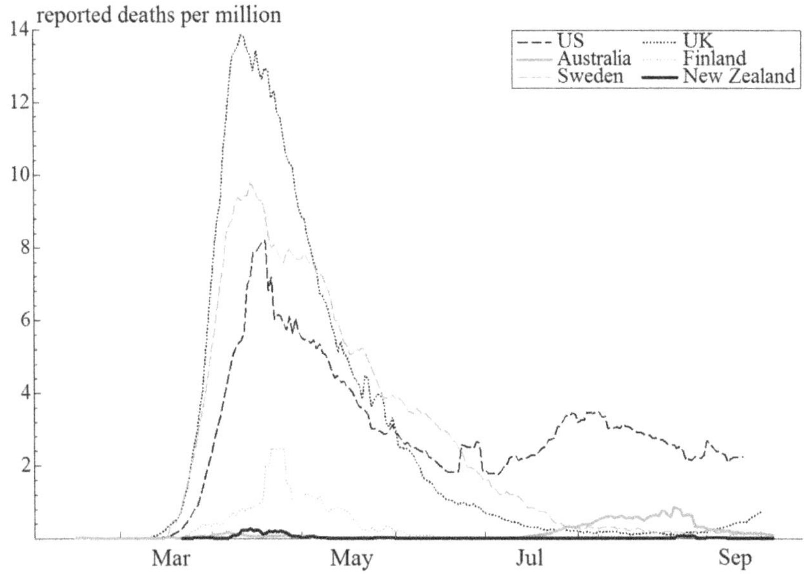

Fig. 14.1 Weekly moving average of reported COVID-19 deaths per million

reducing the spread of the virus. Nobel Prize winning economist Joseph Stiglitz has favourably compared New Zealand's response to COVID-19 with that of the US, noting that New Zealand is a country in which 'there is a high degree of social solidarity–citizens recognize that their behaviour affects others–and trust, including trust in the government' (Stiglitz 2020, p. 17). We make the same point, but in much more detail. We begin by summarising New Zealand's lockdown strategy and then discuss the level of social capital in New Zealand compared with other countries, before discussing how social capital has been important in New Zealand's fight against COVID-19. We then discuss some findings from behavioural and experimental economics that may be suggestive of the conditions under which strict lockdowns become more difficult to enforce, the longer the lockdown lasts.

New Zealand's Lockdown Strategy

New Zealand's first case of COVID-19 was identified on 28 February 2020. On 21 March, the Prime Minister of New Zealand, Jacinda Ardern, announced a four-level alert system and that New Zealand had moved to Alert Level Two. On 23 March, she announced New Zealand had moved to Alert Level Three and would be at Alert Level Four from 26 March.[2] New Zealand remained at Level Four for over a month, moving down to Alert Level Three on 28 April and then to Alert Level Two on 14 May. On 9 June, the country moved down to Alert Level One, remaining at that level until August. New Zealand had no new reported cases of community transmission of COVID-19 between the end of May and 11 August, a period of 102 days. On 11 August, four cases of community transmission of COVID-19 were reported in Auckland. Auckland moved to Level Three at noon the following day and later moved back down the levels, eventually returning to Level One on 8 October. The rest of the country moved to Alert Level Two on 12 August, before returning to Alert Level One on 22 September. Our main focus is on New Zealand's experience during the first period of lockdown, that which occurred between March and June. We refer to this as the 'original lockdown'.

[2] Strictly speaking, New Zealand moved to Alert Level Four at 11:59 p.m on 25 March. In cases where a move to a new level occurred at 11:59 p.m, we report this as moving to the Alert Level the following day.

Level Four lockdown was strict. Schools, universities and non-essential businesses were all closed. People were required to remain at home, unless they were exercising, visiting the supermarket or seeking medical attention. Exercise was required to be taken near your own home. The main change at Alert Level Three was that some additional businesses were allowed to open, children of essential workers could return to school and takeaway meals could be purchased from restaurants and fast-food outlets. Rather than being confined to their own household, people could interact with one other household. However, for much of the population Level Three felt much like Level Four, with one opposition politician describing Level Three as 'a lot like Level Four with KFC [takeaways]' (Newshub 2020a).

Fig. 14.2 shows how strict New Zealand's lockdown was compared to the other five countries in Fig. 14.1. The data are from the Oxford Coronavirus Government Response Tracker (OxCGRT), and the index is based on 17 indicators, such as school closures and travel restrictions. In cases where the restrictions differ across regions in a country, the data are for the region with the strictest restrictions. As can be seen from the figure,

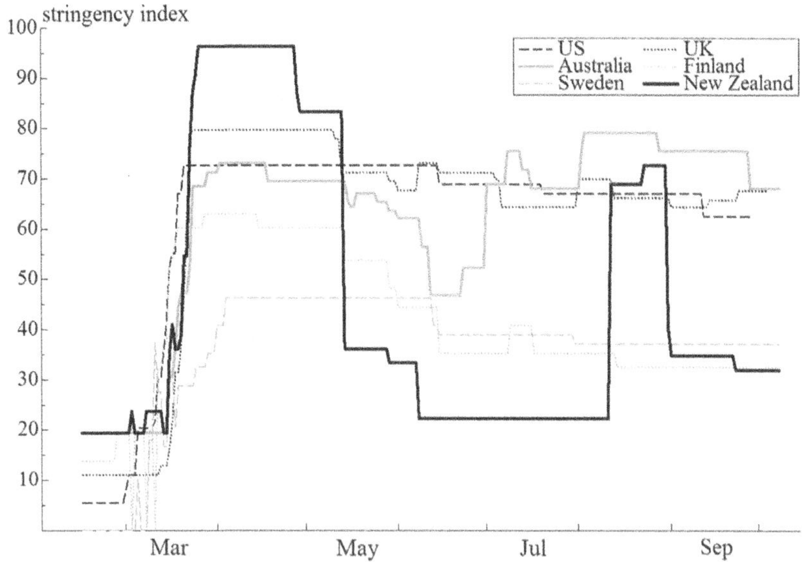

Fig. 14.2 The OxCGRT stringency index

New Zealand's Alert Level Four restrictions were stricter than any of the other countries included in the figure, but once New Zealand returned to Alert Level One, people enjoyed significantly more freedom than the other countries shown in the figure.

Defining and Measuring Social Capital with Reference to New Zealand

As argued in the introduction, we suggest that the high levels of compliance with the requirements of Alert Level Four may be due in part to New Zealand's high level of social capital. Social capital is a notoriously difficult term to pin down, as it can mean different things to different people and definitions have changed somewhat over time (Knowles 2007). In a seminal contribution to the literature, Putnam et al. (1993, p. 167) defined social capital as 'features of social organization, such as trust, norms, and networks that can improve the efficiency of society'. At least one of the notions of trust, norms and networks feature in most definitions of social capital (see Coleman 1998; Putnam 2000; Sobel 2002).

In recent years, the New Zealand Treasury has developed a *Living Standards Framework* to measure wellbeing and to inform policy decisions in New Zealand. This framework includes 12 domains (or measures) of wellbeing and four capital stocks: financial and physical capital, human capital, natural capital and social capital. The focus of our discussion is on social capital. The Treasury (2020) has defined social capital as "[t]he norms, rules and institutions that influence the way in which people live and work together and experience a sense of belonging. [Social capital] includes trust, reciprocity, the rule of law, cultural and community identity, traditions and customs, common values and interests". This is a broader definition than many, but importantly it includes the concepts of trust and cooperation that are central to most definitions of social capital.

Not only is social capital difficult to define, it is also difficult to measure. One commonly used proxy is the extent to which people trust others in their society. Data on trust in New Zealand are collected every two years in the *New Zealand General Social Survey* (GSS). Respondents are asked on a ten-point scale how much trust they place in different groups of people. In 2018/2019 (the data were collected between April 2018 and March 2019), the average score for trust in other New Zealanders was 6.9/10. The average score for trust in parliament was 5.8, for trust in the police was 7.9 and for trust in the health system was 6.9 (StatsNZ 2020).

How does the level of trust in New Zealand compare with other countries? Nationally comparable data has been collected at different points in time in the World Values Survey (Inglehart et al. 2014). The World Values Survey asks people hundreds of questions about their attitudes and beliefs, including a question about generalised trust. This question asks people whether they believe that generally speaking most people can be trusted. The proportion of people who answer 'yes' is a proxy for the level of generalised trust in a country.

Table 14.1 shows the level of generalised trust from the World Values Survey, for a selection of countries. The number reported for each country is that which is most recently available. Not all countries for which data are available are reported in the table, but the highest scoring six countries are all shown, with New Zealand coming in at number six. Not shown in the table is that New Zealand's trust score has been increasing over time: 48 in 1998, 51 in 2009 and 56 in 2014. Also of interest is that the Northern European countries of Norway, the Netherlands and Sweden have the highest levels of generalised trust. Many

Table 14.1 Generalised trust in different countries

Country	*Year*	*Trust %*
Norway	2009	74
Netherlands	2014	66
Sweden	2014	64
China	2014	62
Finland	2009	57
New Zealand	*2014*	*56*
Australia	2014	54
Vietnam	2014	51
US	2014	38
United Kingdom	2009	30
South Africa	2014	24
Argentina	2014	23
Mali	2009	17
Malaysia	2014	9
Zimbabwe	2014	7
Colombia	2014	4
Philippines	2014	3

Source Ortiz-Ospina and Roser (2020)

countries in the world have very low levels of generalised trust, with examples from the table including the Philippines (3%), Colombia (4%) and Zimbabwe (7%). In summary, New Zealand has high levels of generalised trust compared to many other countries, and this has been increasing over time.

Readers may be concerned that when answering survey questions about trust, people may not answer the questions truthfully or that trust may mean different things to different people. In other words, the survey data may be unreliable. However, in support of the reliability of the generalised trust data from the World Values Survey, Knack and Keefer (1997) report the results of an experiment carried out by the *Readers' Digest* magazine. In this experiment, wallets were dropped in a number of different countries, with the wallets containing the name and address of the purported owner, along with the equivalent of $50 in cash. The number of wallets returned in each country was positively correlated with the World Values Survey data on generalised trust, which Knack and Keefer argue should give us some confidence in the reliability of the World Values Survey data.[3]

So far, we have focused on generalised trust; trust in government is also an important component of social capital. The Organisation for Economic Cooperation and Development (OECD) publishes data on trust in different groups for OECD member countries, with the data drawn from the Gallup World Poll. Data on trust in the government for OECD countries, for the period 2016–2018, are presented in Table 14.2. The data show the percentage of the population answering 'yes' when asked if they have confidence in the government. New Zealand has the sixth highest level of trust in the government in the OECD, with 60.7% of the population trusting the government. Trust in government ranges from a high of 82% in Chile to a low of 14% in Greece. The table also reports trust in the police for the countries for which the data are available. Note that these data are measured on a 1 to 10 scale. The data show that trust in the police is also very high in New Zealand compared to other countries.

The data from Tables 14.1 and 14.2 show that compared to many other countries, New Zealanders have a high degree of trust in the government and in each other. In fact, the only countries to rank higher

[3] For further evidence of a positive correlation between experimental measures of trust and survey measures of trust, see Etang et al. (2012).

Table 14.2 Trust in government in OECD countries

Country	*Trust in government*	*Trust in police*
Chile	82.00	
Luxembourg	72.67	6.1
Norway	68.67	7.5
Netherlands	63.33	6.6
Canada	62.67	
New Zealand	*60.67*	*7.7*
Ireland	59.67	6.9
Germany	58.67	6.4
Turkey	56.00	6.5
Denmark	55.67	7.9
Finland	55.00	8.2
Russia	53.33	
Sweden	51.33	7.1
South Africa	47.33	
Australia	45.67	
Portugal	45.67	5.4
Austria	45.33	7.2
Belgium	43.67	6.1
Poland	43.67	5.2
United Kingdom	42.33	6.4
Israel	41.67	7.7
Czech Republic	39.33	4.9
Estonia	39.00	6.0
Costa Rica	39.00	
Japan	38.33	
Iceland	36.50	
Hungary	35.67	5.7
Slovakia	34.67	4.4
France	34.33	5.6
US	33.33	
South Korea	33.00	
Lithuania	31.00	6.0
Spain	28.67	5.4
Mexico	27.67	
Chile	26.67	7.4
Latvia	26.00	5.8
Colombia	25.00	
Slovenia	24.33	5.5
Italy	22.67	5.8
Brazil	20.00	
Greece	14.33	5.0

Source OECD (2020)

than New Zealand for both measures are Norway and the Netherlands. If we also focus on trust in the police, New Zealand does slightly better than both Norway and the Netherlands.

Social Capital and New Zealand's Lockdown

There is evidence that social capital, proxied by generalised trust, is positively correlated with economic growth (see Knack and Keefer 1997), health outcomes (see Knowles and Owen 2010; Islam et al. 2006) and engagement with the political process (see Putnam et al. 1993). We argue that social capital has also been important in New Zealand's response to COVID-19. Keeping a country in lockdown, in a democratic country at least, requires high levels of social capital. The police may have a role to play in enforcing the rules, but if people are determined to avoid the requirements of lockdown, the police would be extremely overstretched. To keep to the plan requires that people act cooperatively, not only to protect their own health, but by staying at home to protect the health of others. People need to have high levels of trust not only in their government, but perhaps more importantly in their fellow citizens. As we have shown, New Zealanders have high levels of trust in each other and in the government.

Public support for the government's COVID-19 response appeared to increase over time during the original lockdown. A Colmar Brunton poll taken in mid-April showed 87% support for the government's response to the crisis, which was higher than 84% in a poll two weeks earlier (The Spinoff 2020). A further Colmar Brunton poll taken towards the end of May showed 92% of New Zealanders approved of the government's handling of the crisis (TVNZ 2020). The poll taken in mid-April also found that 93% of New Zealanders said they were abiding by the lockdown restrictions, with only 6% describing the behaviour of others as poor (compared to 27% two weeks earlier). The percentage of New Zealanders approving of the government's response was higher in mid-April than in other countries; for example, approval was 74% in Canada, 43% in France, 71% in Italy, 69% in Great Britain and 46% in the US (The Spinoff 2020).

In New Zealand, compliance with the requirements of Level Four was high, with only 5,857 breaches of the Civil Defence Emergency and Health Acts reported during Level Four (Newshub 2020b). New Zealand has not witnessed the protests that have occurred in some other countries. Although there were some protests in Auckland when Auckland went to Level Three in August, there were no large-scale organised protests during the original lockdown.

Compliance with lockdown restrictions can be measured with data compiled by Google, based on what people's mobile phones show about their movements, on the extent to which people stayed at home. Fig. 14.3 presents data on the extent to which people's movements fell, compared to a historical average for the same day in the year over previous years. The data are a weekly moving average of the percentage deviation from historical average mobility around five types of location: grocery and pharmacy stores, other stores and recreation centres, transit stations, workplaces and residential homes. The data are graphed for both New Zealand and a selection of other countries. If people generally comply with restrictions, then since New Zealand had the strictest lockdown, we would expect New Zealand to have the largest reduction in mobility, and this is what the figure shows. During the early stages of Alert Level Four, mobility fell by more than half, with mobility increasing as the restrictions were eased. The country with the second-highest stringency index for

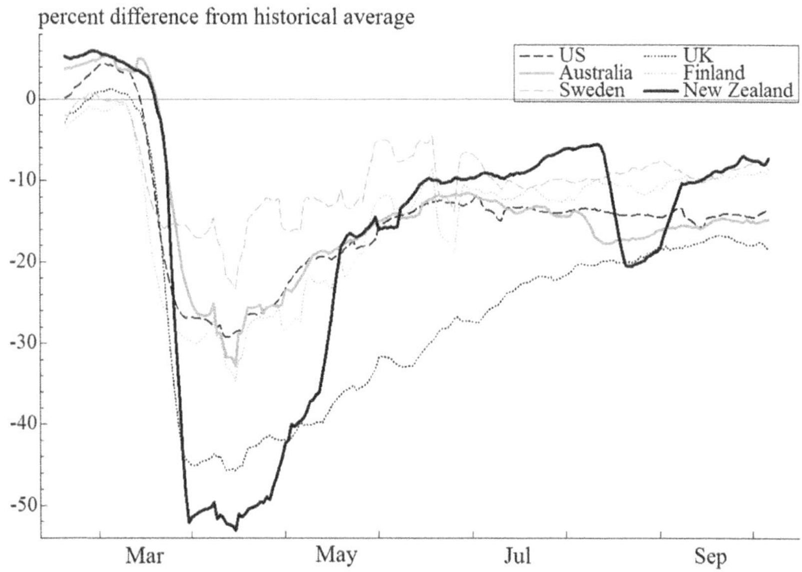

Fig. 14.3 Weekly moving averages of percentage deviations from historical average mobility levels

April in Fig. 14.1 (the UK) also registered the second-highest reduction in mobility in Fig. 14.2. Sweden, a country which introduced minimal restrictions, had only a small drop in mobility. Comparing Figs. 14.2 with 14.3 for April suggests that the reduction in mobility was generally proportional to the severity of the lockdown requirements, with New Zealand having the strictest lockdown. This pattern suggests substantial compliance with the lockdown rules, at least in countries with relatively strict rules, and we suggest that compliance in New Zealand was high due to high levels of social capital.

Sweden is another high-trust country, but one that adopted a very different approach to fighting COVID-19 than did New Zealand. The Swedish government took the view that because of the high levels of trust in Sweden, people could be trusted to make wise decisions about protecting themselves and others from COVID-19, without the need to go into lockdown. Although large-scale events were prohibited and bars and restaurants could provide table service only, private businesses were largely able to stay open. People were encouraged to stay at home if unwell and to limit social interaction where possible, but there were no strict rules around this (Anderson et al. 2020). As Fig. 14.2 shows, mobility did fall in Sweden, but not by as much as countries that had some form of lockdown. As noted in the introduction, as of October 2020 Sweden's death rate is much higher than New Zealand's (581.15 per million compared to 5.12 per million). New Zealand and Sweden represent two very different approaches in countries where social capital has been known to be high. Note also that the two countries with a higher trust ranking than New Zealand in Tables 14.1 and 14.2, the Netherlands and Norway, both have smaller values of the stringency index than New Zealand in late March and April: a value of 80 for the two European countries, compared with a value of 95 for New Zealand. The percentage deviations in mobility for the Netherlands and Norway in April are correspondingly small: around 30% for the Netherlands and 40% for Norway, compared with around 50% for New Zealand.

It is also possible to conduct a more formal statistical analysis of the association between lockdown severity and mobility using data from a wider range of countries, but such an exercise is beyond the scope of this chapter. We do not claim that the relationship between the severity of lockdown restrictions, changes in behaviour and changes in the incidence of infectious disease is a simple one. For example, over May–July, mobility in Australia was almost as high as in New Zealand, despite the fact that Australian restrictions were more severe.

Lessons from Behavioural Economics

We now turn our attention to some lessons from behavioural economics as to what might have happened to compliance if the lockdown had continued for longer. The propensity of people in a society to observe social norms, either in following lockdown rules or in contributing to charitable activities, could be driven by a number of underlying behaviours that come under the heading of social capital. For the last three decades or so, economists have been using laboratory experiments to investigate a number of these behaviours, including (i) the inclination to cooperate and (ii) generosity. The inclination to cooperate has been explored through 'public goods games' in which a small group of individuals is given a collective task generating a collective reward, and the income of each individual depends not only on their own effort, but also on the effort of others; see Chaudhuri (2011). The rules of the game are constructed so that the individually rational, selfish strategy is to 'free ride', that is, to avoid making any effort, as long as you can get away with it. The propensity for generosity is explored through variations on the 'Dictator Game' in which individuals (or sometimes groups of people) must allocate a certain sum of money between themselves and another individual (or group); see Engel (2011).

Although experimental behaviour varies according to the characteristics of the participants, the specific rules of the game and the way in which the game is framed, there are some robust general results. Firstly, most public goods game participants are not natural free-riders, but 'conditional cooperators': they start out by making an effort and continue like this as long as they see others also making an effort. This may explain why there was an increase in the number of breaches the longer the original lockdown continued; when people see evidence of others not keeping the rules, they are less likely to keep the rules themselves. Secondly, most Dictator Game participants are not completely selfish: they will allocate at least some amount of money to others. But thirdly, there is almost always a substantial minority of public goods game participants who free ride, and a substantial minority of Dictator Game participants who are completely selfish.

There is also evidence that most people are hard-wired to punish free-riding and selfishness, and that achieving cooperation depends at least as much on the threat of punishment as it does on instinctive good will or generosity. The propensity to punish free-riding is connected to a sense of fairness that is observed in one form or another in a wide range of human societies, and also in other species, although there is variation in the propensity to punish across different cultures. See Oosterbeek et al. (2004), Gabay et al. (2014) and Brosnan and De Waal (2014). Punishment can take a number of forms, but even verbal censure appears to be effective in some settings (Ellingsen and Johannesson 2008). Conditional cooperation may be motivated by a sense of fairness, and the fact that New Zealanders have been prepared to report breaches by others is evidence of the propensity to punish free-riding and enforce fairness norms.

What factors influence the levels of generosity and fairness in countries like New Zealand, especially in a time of crisis? First of all, experiments indicate that leading by example—the public demonstration of generosity or cooperation by those in a position to lead—generates higher levels of cooperation. Moreover, even in the absence of a visible example, appropriate verbal encouragement by leaders can stimulate cooperative behaviour. The catch is that this only works if the leader is a human being and not a machine, so having political leaders who can demonstrate a credible degree of humanity will be an advantage. Finally, cooperation is more common in groups that have formed voluntarily and that can choose their own leaders. New Zealand is a democracy with an unusually large number of both immigrants and emigrants, so an unusually large fraction of people in New Zealand have chosen to be here.

A common feature of public goods game experiments is that when the game is repeated, the level of cooperation between participants tends to decline over time (Ledyard 1995). Neugebauer et al. (2009) present experimental evidence that suggests that this phenomenon is a consequence of the conditional cooperation described above. Among conditional cooperators, non-cooperative behaviour is infectious, and in many situations, the corresponding R-value is greater than one. In the context of a pandemic, this means that the epidemiological R-value can increase over time, even if nothing else changes, which makes the case for 'going hard and going early' even stronger. The longevity of cooperative behaviour during the COVID-19 pandemic has not been tested in New Zealand, because severe lockdown restrictions were introduced before the prevalence of the disease was very high. In other countries, there was either no severe lockdown or a severe lockdown was introduced only after prevalence was quite high. This meant that in New Zealand—but not elsewhere—restrictions could be lifted before there was any possibility of behaviour becoming less cooperative. In contrast, Australia has had to maintain lockdown restrictions for longer: the value of the Australian stringency index over July–September was slightly higher than it was in April (see Fig. 14.2). Nevertheless, Australian mobility was *higher* over July–September than it was in April (see Fig. 14.3). This suggests that compliance with the Australian restrictions might be declining over time, which is consistent with the evidence from behavioural economics.

Conclusion

In summary, New Zealand is fortunate in having high levels of trust, both in the government and in fellow citizens compared to other countries. New Zealand's original lockdown was one of the strictest in the world, but as we have shown levels of compliance were high, and the level of public support for the measures taken by the government was extremely high. This high level of compliance may well be due to the high level of social capital in New Zealand. Many of the countries with levels of trust similar to those in New Zealand did not impose such severe restrictions, so the trust was not tested as much. However, lessons from experimental economics suggest that when people observe lower levels of compliance by others, they are less likely to comply themselves. If New Zealand's lockdown had continued for longer, it is possible compliance would have become less common, as seems to be the case in Australia. As New Zealanders became aware that some others were not sticking to the rules, they may have been less likely to stick to the rules themselves.

References

Andersen, Asger L., Emil T. Hansen, Niels Johannesen and Adam Sheridan. 2020. Pandemic, shutdown and consumer spending: Lessons from Scandinavian policy responses to COVID-19, Working Paper, arXiv:2005.04630v1.

Brosnan, Sarah F. and Frans B. M. de Waal. 2014. Evolution of responses to (un)fairness. *Science* 346 (6207): 1251776.

Chaudhuri, Ananish. 2011. Sustaining cooperation in laboratory public goods experiments: A selective survey of the literature. *Experimental Economics* 14 (1): 47–83.

Coleman, James S. 1998. Social capital in the creation of human capital. *American Journal of Sociology* 94: 95–120.

Ellingsen, Tore, and Magnus Johannesson. 2008. Anticipated verbal feedback induces altruistic behavior. *Evolution and Human Behavior* 29 (2): 100–105.

Engel, Christoph. 2011. Dictator games: A meta study. *Experimental Economics* 14 (4): 583–610.

Etang, Alvin, David Fielding, and Stephen Knowles. 2012. Are survey measures of trust correlated with experimental trust? Evidence from Cameroon. *Journal of Development Studies* 48 (12): 1813–1827.

Gabay, Anthony S., Joaquim Radua, Matthew J. Kempton and Mitul A. Mehta. 2014. The Ultimatum Game and the brain: A meta-analysis of neuroimaging studies. *Neuroscience and Biobehavioral Reviews* 47: 549-558.

Inglehart, Ronald, Christian Haerpfer, Alejandro Moreno, Christian Welzel, Kseniya Kizilova, Jaime Diez-Medrano, Marta Lagos, Pippa Norris, Eduard Ponarin and Bi Puranen et al. (eds.). 2014. World values survey: All rounds—Country-pooled datafile version. https://www.worldvaluessurvey.org/WVS DocumentationWVL.jsp. Madrid: JD Systems Institute.

Islam, M. K., Juan Merlo, Ichiro Kawachi, Martin Lindstrom and Ulf-G. Gerdtham. 2006. Social capital and health: Does egalitarianism matter? A literature review. *International Journal for Equity in Health* 5 (3): 1–28.

Jefferies, Sarah, Nigel French, Charlotte Gilkinson, Giles Graham, Virginia Hope, Jonathan Marshall, Caroline McElnay, Andrea McNeill, Petra Muellner, Shevaun Paine, Namrata Prasad, Julia Scott, Jillian Sherwood, Laing Yang and Patricia Priest. 2020. COVID-19 in New Zealand and the impact of the national response: A descriptive epidemiological study. *The Lancet Public Health* 5 (11): e612e623. https://www.sciencedirect.com/science/article/pii/S2468266720302255. Accessed 16 November 2020.

Knack, Stephen, and Philip Keefer. 1997. Does social capital have an economic payoff? A cross-country investigation. *Quarterly Journal of Economics* 112: 1251–1288.

Knowles, Stephen. 2007. Is social capital part of the institutions continuum and is it a deep determinant of development? In *Advancing Development: Core Themes in Global Economics*, ed. George Mavratos and Anthony Shorrocks, 197–223. London: Palgrave Macmillan.

Knowles, Stephen, and P. Dorian Owen. 2010. Which institutions are good for your health? The deep determinants of comparative cross-country health status. *Journal of Development Studies* 46 (4): 701–723.

Ledyard, John O. 1995. Public goods: A survey of experimental research. In *The handbook of experimental economics*, eds. John H. Kagel and Alvin E. Roth, Princeton, NJ: Princeton University Press.

Neugebauer, Tibor, Javier Perote, Ulrich Schmidt, and Malte Loos. 2009. Selfish-biased conditional cooperation: On the decline of contributions in repeated public goods experiments. *Journal of Economic Psychology* 30 (1): 52–60.

Newshub. 2020a. Coronavirus: Alert level 3 'a lot like level 4 but with KFC'—Judith Collins. https://www.newshub.co.nz/home/politics/2020/04/coronavirus-alert-level-3-a-lot-like-level-4-but-with-kfc-judith-collins.html. Accessed 21 October 2020.

Newshub. 2020b. Coronavirus: Worst districts for lockdown breaches revealed by police. https://www.newshub.co.nz/home/new-zealand/2020/04/coronavirus-worst-districts-for-lockdown-breaches-revealed-by-police.html. Accessed 21 October 2021.

OECD. 2020. How's life, OECD iLibrary. https://doi.org/10.1787/888934083050. Accessed 21 October 2020.

Oosterbeek, Hessel, Randolph Sloof, and Gijs Van De Kuilen. 2004. Cultural differences in ultimatum game experiments: Evidence from a meta-analysis. *Experimental Economics* 7 (2): 171–188.

Ortiz-Ospina, Esteban and Max Roser. 2020. Our world in data: Trust. https://ourworldindata.org/trust. Accessed 21 October 2020.

Putnam, Robert D., Robert Leonardi and Raffaella Y. Nanetti. 1993. *Making democracy work: Civic traditions in modern Italy*. New Jersey: Princeton University Press.

Putnam, Robert D. 2000. *Bowling alone*. New York: Simon and Schuster.

Sobel, Joel. 2002. Can we trust social capital? *Journal of Economic Literature* 40: 139–154.

Statista. 2020. Coronavirus (COVID-19) deaths worldwide per one million population as of October 20, 2020, by country. https://www.statista.com/statistics/1104709/coronavirus-deaths-worldwide-per-million-inhabitants/. Accessed 21 October 2020.

StatsNZ. 2020. Wellbeing statistics: 2018. https://www.stats.govt.nz/information-releases/wellbeing-statistics-2018. Accessed 21 October 2020.

Stiglitz, Joseph. 2020. Conquering the great divide. *Finance and Development*, September 2020: 17–19.

The Spinoff. 2020. Public backing for NZ COVID-19 response rises to 87%—New poll. https://thespinoff.co.nz/politics/23-04-2020/public-backing-for-nz-government-covid-19-response-rises-to-87-new-poll/. Accessed 21 October 2020.

The Treasury. 2020. Our living standards framework. https://treasury.govt.nz/information-and-services/nz-economy/higher-living-standards/our-living-standards-framework. Accessed 21 October 2020.

TVNZ. (2020). Kiwis overwhelmingly agree Government responded appropriately to COVID-19—1 NEWS poll. https://www.tvnz.co.nz/one-news/new-zealand/kiwis-overwhelmingly-agree-government-responded-appropriately-covid-19-1-news-poll. Accessed 21 October 2020.

CHAPTER 15

Vulnerability of Children in Fiji: The Impact of COVID-19

Litea Meo-Sewabu

This chapter focuses on vulnerability of children specifically related to the impact of COVID-19 in Fiji. Child protection literature emphasises the fact that children by nature are considered a vulnerable group based on a number of factors including cognitive reasoning. Harbach (2019) states that children are "unable to provide for their physical and material needs" (p. 493). Harbach adds that "they are at risk of harm because of the way they think, process and make decisions" (p. 493). In addition, their dependence on adults and their socialization and development within and through different social institutions adds to the risks and their vulnerability to violence, abuse and exploitation.

Research across the Pacific and in Fiji has discussed vulnerabilities of children and the protection that will be explained in this chapter. This chapter first outlines the dynamics of family demographics and the cultural setting that contributes to these vulnerabilities, and then it looks at how these vulnerabilities have been exacerbated in the face of COVID-19.

L. Meo-Sewabu (✉)
The University of the South Pacific, Suva, Fiji
e-mail: litea.meosewabu@usp.ac.fj

S. Ratuva et al. (eds.), *COVID-19 and Social Protection*,
https://doi.org/10.1007/978-981-16-2948-8_15

The chapter attempts to answer two key questions. First, what makes children so vulnerable in the Fiji context? What factors contribute to this and why? The second key question asks; what are the social protection issues for children in Fiji? Both questions will then be addressed in the context of COVID-19.

Background

Fiji has two dominant cultures, the i'Taukei (Indigenous Fijians) and the Indo-Fijians, who are both politically referred to a Fijians. Children in both cultures learn to respect authority from such a young age, and hence they are socialized not to question or speak back to authority and not to question seniority. This traditional culture teaches children to become respectful and to learn the ways of being within a traditional setting. Within these settings, children beginning from such a young age also have roles including household tasks that are pertinent in contributing to the wellbeing of a family, extended family and community (Ravuvu 1983; 1987; Schofield 2007). Within the traditional iTaukei context, raising the child is the role not only of the biological parents, but also the maternal and paternal links of the parents, which reinforces a child's moulding process to behave and act in a certain way. The parent's relatives then have just as much a right as the biological parents to teach, mould as well as discipline the child accordingly. This indirectly leaves the child at such a vulnerable stage where they cannot question authority nor raise any concerns or be protected from numerous elements that they can be exposed to with and by those that are supposed to protect them.

The consequences for children not following the norms brings about forms of punishment that can be violent, often victimizing the child (Plange 2002; Vakaoti et al. 2002; Save the Children 2006; Vakaoti and Finekaso 2002). In addition, in both cultures the "Girl Child" is socialized and expected to carry out definitive roles within their families and community, often resulting in forms of discipline otherwise (Save the Children 2006).

In summary, the background information on how children in both cultures are socialized already creates the potential for vulnerabilities. The global pandemic compounded these vulnerabilities and either triggered or worsened conditions for already vulnerable children which will be explained in this chapter.

Demography

There are 322 islands that make up the Fiji Islands; 110 of these islands are inhabited. Fiji is part of the Melanesian group of islands in the Pacific Ocean and is classified as an upper-middle income developing country. According to the 2017 census, Fiji's population was 884, 887 (Bureau of Statistics, Fiji 2017a). Fiji consists of i'Taukei (Indigenous Fijians) (57%) and of Fijians of Indian descent (38%), with other minority groups of Pacific Islanders, mixed race, Chinese and Europeans making up the remaining demographical breakdown. The 2017 census also highlighted that 44.1% lived in rural areas, with an increase in population in the towns and cities. With the urban drift happening since the 1980s, the main city Suva and its peri-urban centres such as the Suva-Nausori corridor, Lami, Vatuwaqa and Raiwaqa have grown astronomically, with many densely populated squatter settlements (Bureau of Statistics, Fiji 2017b).

The census also reiterates that Fiji has a youthful population, with 68% of the population aged less than 40 years. Adolescents aged 10–24 years make up about 26% of the population, estimated at 227,300 887 (Bureau of Statistics, Fiji 2017a). In addition, teenage pregnancy is high, with approximately 6% of births to adolescents aged less than 18 years.

According to the Fiji Census, the largest number of children lived in the Ba and Naitasiri provinces; 10% and 7%, respectively. Ba is the most populous province and consists of the areas of Ba, Magodro, Nadi, Nawaka, Tavua, Vuda, Vitogo, Lautoka city and the Yasawa islands (Bureau of Statistics, Fiji 2017b).

According to a United Nations International Children's Emergency Fund (UNICEF) study, international data shows that the average household size is about two to four persons, whereas Fiji data shows that average households in Fiji have about 5–10 or more persons residing in a household (UNICEF 2007). The relatively high number of people under one household presents other vulnerabilities for children that potentially became more overwhelming in the face of COVID-19 and that may have increased vulnerability of children exponentially during the lockdown period.

In addition to understanding the demographics in Fiji, it is also important to note the cultural factor of the Vanua and the family web provides the opportunity for perpetrators to cause harm to already vulnerable children. In addition, security of children during the lockdown period was questionable as news coverage in the local media indicated the increase in violence against children and exposure to harm that were further compounded by COVID-19.

The Vanua and the Family Web

Vanua within the Fijian worldview underpins the Fijian ways of being. Ravuvu (1987) explains that culturally:

> the word vanua (land) embodies the values and beliefs which people of a particular locality have in common. It includes their philosophy of living and their beliefs about life in this world and in their supernatural world … for to live well in the world one has to live according to the vanua beliefs and values. (pp. 14–15)

Reference to health and wellbeing is very much underpinned by these worlds of the natural and the supernatural. Nabobo-Baba (2006) states further that there is a strong link between custom, culture and epistemology. She emphasized that a Fijian worldview is based on three related dimensions: *lagi* (the heavens), *vuravura* (the earth) and *bulu* (the underworld or spirit world).

As discussed earlier, the socializing and discipline of children is not limited to the biological parents alone, but is also the role of the extended family. The extended family roles are part of the social norms expected within the Vanua. The belief is that not honouring nor participating in these roles has implications in the supernatural world and therefore is not to be taken lightly (Nabobo-Baba 2006).

The child also understands as a result of their socialization that there are multiple authority figures within their household and questioning these authorities has consequences. Therefore, they are often in a very vulnerable environment, viewed however within the Vanua as a norm to show respect for seniority and their elders.

Based on these facts of multiple authority figures and not questioning authority, children are then often positioned in situations where perpetrators can abuse a child and the child is not protected, hence their security is breached by those within their extended family.

In the traditional Vanua setting, this system would often protect them from vulnerabilities, however as the world has become globalised, exposure to other media sources as well as the disruption of the Vanua values and belief systems by outside forces has left children in an even more vulnerable state. These Vanua values and belief systems are further challenged by children entering institutions such as school, sports and exposure to other worldviews that often come into conflict with how they have been socialized. This presents a dilemma for children when questioning opposing views that can disrupt their ways of being within the Vanua. Hence, the extended family web that assumes the role of protecting the child also exposes the child to more vulnerable consequences when questioning views or going against the cultural norms.

The extended family web also differs in the Fiji context, with international studies showing that about 25% of perpetrators are known to the victims, whereas a recent study in Fiji indicated that about 41% of perpetrators are family members, with more than 50% known to the child (Ministry of Women, Children and Poverty Alleviation 2020). This illustrates that while the family web within the Vanua is supposed to protect children, on the flip side it also provides the opportunity for perpetrators, who in the face of COVID-19 are multiplied as the extended family web is required to stay within a confined space for prolonged periods during lockdown. With the implications stated in terms of socialization within the two cultures, the demographics of households in Fiji and the Vanua and family web issues, what then does this mean in terms of vulnerability of children in Fiji in the face of COVID-19?

VULNERABILITYOF CHILDREN AND COVID-19

To begin this section, I will first define the child and unpack the forms of abuse that children can experience, before exploring the vulnerability of children in the context of COVID-19. A child is defined by the United Nations Convention on the Rights of the Child (UNCRC 1989) as "any human being under the age of 18 years" (1999). Violence against children is defined as, "The intentional use of physical force or power, threatened or actual, against a child by an individual or group that either results in or has a likelihood of resulting in actual or potential harm to the child's health, survival, development and dignity". This includes "all forms of psychological and emotional ill-treatment, sexual abuse, neglect and exploitation, injury, death, psychological harm, mal-development or deprivation" (WHO 2002, p. 5; also see Etienne G. Krug et al. 2002).

The Division of Violence Prevention at the National Centre for Injury Prevention (CDC 2020) has identified four common forms of child abuse as follows:

Physical abuse: This is the application of physical force, which includes hitting, kicking, shaking, burning and other acts or threats of the use of force against a child.

Sexual abuse: This entails seducing, inducing or coercing a child to engage in sexual acts of all kinds. It includes fondling, penetration and exposing a child to sexual acts.

Emotional abuse: This usually includes actions that cause harm to a child's worth or emotional wellbeing. It includes shaming, name calling, rejection, withholding love and threatening.

Neglect: This entails the inability or failure to meet a child's physical and emotional needs, for example, health and medical care, food and clothing.

Fiji's Ministry of Women, Children and Poverty Alleviation (MWCPA), Child Service Unit identified "Neglect" as the most common form of abuse in Fiji. Underlying causes for this include absentee parent/guardians, step-parenting issues, lack of supervision of children and children handed over to other relatives at the death of a biological mother, as well as alcohol abuse within the home-setting (MWCPA 2020).

Implications of COVID-19

As COVID-19 hit in Fiji in March 2020 and lockdown was enforced, the home became a highly volatile space in which violence and abuse was experienced. In the Fiji setting, the ***home is a shared place of family(ies)***, with a web of complex relationships and interactions as previously explained (Koya-Vaka'uta 2017).

The family, in some cases extended family of inter-generational membership, is not an entity by itself and detached from the community as prevails in developed countries. It relates to and interacts with the community, and this interaction is relatively more dynamic in villages and establishes a relationality characteristic of Pacific Island societies and cultures.

In the face of COVID-19, there were several factors that added to the vulnerability of children. First, as COVID-19 hit and global markets began to crash, many people globally lost their jobs. These additional stressors of job loss and associated factors further add to the vulnerabilities explained in the following sections. Second, the fact that they are in a confined space for a prolonged period with the extended family web exposes the child to a number of uncertainties and provides opportunities where children are most at risk.

In Fiji, the tourism industry that employed almost a quarter of Fiji's workforce experienced massive job losses. In addition to this, most workers who were already on the minimum wage and who worked within both the formal and informal sector were heavily impacted. Losing work or having their hours of work reduced meant that there was little to no income to pay for basic living costs and food, but also rent. Goods had to be returned or confiscated as people could not pay for them and the shame and associated guilt became a real phenomenon experienced by many families across the globe and in Fiji.

Compounded by the fact that most of the children are going without food as families can no longer provide for them. An article reported by Vakasukawaqa (2020) stated that children in 30 informal settlements in Lami have to go without food as the breadwinners in these families lost their jobs due to COVID-19. She further states that most of these households have more than 10 people residing in them and that they are a group that were already living below the poverty line prior to COVID-19. The COVID-19 situation has pushed most families who were already vulnerable over the edge, further impacting the lives of those that are most vulnerable in these communities, which are usually children, the elderly and women.

Another factor adding to the stressors of job losses was the fact that most parents could not afford to buy food for their children's lunch as schools were anticipating opening once again. As schools across Fiji resumed in June, the Minister for Education received backlash from the public after she made a plea that the least that parents can provide was lunch for their children when they go back to school (Chand 2020). Families across Fiji who were already at a loss due to COVID-19 and already on shoestring budgets or none at all found the statements made by the Minister offensive, demonstrating very little empathy at such a crucial time globally and for the nation. Therefore, the statement by the Minister was received with a lot of criticism specifically as families and communities were slowly coming to grips with their new reality and facing their losses. In response, civil society organizations and non-government organizations worked together to ensure that students could have food, providing free lunches for students across Fiji (Nasiko 2020). School communities also worked together with school parent teacher associations and wider communities first to identify children with parents who had lost jobs or were impacted by COVID-19, and then to offer assistance by providing food, school supplies and other means to assist families who are most vulnerable. This is a form of social protection that is an excellent example of how the informal sector came into operation to assist an already vulnerable group (Ratuva 2010). In this context, the key relationships that exist and the social capital that thrives within the Vanua played a crucial role in putting things in motion for most communities in Fiji to work collectively to assist each other at such times.

Secondly, the global pandemic has impacted global markets and has led to a lot of job losses. Fiji was no exception to this experiencing one of its biggest losses in the tourism industry. Tourism in Fiji makes up about 30% of Fiji's GDP and employs about 119,000 Fijians (Investment Fiji 2020). This sector suffered a tremendous loss as borders closed and travel was at a halt globally. Hotel workers, airline workers and other services associated with the tourism industry faced exponential losses. Workers now without a source of income either had to look for other work, which was already scarce, or had to be creative, often finding skills that were hobbies to be useful for sourcing income. As the world came to grips with the fact that COVID-19 was unpredictable and was bound to stay for a much longer period, most families had to revisit their plans and make drastic moves. Living within the urban centres became more expensive and with little to no income, meeting expenses became a struggle for most. Families soon started moving back to their villages and settlements as well as moving in with other families as rent and costs of living in urban centres become unaffordable. For most families, the move back to the rural areas or reverse migration meant that household numbers in rural areas increased dramatically. Mitchell (2020) refers to this as an "Exodus" as families move back to the villages or their maternal village. This exodus, he states, can ultimately impact health and wellbeing as well as mental outlook on things, both for those moving into the villages and settlements as well as for those who have remained in these villages and settlements who have now to share their homes with extended family members from the urban centres.

These factors and associated stressors have added to the elements that leave the most vulnerable in our communities more susceptible to harm and to conditions that they cannot control. The family web within the Vanua becomes extended even further where children are exposed to multiple other authority figures that they suddenly must also answer to.

The added mental stress of job losses, the associated shame and added stress of finding a new home is not an easy process. Most of these families move back to their villages where they share living spaces with other extended family members. These living spaces become incubators of stressors for families in which children are exposed to elements leaving them vulnerable to experiencing the brunt of the stressors.

Another added factor is the lockdown that occurred during COVID-19. In Fiji, the lockdown period occurred for over three months, where there was minimal movement, streets and towns were deserted and curfews were put in force. When the curfews were first implemented and breaches were made, the initial cases were dismissed due to the fact that the Public Health Act of 1928 gives the authority to the Minister for Health rather than the Prime Minister to make such a ruling in the face of a global health pandemic (Rovoi 2020). The lockdown required that all citizens were indoors, and this meant that households that were full had to have additional people crammed into confined spaces for prolonged periods compounding the issue of vulnerability amongst children.

The Issue of Child Neglect and COVID-19

Numerous studies in Fiji have indicated several factors leading to child abuse. These include the fact that child violence and abuse in its different forms continue to exist in Fiji. However, amongst all forms of child abuse, *child neglect* is currently the most predominant. Child sexual abuse persists, and anecdotal evidence through the dailies indicates that these abuses were occurring during the lockdown period (Kumar 2020). This in fact reinforces the reality of the assumptions made earlier about the vulnerability and abuse of children during the lockdown periods.

According to the study by MWCPA (2020), the key drivers of child abuse include *opportunity* and *security*. *Opportunity* relates to the close access/relationship by the perpetrator to children provided by the home-setting and even the community and village. *Security* includes the perpetrator's perception that the abuse may neither be found nor reported due to being covered under the secure blanket of tradition and family values and even if reported, it would most likely be withdrawn from legal prosecution.

Conclusion

This chapter explores the factors that relate to the vulnerability of children to child abuse as a direct impact of COVID-19. It discusses the issues of the Vanua and the family web as a disrupted space that once was a place of the safe exploration and confirmation of identity and socialization into the ways of being within the Vanua and the extended family web: a structure that kept families safe and yet now provides spaces where children are exposed to harm and are vulnerable to abuse as they defy the norms and values and belief system of the Vanua. As discussed in the chapter, Fiji has two main ethnic identities, and for both cultures the girl child is socialized in a certain way and defined by various roles and responsibilities that in both communities contribute to the wellbeing of the family as a whole. This easily can be a bubble where norms are not questions, but rather become a part of their value and belief system. As children become parts of institutions such as schools where there are diverse cultures and where children get to learn about various rights under the laws of a country, worldviews then become disrupted and questioned resulting in conflicts and chaos that goes against the norms in which they have been socialized. Going against the norms has consequences that lead to abuse. Child neglect is the form of abuse that is most prominent in Fiji and as explained, this has become worse as the exodus or movements of groups of people back into their villages and settlements have further strained villages and communities that are already vulnerable. Children within these environments are then exposed to multiple factors that were aggravated further by COVID-19. However, there are factors that have been visible in maintaining the wellbeing of communities. Contributions and the re-emergence and reinforcement of the informal economy have been forms of social protection that have united many communities as well as provided everyday citizens the opportunity to be of assistance to the most vulnerable in the community. There is still work to be done in terms of agencies working together and church groups as well as institutions all working together to keep our most vulnerable safe.

References

Bureau of Statistics. 2017a. Population and demographics. https://www.statsfiji.gov.fj/index.php/statistics/social-statistics/population-and-demographic-indicators. Accessed September 5, 2020.

Bureau of Statistics. 2017b. 2017 Population and housing census. Release 1: Age, sex, geography and economic activity: Published January 5, 2018. https://www.statsfiji.gov.fj/index.php/census-2017/census-2017-release-1. Accessed September 5, 2020.

Chand, Anish. 2020. Minister: The least parents can do is provide lunch. *Fiji Times*. https://www.fijitimes.com/minister-the-least-parents-can-do-is-provide-lunch/. Accessed September 10, 2020.

Centers for Disease Control and Prevention (CDC). 2020. What are child abuse & neglect? National Centre for Injury Prevention and Control, Division of Violence Prevention. https://www.cdc.gov/violenceprevention/childabuseandneglect/fastfact.html. Accessed September 2, 2020.

Etienne G. Krug, James A. Mercy, Linda L. Dahlberg, and Anthony B. Zwi. 2002. The world report on violence and health. *The Lancet* 360 (9339): 1083–1088, ISSN 0140-6736, https://doi.org/10.1016/S0140-6736(02)11133-0. http://www.sciencedirect.com/science/article/pii/S0140673602111330.

Harbach, Meredith Johnson Harbach. 2019. Childcare, vulnerability, and resilience, 37 Yale L. & Policy Rev. 459.

Investment Fiji. 2020. Sector profile: Tourism. https://www.investmentfiji.org.fj/pages.cfm/for-investors/sector-industry-profiles/tourism.html#:~:text=In%202018%2C%20approximately%20870%2C309%20visitors,Gross%20Domestic%20Product%20(GDP).

Kumar, Vishaal. 2020, October 4. Mental pandemic alert. *Fiji Times*. https://www.fijitimes.com/mental-pandemic-alert/. September 10, 2020.

Koya-Vaka'uta, Frances. 2017. Rethinking research as relational spaces in the Pacific: Pedagogy and praxis. In *Relational hermeneutics: Decolonizing the mindset and the Pacific Itulagi*. Edited by Upolu Luma Vaai and Aisake Casimira. University of the South Pacific: 65–84.

Ministry of Women, Children & Poverty Alleviation. 2020. *Violence against children in Fiji. Suva* MWCPA *(Pending cabinet decision for release)*.

Mitchell, John. 2020. Behind the news: The Exodus. *Fiji Times*. https://www.fijitimes.com/behind-the-news-the-exodus/.

Nabobo-Baba, Unaisi. 2006. *Knowing and learning: An indigenous Fijian approach*. Suva: Institute of Pacific Studies, USP.

Nasiko, Repeka. 2020. Free lunch for 8000 students. *Fiji Times*. https://www.fijitimes.com/free-lunch-for-8000-students/. September 10, 2020.

Plange, Nii-K. 2002. *Pacific child protection project: Manual for assessment of child protection practices with participatory methods*. Department of Sociology, University of the South Pacific.

Ratuva, Steven. 2010. Back to basics: Towards integrated social protection for vulnerable groups in Vanuatu. *Pacific Economic Bulletin* 25 (3): 40–63.

Ravuvu, Asesela. 1983. *Vaka i taukei: The Fijian way of life*. Suva: Institute of Pacific Studies of the University of the South Pacific.
Ravuvu, Asesela. 1987. *The Fijian Ethos*. Suva: Institute of Pacific Studies, University of the South Pacific.
Rovoi, Christine. 2020. Fiji government at odds with magistrate over COVID 19 curfew ruling. RNZ. https://www.rnz.co.nz/international/pacific-news/414397/fiji-govt-at-odds-with-magistrate-over-covid-19-curfew-ruling.
Save the Children. 2006. *Commercial sexual exploitation and sexual abuse of children in Fiji: A situational analysis*. Fiji: Save the Children.
Schoffel, Penny. 2007. *Elimination of all forms of discrimination and violence against the girl child: Situation paper for the Pacific Region*. UNICEF.
United Nations Convention on the Rights of the Child. 1999.
United Nations Convention on the Rights of the Child (UNCRC). 1989. Children: Child abuse, the United Nations Convention on the Rights of the Child and the Criminal Law. Retrieved from https://www.ohchr.org/en/professionalinterest/pages/crc.aspx.
United Nations International Children Emergency Fund (UNICEF). 2007. Fiji: A situational analysis of children, youth & women, government of Fiji with the assistance of UNICEF 2007. https://www.unicef.org/pacificislands/Fiji_SitAn.pdf.
Vakaoti, Patrick and Finekaso, Gaylene. 2002. Country report on child development in Fiji (Part of overview of child protection practices in Fiji, Vanuatu and Samoa). AusAID Pacific Children's Programme.
Vakasukawaqa, Arieta. 2020. Kids without meals. *Fiji Times*. https://www.fijitimes.com/kids-without-meals/.
World Health Organization. 2016. *INSPIRE: Seven strategies for ending violence against children*. Geneva, Switzerland: World Health Organization.
World Health Organization. 2002. World report on violence and health. Geneva: World Health Organization; 2002. Violence—a global health problem; 3–19.
World Health Organization. 1999. *Report of the consultation on child abuse prevention*. WHO Geneva, March 29–31.

CHAPTER 16

Conclusion

Steven Ratuva

In the introduction to this book, we used the analogy of H. G. Wells' *The war of the worlds* in which Martians invaded Earth, but were eventually destroyed by microbes similar to the COVID-19 virus. The irony here is that in the fictional story Earth-based pathogens helped save humanity from marauding aliens, but the real life version is vastly different—humans have to save ourselves from the destructive COVID-19 virus. So far, there have been mixed results regarding how we have used human ingenuity to defeat the virus. Some countries such as Aotearoa New Zealand and Fiji, both of which feature in the book, have been successful in eradicating and controlling the virus, while some like the United States (US) and many European countries have struggled to keep up with the spreading infection. Many countries in the Global South, which were earlier identified as potential hotspots, have done considerably better than industrialized and technologically advanced states. One of the reasons for this is the use and extensive prevalence of community-based social protection systems and reliance on social solidarity economies.

S. Ratuva (✉)
Faculty of Arts, University of Canterbury, Christchurch, New Zealand
e-mail: steven.ratuva@canterbury.ac.nz

S. Ratuva et al. (eds.), *COVID-19 and Social Protection*,
https://doi.org/10.1007/978-981-16-2948-8_16

Pandemics are not new and even as we eradicate this particular viral strain, a new pandemic is bound to re-emerge in another form, requiring new scientific and social responses. The unique lesson and moral directive from this COVID-19 pandemic is for us to re-examine not just our relationship with nature, but also our own dislocated human relationships and unequal social structures. COVID-19 has exacerbated economic inequality, deepened food insecurity, worsened health disparity and further marginalized the wellbeing of poor communities around the world. Those people hardest hit by the pandemic are also the very same people who are at the lost strata of global priorities when it comes to access to vaccination, unless the World Health Organization and other empathetic institutions and countries embark on a massive global strategy of vaccine access. Devising local means of social protection and building a strong social and solidarity economyas a basis for empowerment and resilience building must be a priority, especially at a time when the market economy is in crisis.

This book has provided snapshots of some of the internal mechanisms of community-based responses both to internally induced and externally generated calamities. As with the epidemiological perspective of COVID-19 and social protection by Basu in Chapter 2, one of the common themes in the chapters is the way in which the pandemic has exacerbated existing inequalities and social discontent. The chapter argued for the strengthening of social protection measures to protect vulnerable members of society from poverty-related adverse life events and circumstances, which could be determinants of infectious diseases and poor health. Pandemics such as COVID-19 must not be seen in isolation as a biological condition, but as part of the larger social milieu. The social impact of COVID-19 transcends culture, nationality and gender, although the specific manifestations linked to the specific conditions vary from context to context. For instance, many women experienced heightened domestic violence as a result of lockdown, as Crichton-Hill showed in Chapter 3. For those already facing food insecurity, as Martin-Neuninger shows in Chapter 4, the problem is worse than ever before. The pandemic thus became a double jeopardy for groups already oppressed during 'normal' situations.

Youths were impacted in different ways, but because they had a sense of resourcefulness and vigour, were able to overcome their difficulties, despite the lockdowns and restrictions and lack of access to face-to-face formal education, as Vakaoti discussed in Chapter 5. Despite the physical isolation, people used information technologies and communication systems very effectively and strategically to engage with each other, as Ross showed in Chapter 6. But again, even in communication, inequality in terms of access and control was a barrier to the less privileged members of society. Among the less privileged members of society are indigenous peoples who have to bear the brunt of multiple levels of colonial and post-colonial oppression and discrimination, as shown in Chapter 7 by Henderson, Martin, Whiteman, Manning, Reyhner and Steeves. COVID-19 was a great opportunity for indigenous communities to show the world the resilience of their way of life and will to overcome multiple layers of hurdles in the face of COVID-19 and other social, economic and political calamities they have suffered for years. In addition, the elderly also constitute an important vulnerable community, and as Plange pointed out in Chapter 8, reliance on the social and solidarity economywas a way of ensuring resilience and empowerment.

The impact of the pandemic differed from country to country in some ways, but by and large, there were broad similarities in terms of the types of social protection programmes. The state, as Espesor shows in Chapter 9 in the case of the Philippines, is still an important player providing social protection programmes for the poor. This is certainly the case in many other countries in the world. On the other hand, indigenous-based social solidarity systems tend to be more embodied in the community ethos and structures compared to state-based social protection systems. But, as Scobie argues in Chapter 10 in the case of Aotearoa New Zealand, this requires a system of indigenous accountability that is people-centred, sustainable and empowering. At the same time, the power of community mobilization remains a force to reckon with as the stress of COVD-19 and the demand for alternative forms of wellbeing programmes increases. As Finau and Kant discuss in Chapter 11, the use of traditional means of exchange using virtual means of communication has become a new mode of empowering cultural reinvention in the Pacific. For countries still under colonial rule, the fight against COVID-19 is part of the broader process of liberation. As Blesia, Lokden and Sulelino discussed in Chapter 12, the students of West Papua faced strains of lockdowns and restrictions, yet were able to use their local systems of innovation to overcome the hurdles.

The capacity of countries to respond to the pandemic is not so much due to the level of industrialization and technological advancement, as

Willis showed in the case of the US in Chapter 13. The lessons of the US show that there are important political, social and economic factors that impact a country's capacity to respond effectively to the pandemic, and the country did very badly in all those areas. In comparison, Aotearoa New Zealand performed admirably, as Fielding and Knowles discuss in Chapter 14. One of the reasons was the significance of social capital, in particular the cooperative and compliant nature of the population. In an implicit way, responses to COVID-19 emphasize the message of building a more resilient society for future generations. This is the focus of Meo-Sewabu's Chapter 15 on the impact of COVID-19 on children and possible responses.

The chapters are arranged not in a conventional way with similar themes bunched together predictably, but in an alternate manner to ensure that the different themes and narratives are in dialogue with each other so that readers are taken for a ride through a varied and unpredictable landscape. This is meant to maximize the sense of variation and provide connections between seemingly different themes. One of the realities of COVID-19 is the way it has created a condition where people are able to discern the interrelatedness of issues at different levels of society. The book tries to emulate this multi-layered interrelationship in a rather simple way.

Social Protection and Social and Solidarity Economy: Emerging Issues

A number of significant issues relating to social protection and the social and solidarity economy have emerged in the book. One of the first issues is that social protection needs to be reconceptualized in a much more critical, nuanced and participatory way to ensure that it is people friendly, empowering and sustainable. Often, social protection is perceived as a short-term response to sudden calamities, usually with the hope that this will buy time while a more long-term solution is identified. While this assumption does make sense in situations where there is a sudden onset of crisis, the reality is that future calamities are bound to happen and take various forms, and thus it is important to be prepared for any eventualities through innovative means of anticipatory social protection. One way of doing this, as a few chapters have suggested, is to build up and strengthen the social and solidarity economy, which is community-based, empowering and sustainable. COVID-19, as we have seen in the preceding chapters, has taught us this critical lesson. The paralysis of the market economy has rendered dominant neoliberal values impotent as far as the poor and even the middle class are concerned, and the search for alternatives is imperative.

Secondly, one of the favourable lessons we have learnt from COVID-19 is how humanity has taken centre stage and, in some cases, 'displaced' market norms of profit making and privatization. The challenge is how this transformation can be institutionally entrenched and permanently sustainable. This is not easy because market structures and ideologies are still dominant and will re-exert themselves aggressively once they have been able to re-energize themselves again through state subsidy. The state in capitalist countries such as the US and even in Aotearoa New Zealand has played a rather complex leveraging game in simultaneously ensuring the survival of the market economy as a first priority and social protection for the underprivileged as a second option. Nevertheless, the gains from the 'shift' towards the realm of humanity must be defended and sustained through state legislations, pressures by civil society and international humanitarian organizations and mass people's campaigns. A '#BlackLivesMatter' or '#MeToo' type of campaign is needed worldwide to keep the focus on the centrality of humanity in economic development, wellbeing policies and social protection over the primacy of capital.

The third issue is how COVID-19 has created conditions for communities to generate and share with others their resilience experiences and norms. This is an extension of the point above, in particular how the central role of human wellbeing in policies and legislations can be shared widely, expanded and nurtured to become an established component of mainstream economic and political structures. Some of the chapters have identified indigenous and community modes of wellbeing responses, and some of these lessons relating to mutual support and accountability can be shared across communities and even countries. In a globalized world, models of community-based social protection can be portable and accessible to others.

Perhaps the last major issue that emerged is the need to deepen, expand and institutionalize the social and solidarity economyas a long-term measure against future crises. The term social and solidarity economy is referred to in different ways in different contexts; some call it 'moral economy', and some refer to it as 'wellbeing economy'. In 2019, the Aotearoa New Zealand Government passed a 'wellbeing budget', which was based on addressing some of the structural issues of poverty, inequality, health disparity and other aspects of wellbeing. Since COVID-19, many semi-subsistence economies around the world focused on their traditional modes of production, land ownership and kinship relations as a basis for survival. The social solidarity economy is not an introduced system, but a pattern of relationships and production, which has been part of people's lives for centuries. For many people who have been forced off their land by colonial land grabbing, absorbed into the capitalist economy as sources of cheap labour or who are lacking the opportunities to survive on a daily basis in a market economy, seeking means of survival is a challenge. This is why it is important to seek alternative means of social protection programmes and social and solidarity economy systems, which are sustainable and empowering.

This book is a work in progress and provides just a snapshot of responses to COVID-19 at a time when the pandemic is still at its height. Yes, there is light and hope at the end of the tunnel as vaccination begins but concerns are already being raised about the role of intellectual property monopolies in using the opportunity to maximize profit rather than using the vaccine for the good of humanity. Two years from now, hopefully COVID-19 will be eradicated and the world will be a different place altogether. People, through their experiences of the pandemic and newfound culture of resilience, will see each other and their planet differently, perhaps more empathetically. It is hoped that this will be the subject of the next volume.

Index

S. Ratuva et al. (eds.), *COVID-19 and Social Protection*,
https://doi.org/10.1007/978-981-16-2948-8

R

S

The manufacturer's authorised representative in the EU is Springer Nature Customer Service Centre GmbH, Europaplatz 3, 69115 Heidelberg, Germany. If you have any concerns regarding our products, please contact ProductSafety@springernature.com

Printed and bound by CPI Group (UK) Ltd, Croydon, CR0 4YY
30/09/2026
02225321-0010